D1606699

# FROM CRITIC
## TO
# CONVERT

# FROM CRITIC TO CONVERT

## A CRITIC CHALLENGES HIS WAY TO MORMONISM

# WILLARD MORGAN

Copyright © 1995 By
HORIZON PUBLISHERS & DISTRIBUTORS, INC.

All rights reserved. Reproduction in whole or any parts thereof in any form or by any media without written permission is prohibited.

Second Printing: November, 1995

International Standard Book Number:
0-88290-517-1

Horizon Publishers' Catalog and Order Number
1051

Printed and distributed
in the United States of America by

Horizon
Publishers
& Distributors, Incorporated
P.O. Box 490 Bountiful, Utah 84011-0490

# Acknowledgment

My deepest gratitude is extended to Dr. Daniel H. Ludlow (emeritus dean, BYU Religious Education), Dr. Fred C. Pinnegar (BYU English Department), Terry Moyer, and Jamie Haubner for their encouragement and patient critiquing of this effort. Without them, I would never have dared submit it for publication. Also, I appreciate LeRoy Simmons encouraging me to use a word processor instead of the old manual typewriter I enjoyed. Without a computer I would still be in the first chapter. Susan and Roy Johnson and their daughter, Barbara, should also be heartily thanked. For hours at a time Susan mainly, but Roy and Barbara also, stuck with me as we worked out glitches in the transferring of my primitive software to her hard drive so her laser printer could perform.

In addition I would like to thank my other friends, both inside and outside of the LDS Church, for their emotional support and good-natured goading to finish what some of them had suggested I undertake in the first place. Most of all, I would like to express my deepest appreciation to my wife, Barbara, and to our seven wonderful children and their spouses, not only for their enthusiastic encouragement, but for the hundreds of hours of my absence from their lives as I prayerfully worked at the keyboard and the books. Without their willingness to sacrifice much of our time together, and their faith in this effort as being inspired by our Father in Heaven, little would have been done. I have dramatically discovered that extensive writing is not a one-person undertaking, nor is it an overnight, easily accomplished, off-the-top-of-the-head achievement.

My thanks would not be complete without mentioning Duane Crowther for the great amount of patience he had with me as we discussed this effort on the phone and in the offices of *Horizon Publishers*. Lorin May, a wonder-working editor at *Horizon,* especially needs to be thanked for the editing he did which I believe made this manuscript much better. They and the receptionists at *Horizon* truly made me feel at home as I nervously submitted my manuscript and returned again and again to discuss it. Thank you all for what you have shared with me in this thoroughly enjoyable work.

Bill Morgan

# Preface

For 58 years Ilma Lowe was faithful in her religion. But, for decades she had also been praying for a prophet to awaken the hearts and minds of church leaders.

One day a pair of neatly groomed young men knocked at her door. Time after time the friendly Mormon missionaries visited her, but they never once mentioned anything about a prophet.

After one of their meetings, a note inadvertently left on her kitchen table caught her eye. On it was written, "suggested date of baptism." She hastily threw things into her suitcases and left. For six weeks Ilma stayed with relatives while she hid from the elders.

Shortly after she returned, the amiable duo once more appeared and left the book, *Meet the Mormons*. When they asked about coming back, Ilma mumbled, "In three or four weeks."

Thumbing through the book the next day she noticed the account of Joseph Smith's first vision and of the restoration of the gospel of Jesus Christ including its Book of Mormon. Dropping to her knees, she exclaimed, "O Lord forgive me, I have been so blind."[1]

Ilma had no problem accepting Joseph Smith as a prophet of God when she was finally introduced to him. However, in my own conversion experience, believing he was a prophet was my biggest stumbling block. If Joseph Smith was truly a prophet then everything that he taught about the gospel of Jesus Christ was from a divine source. His story about visitations from Deity and from angels, a centuries-old gold text written by ancient prophets and containing the account of Jesus Christ coming to the Western Hemisphere, mankind's premortality, eternal family relationships—difficult concepts for me to believe at first—must be true.

Jesus has left us a clue in the discerning of true as well as false prophets: "Ye shall know them by their fruits" (Matthew 7:16-20). By carefully inspecting some of Joseph Smith's fruits—especially the Book of Mormon—I have learned that he has more good fruit that can easily be examined than does any other prophet who has ever lived.

Like the apostle Thomas and many others, I had to be shown that Joseph Smith was who he said he was; otherwise the experiences he said he had probably did not occur, and the principles he taught could not have come from on high. "Doubting Thomas" was shown that Jesus was literally resurrected when he was permitted to handle him and see for himself. By handling the Book of Mormon, and learning through prayerful study that it is true, I eventually gained a testimony through the Spirit that Joseph Smith was indeed the Lord's prophet of the restoration. That testimony, in turn, has helped me to also know that Jesus is the Christ, the Savior of the world.[2]

# Contents

# 1
# Searching for Truth

## A Child's Search

Though I didn't realize it at the time, my quest for a prophet began early. When I was a boy, California's fourth-grade social studies curriculum was the Golden State's history, which had its European roots in the Spanish conquest of the Americas. It was then that I first heard the tongue tangler, "Quetzalcoatl." Long ago, according to the Aztec wise men, Quetzalcoatl, a fair-skinned, bearded god, came from the sky and taught the secrets of happiness. Before leaving the land, he made a sacred promise to someday return.

Hundreds of years later, the streets of Tenochtitlan thundered with excitement as rumors spread that the long awaited Quetzalcoatl had at last returned. Their light-complexioned, bearded legend had arrived from across the blue waters in a gigantic winged canoe.

It wasn't long, though, before the man they had believed was their god betrayed their trust. With only a handful of conquistadors and some natives anxious to help bring about the downfall of their hated overlords, Hernando Cortez conquered hundreds of thousands who had at first welcomed him with gifts of gold and splendid feathers.

Memories of another who had taught his people to live righteously, and who had also promised to return, flashed through my mind. Strange how alike the two commitments were. Many times—even at that tender age—I had wondered if Jesus had journeyed to other places. Why would the Savior and creator of the entire world limit himself to a thin strip of rocks and sand at the eastern edge of the Mediterranean? Could the legendary Quetzalcoatl have been him? Jesus demonstrated his knowledge of flying by ascending into heaven. It would be no trick at all for him to travel to other parts of the world—perhaps instantaneously. How could I know if Quetzalcoatl was indeed Jesus Christ? Dismissing the thought as just another unanswered question, I went on being a boy.

When we were youngsters, my sister Pat and I sporadically attended Protestant Sunday schools with our mother in Los Angeles, California. Though she was a Bible reader, Mother never identified herself with any particular denomination during our early years. Daddy seldom attended church, except for weddings and funerals.[1] Our parents and grandparents, "Dee Dee" and "Umptah," with whom Pat and I lived for two years, were once active in Freemasons and Eastern Star. Available in our home were colorfully illustrated Bible stories, which Mother made sure we knew. We learned the Lord's Prayer and the 23rd Psalm at a Los Angeles boarding school we attended for a year in our early primary grades. That was the extent of our Christianity. It was solid enough, though, to cement a deep faith within me of Jesus Christ and the Bible.

Even in those earliest years I often wondered why God didn't speak through prophets anymore, and why more scriptures had not been written. I also questioned why there would be only one God. If there were one, why couldn't there be, or why couldn't he make, another? If there were no others like him, wouldn't he be lonely? My many questions earned me the nick-name "Question Box" from my parents.

## Prayerful Agnostic

Despite my Christian upbringing and meandering search for truth, during high school my faith began to slip and it continued to grow colder. After graduating from high school, I worked on a turkey ranch in the Mojave Desert. There in Victorville I enjoyed the friendship of a Methodist youth group and was baptized into that persuasion. However, after leaving the area, my belief began eroding again. A year or two later I was again sprinkled into Fontana, California's Community Church as good people there friendshipped me back to the Bible.

Following my discharge from the U.S. Coast Guard, where my religious devotion again had slid, I moved in with my parents again and enrolled at the University of California at Riverside. Largely because of the cynical attitude about religion among many professors and students, my belief in Christ crumbled almost completely.

Because of my childhood faith, my heart continually talked with God but my mind doubted that he was out there. I had become a prayerful agnostic, and was leaning toward atheism. I didn't know if there was a God, though I rather doubted it. I didn't know if Jesus was really a miracle man or if his followers simply made him look that way. To me, the Bible had become a mere collection of folktales about mythical people who may or may not have lived. I felt that man was the creator of God.

## The Awesome Mystery

Death's specter, which eventually motivated me to seek truth, first intruded into my life while I was in the sixth grade. My mother's brother, Ben, died. Cigarette embers ignited his mattress as he drifted off to sleep. Two years younger than Mother and twenty-five years older than me, he was nevertheless one of my best friends. As I tearfully trudged around the putrid ashes of what had once been his home at the back of Dee Dee and Umptah's house, I kept glancing around, half-way expecting to see him standing by the blackened dog pen. It was a terrible mistake, a rotten joke. "Uncle Ben can't be dead!" I cried through my aching throat. "Why?" I sobbed. "Why did he die? Why are you punishing him, God? He never hurt anyone."

Mother and Daddy tried comforting me with, "Death is merely falling asleep." But how did they know? They had never died. All I had to go on were the words of prophets who themselves died thousands of years ago. And yet I had so many questions and fears they never addressed in the Bible. Where was a living prophet who could explain?

While I was serving in the Coast Guard, Dee Dee and Umptah died within a few months of each other. They were like second parents. Again death's mystical shadow confronted me.

Night and day the terrible image of the grave haunted me. "I am going to die!" Walking into a cemetery or by a mortuary was a ghoulish agony. Constantly before me was the macabre thought: Someday they're going to stuff me inside a stifling coffin and close the lid! They're going to put me in a hole and I'll be smothered with dirt! Rigor mortis will stiffen my body! What if they make a mistake and I'm alive inside that inky vacuum? It has happened before.

A morbid ditty was unceasing in its rhythmical reminder:

Have you ever thought when the hearse goes by
That you might be the next to die?
They seal you in a wooden box
And cover you deep with dirt and rocks.
The worms crawl in, the worms crawl out,
The worms play pinochle in your snout.

The humor had long since vanished. That was talking about me!

I was forced to ask myself: What becomes of us after we die? What if there is a hell? What if there *are* eternal fires where the wicked are continually burning but are never consumed? It was hell just thinking about it. I feared I might have to spend the rest of eternity in hell if I didn't straighten myself out. But straighten out to what?

Again, the questions—the unending eternal questions. The older I became, the more my fear crescendoed. What was wrong with me? Such thoughts didn't seem to bother anyone else. Was I becoming insane? Somehow, somewhere, for the sake of my emotional health and mental stability, I had to find answers.

## Getting Religion

Becoming "religious" seemed the obvious solution. My experiences in religion during my teen years had been with youth and young-adult groups; I hadn't really devoted myself to a changed way of life, though I had been baptized and had frequently prayed. I agreed that if I became religious, it wouldn't be a bad life. I would have to change some things, but that would be all right if there really was a lower world. If Satan's nether regions existed, heaven would probably exist too. I decided that proving to God that I was on his side would guarantee my admittance into his paradise and I would escape hell; and if there were no heaven nor hell, the religious life still wouldn't be a waste of time. The few "churchy" people I had known seemed to be happy, though I had thought them to be weird.

However, my decision created a new dilemma: if I became religious, which religion should I join? None of the ministers whom I had known even claimed to have the complete truth within their church's doctrine. They would tell me that it didn't matter which religion I belonged to as long as I believed in Christ. Yet it was obvious to me that because there were so many different denominations within Christianity, they didn't all teach the pure gospel that Christ taught. If, at the time I had known about Harry Emerson Fosdick, a noted Protestant preacher, I would have agreed with his conclusion: "If Jesus should come back to earth now, hear the mythologies built up around him, see the creedalism, denominationalism, sacramentalism, carried on in his name, he would certainly say, 'If this is Christianity, I am not a Christian.'"[2]

Yet aside from a Roman Catholic catechism class I'd taken with a girlfriend, the only religious orientation I had ever received was the Protestantism I had experienced as a youth and young adult. Which of the hundreds of religions was the one God recognizes? Where was the prophet who could tell me? Most of the concepts the Catholic priest had taught, such as the mystery of the Trinity and transubstantiation, hadn't sounded right to me at all. Furthermore, Catholic practices such as elevating Mary and other Saints to a mediator status between God and man, giving icons and relics a sacred place on the altar, using holy water, priests and nuns living cloistered and celibate lives, Joseph and Mary remaining virginal throughout their marriage, were simply too foreign to my Protestant up-bringing.

Foreign, that is, except for the notion that Christ had founded a church organization that was administrated by men who held his priesthood authority. The Catholic priest had explained that Jesus ordained his apostles: "Ye have not chosen me, but I have chosen you, and ordained you." If Jesus Christ was not a myth, the priesthood concept—the authority to act for God—made sense to me. But I couldn't figure out where, if he had a priesthood within a church, would that priesthood and institution be found today? Do the Catholics have the priesthood? If so, which Catholic group—Eastern or Roman? Who can validly perform the ordinances and rites of Christianity? Who is authorized by God to represent him and preach his word? If, in fact, there was a God?

Prayers continually flowed from my agnostic heart as I pleaded for answers. But answers didn't seem to come.

# Mt. Rubidoux

Not far from my parents' Fontana home, sixty miles east of Los Angeles, the tip of beautiful Mt. Rubidoux rises on the horizon. Perhaps because of its natural setting and because of the Easter sunrise services conducted there, the impression came to me that Mt. Rubidoux might be a more sacred place than our home to further my quest. Desperately, I wanted answers. I would do anything to know—even offer a prayer on a mountain top.

Making up my mind to kneel on a hilltop didn't happen overnight. A lot of foot dragging preceded it. It's not every day that a guy hikes up a mountain to pray.

Eventually the day came when I decided to do it. Swallowing my pride, I hopped into my '42 Ford sedan and backed out of the driveway. Jubilantly I plunged down the road as I realized I was finally going to go through with it. But the closer I got to the hill the lighter my foot became. The car was nearly tractoring along the highway when Mt. Rubidoux loomed ahead. Half hoping something would stop me, I found excuses to tour the countryside. I made sure I saw *all* of it. As the day wore on, though, I had to face my reason for being there: was I going to Mt. Rubidoux or wasn't I?

Parking the car, I forced my feet to plod up the path until I came to a lonely place amidst the trees and brush. Looking in all directions I fidgeted, circled to see if anyone was watching, began to kneel, stood up, then stumbled back down the hill.

It was embarrassing. How pitifully dramatic: praying on a hillside like some biblical wise man. Who did I think I was—Moses? I lost courage and quietly made my way back home, hoping my resolve would be stronger another day.

A week or two later I again trudged the trail to the same secluded spot. Kneeling, I spilled myself out to Someone.

# 2
# The Beginning of Answers

At the time I was disappointed in the results—it seemed that I had received no answer. However, as I look back, I see that answers began coming in unexpected and unrecognized ways. Shortly after coming off the mountain, I attempted to become religious, though it was a struggle. Someday I would have to change—it might as well be now. There was nothing to lose except my personality and friends. Because they were not used by the few religious people I had admired, I supposed that cigarettes, beer, bars, poker parties, girlie magazines, profanity and other things had to go.[1] I would probably have to start attending church again and give up Sabbath breaking.

## Missionaries

I was lounging in my bedroom one hot afternoon in June when my mother poked her head through the door. "Bill, there are some *young men* here to see you," she said, in the sarcastic singing tone she often used when salesmen rang the bell. She returned to the kitchen before I could ask who they were.

Walking through the living room I saw what looked like two older teenagers in suits standing inside the front door, their hats in their hands. The short blond one stepped forward and extended his hand. "Hello, I'm Elder Green and my companion is Elder Johnson. We're missionaries from The Church of Jesus Christ of Latter-day Saints."

I greeted them with handshakes and raised eyebrows. "Elder?" I thought elders were older, bearded, wise patriarchs of ancient religious orders. That description certainly doesn't fit you."

Elder Green smiled. "Your friend Heidi Kopp said you might want to talk with us."

I tried not to roll my eyes as I smiled and shook my head in disbelief. Heidi was one of those rare religious people I actually admired. I wondered how she knew I was getting interested in religion.

23

"We would like to share a message about Jesus Christ with you and your family if you have time," Elder Green said.

"How much is this going to cost me?" I asked with a suspicious grin.

"Not a thing. Honest."

"So often people come to the door wanting a handout," I explained. Mother was home but my dad was still working. I walked over to the kitchen door and asked, "Mother, do you want—"

"Maybe later. I'm pretty busy now," she said slamming the refrigerator door.

"Sure, I'll talk to you for awhile," I said to the missionaries as I motioned toward the couch.

"Actually, would it be possible for us to sit at the dining room table? It would be easier to talk there where we can show you some things about Christ."

At first their smiling faces threw me off. I felt fidgety because they seemed to come on like super-salesmen. But it didn't take long to warm up to these polite young men as we got acquainted. They were younger than I was, but seemed mature and genuinely interested in me. The tall, dark-haired one—Elder Johnson—only spoke when I asked him questions. He was from Miami and hadn't been a missionary for very long. Elder Green was from Provo, Utah.

"It's interesting that you're from Utah, Elder," I said. "I thought everyone there was a Mormon."

He gave an embarrassed laugh as he briefly glanced at his companion. "I'm sorry, Bill, I guess we should have explained: we *are* Mormons. We didn't use the word 'Mormon' when we introduced ourselves because that's only a nickname."

My enthusiasm faded. I had no interest in listening to representatives of a bunch of uneducated, polygamous ranchers in Utah who were led across the plains by Brigham Young and his many wives. Heidi had said she was LDS, not *Mormon*. But I knew she wouldn't like it if I threw them out. I stammered for a few moments and decided to not make an issue of it.

"So you're missionaries?" I finally said. "I thought missionaries were older folks who go off to the jungles and convert cannibals."

We talked for a few more minutes and I felt my negative emotions melt away. They were very likeable, surprisingly normal people, so I figured we could discuss their religion for a few minutes and then part as friends. But when Elder Green asked if one of them could offer a prayer, I realized that they were getting ready for a serious discussion. When Elder Johnson finished praying I decided to get all of my questions out of the way so they couldn't indoctrinate me too much.

"Just out of curiosity, why do you call yourselves Latter-day Saints? I thought saints were dead men and women who were canonized by the Catholic Church because they had lived good lives and had performed miracles."

"Back in New Testament times, common, everyday members of the Church of Jesus Christ were known as saints," Elder Green explained. "Paul wrote his epistles to the saints in Corinth, the saints at Ephesus, etc. No one had been canonized. Comparatively few had performed any dramatic miracles. They referred to one another as saints whether or not they were good or bad.

"Which brings us to the reason that we're here. We would like to give you a short message about Jesus Christ and our Father in Heaven, if that's all right."

"I . . . I guess so," I stuttered.

# The God of Israel

Although I listened reluctantly at first, I soon became captivated. Using the Bible as their reference and a pad of paper upon which to make notes and drawings, Elder Green began a riveting discussion about Deity. He showed that Jesus and his Father are two separate persons—not merely one as I had been led to believe in my youth.

It was not difficult for him to show this was true. Very well-known incidents from the Bible seemed to clearly demonstrate that. When a voice announced from the heavens at his baptism and at the Transfiguration mount, "This is my beloved Son, in whom I am well pleased," Jesus was not playing ventriloquistic tricks (Matthew 3:11; 17:5). Someone else—his Father—had spoken.

When he prayed, Jesus talked with another being, not with himself. He said, "Our Father which art in heaven, hallowed be *thy* name" (Matthew 6:9-13). In that same prayer he implied that all of us are his brothers and sisters. Rather than *my* Father, he had said, *"Our* Father." Later, in the garden, after his resurrection, Jesus told Mary that he was going to "ascend unto *my* Father, and *your* Father; and to *my* God, and *your* God" (John 20:17). Paul also taught that "the head of Christ is God" (I Cor. 11:3).

I had often wondered about the dialogue prior to the creation of Adam. God said, "Let *us* make man in *our* image, after *our* likeness." To whom was he speaking? Himself? (Genesis 1:26-27).

On another occasion Jesus explained that "my Father is greater than I," meaning, of course, that his Father is a superior being to his Son (John 14:28). Jesus revealed, "I came down from heaven, not to do my will, but the will of him that sent me" (John 6:38). The doctrine the Lord taught was not his, "but his that sent me" (John 7:16). He did nothing of himself, "but as my Father hath taught me" (John 8:28).

During the agony of being stoned to death, Stephen saw Jesus standing next to his Father: "Behold, I see the heavens opened, and the Son of man standing on the right hand of God" (Acts 7:55-56).

I later read the conversion story of a former minister (I held ministers in the highest esteem) who suddenly came to the same realization I did about the true godhead—that the Father, Son, and Holy Ghost are three personalities—not a mysterious one. The minister had left "the world of ecclesiastical babel" because he did not believe the doctrine of the Trinity as well as other long accepted teachings in his church. After hearing a Brigham Young University professor discuss the godhead one day,

> the problem with the Trinity very quickly and quite inexplicably began to dissolve. On that day I was introduced to Heavenly Father and found him to be real, personable, warm, and quite capable of anger and love and joy and pain. I left the conference pleasantly dazed but fully aware that I had had a spiritual encounter. Truth had won out.[2]

The missionary's description of the Mormon God was a believable God. To me he seemed to be the true God of the Bible. But was the God of the Bible true?

Despite the fact that what he said seemed to be correct and logical, I wasn't about to accept that view just because a couple of young men in suits told me it was true. "Your explanation about God seems valid, but I'm no theologian. How do you know you have a true interpretation about him and not merely an opinion?" I asked.

# Joseph Smith's First Vision

Elder Green then told me the most fascinating, yet unbelievable, story I had ever heard. It was about a boy prophet named Joseph Smith, Jr. and his search for truth. In his own words he tells about a remarkable experience he had after praying in a grove of trees:

> Some time in the second year after our removal [from Vermont] to Manchester, [New York], there was in the place where we lived an unusual excitement on the subject of religion. It commenced with the Methodists, but soon became general among all the sects in that region of country. Indeed, the whole district of country seemed affected by it, and great multitudes united themselves to the different religious parties, which created no small stir and division amongst the people, some crying, 'Lo, here!' and others, 'Lo, there!' Some were contending for the Methodist faith, some for the Presbyterian, and some for the Baptist.
>
> For, notwithstanding the great love which the converts to these different faiths expressed at the time of their conversion, and the great zeal manifested by the respective clergy, . . . when the converts began to file off, some to one party and some to another, it was seen that the seemingly good feelings of both the priests and the converts were more pretended than real; for a scene of great confusion and bad feeling ensued—priest contending against priest, and convert against convert; so that all their good feelings one for another, if they ever had any, were entirely lost in a strife of words and a contest about opinions.
>
> I was at this time in my fifteenth year. My father's family was proselyted to the Presbyterian faith, and four of them joined that church, namely my mother, Lucy; my brothers Hyrum and Samuel Harrison; and my sister Sophronia.
>
> During this time of great excitement my mind was called up to serious reflection and great uneasiness; but though my feelings were deep and often poignant, still I kept myself aloof from all these parties, though I attended their several meetings as often as occasion would permit.
>
> . . . In the midst of this war of words and tumult of opinions, I often said to myself: 'What is to be done? Who of all these parties are right; or, are they all wrong together? If any one of them be right, which is it, and how shall I know it?'

While I was laboring under the extreme difficulties caused by the contests of these parties of religionists, I was one day reading the Epistle of James, first chapter and fifth verse, which reads: *If any of you lack wisdom, let him ask of God, that giveth to all men liberally, and upbraideth not; and it shall be given him.*

Never did any passage of scripture come with more power to the heart of man than this did at this time to mine. It seemed to enter with great force into every feeling of my heart. I reflected on it again and again, knowing that if any person needed wisdom from God, I did; for how to act I did not know, and unless I could get more wisdom than I then had, I would never know; for the teachers of religion of the different sects understood the same passages of scripture so differently as to destroy all confidence in settling the question by an appeal to the Bible.

At length I came to the conclusion that I must either remain in darkness and confusion, or else I must do as James directs, that is, ask of God . . . concluding that if he gave wisdom to them that lacked wisdom, and would give liberally, and not upbraid, I might venture.

So, in accordance with this, my determination to ask of God, I retired to the woods to make the attempt. It was on the morning of a beautiful, clear day, early in the spring of eighteen hundred and twenty. It was the first time in my life that I had made such an attempt, for amidst all my anxieties I had never as yet made the attempt to pray vocally.

After I had retired to the place where I had previously designed to go, having looked around me, and finding myself alone, I kneeled down and began to offer up the desires of my heart to God. I had scarcely done so, when immediately I was seized upon by some power which entirely overcame me, and had such an astonishing influence over me as to bind my tongue so that I could not speak. Thick darkness gathered around me, and it seemed to me for a time as if I were doomed to sudden destruction.

But, exerting all my powers to call upon God to deliver me out of the power of this enemy which had seized upon me, and at the very moment when I was ready to sink into despair and abandon myself to destruction—not to an imaginary ruin, but to the power of some actual being from the unseen world, who had such marvelous power as I had never before felt in any being—just at this moment of great alarm, I saw a pillar of light exactly over my head, above the brightness of the sun, which descended gradually until it fell upon me. It no sooner appeared than I found myself delivered from the enemy which held me bound. When the light rested upon me I saw two Personages, whose brightness and glory defy all description, standing above me in the air. One of them spake unto me, calling me by name and said, pointing to the other—*This is My Beloved Son. Hear Him!*

My object in going to inquire of the Lord was to know which of all the sects was right, that I might know which to join. No sooner, therefore, did I get possession of myself, so as to be able to speak, than I asked the Personages who stood above me in the light, which of all the sects was right (for at this time it had never entered into my heart that all were wrong) —and which I should join.

I was answered that I must join none of them, for they were all wrong; and the Personage who addressed me said that all their creeds were an abomination in his sight, that those professors were all corrupt; that: 'they draw near to me with their lips, but their hearts are far from me, they teach for doctrines the commandments of men, having a form of godliness, but they deny the power thereof.'

He again forbade me to join with any of them; and many other things did he say unto me, which I cannot write at this time. When I came to myself again, I found myself lying on my back, looking up into heaven. When the light had departed, I had no strength; but soon recovering in some degree, I went home.

(Joseph Smith History 1:5-20)

Joseph Smith's story seemed glorious yet too far out to be true. "You've got to be kidding!" I smirked. "Seeing God in our day and age?"

Elder Green didn't seem bothered by the comment, as though he had heard it hundreds of times before. He looked at his closed Bible as he quietly responded, "Stephen had a similar experience when he stared into heaven and saw Jesus and his Father in the midst of a glorious light" (Acts 7:51-59). The elder was right, but I'd thought such remarkable things only happened in Bible times. I kept my mouth shut while the missionary continued.

A few days after his vision, Joseph told a Methodist minister about his sacred vision, believing that he, of all people, would be enthused:

. . . I was greatly surprised at his behavior; he treated my communication not only lightly, but with great contempt, saying it was all of the devil, that there were no such things as visions or revelations in these days; that all such things had ceased with the apostles, and that there would never be any more of them.

I soon found, however, that my telling the story had excited a great deal of prejudice against me among professors of religion, and was the cause of great persecution, which continued to increase; and though I was an obscure boy, only between fourteen and fifteen years of age, and my circumstances in life such as to make a boy of no consequence in the world, yet men of high standing would take notice sufficient to excite the public mind against me, and create a bitter persecution; and this was common among all the sects—all united to persecute me.

(Joseph Smith History 1:21-22)

I could somewhat relate to the Methodist minister. The story just seemed too unbelievable to be true. "Why wouldn't a man of God—a minister—believe Joseph's story if it was the truth?" I challenged the elders.

Elder Green showed me that even Jesus was chased out of Nazareth's synagogue by the rabbi and Jesus's supposed friends when he told them that Isaiah 61:1-2 was fulfilled in him. When Jesus went "to his own country [Nazareth] he taught them in their synagogue, so that they were astonished, and said, 'Where did this man get this wisdom and these mighty works? Is not this the carpenter's son? Is not his mother called Mary? And are not his brothers James and Joseph and Simon and Judas? And are not all his sisters with us? Where then did this man get all this? And they took offense at him" (Luke 4:16-24; Matt. 13:53-58; Revised Standard Version).[3]

That scripture took the wind out of my sails. I didn't have an answer for it so I let them continue Joseph Smith's account:

It caused me serious reflection then, and often has since, how very strange it was that an obscure boy of a little over fourteen years of age, and one, too, who was doomed to the necessity of obtaining a scanty maintenance by his daily labor, should be thought a character of sufficient importance to attract the attention of the great ones of the most popular sects of the day, and in a manner to create in them a spirit of the most bitter persecution and reviling. But strange or not, so it was and it was often the cause of great sorrow to myself.

However, it was nevertheless a fact that I had beheld a vision. I have thought since, that I felt much like Paul, when he made his defense before King Agrippa, and related the account of the vision he had when he saw a light, and heard a voice; but still there were but few who believed him; some said he was dishonest, others said he was mad; and he was ridiculed and reviled. But all this did not destroy the reality of his vision. He had seen a vision, he knew he had, and all the persecution under heaven could not make it otherwise; and though they should persecute him unto death, yet he knew, and would know to his latest breath, that he had both seen a light and heard a voice speaking unto him, and all the world could not make him think or believe otherwise.

So it was with me. I had actually seen a light, and in the midst of that light I saw two Personages, and they did in reality speak to me; and though I was hated and persecuted for saying that I had seen a vision, yet it was true; and while they were persecuting me, reviling me, and speaking all manner of evil against me falsely for so saying, I was led to say in my heart: 'Why persecute me for telling the truth? I have actually seen a vision; and who am I that I can withstand God, or why does the world think to make me deny what I have actually seen? For I had seen a vision; I knew it, and I knew that God knew it, and I could not deny it, neither dared I do it; at least I knew that by so doing I would offend God, and come under condemnation.[4]

(Joseph Smith History 1:23-25)

In answer to my earlier question about how the missionaries knew their interpretation about God was valid, Elder Green explained, "Because Joseph Smith was a prophet and had actually seen and talked with two heavenly beings—the Father and his Son—the LDS view of God is true. It is not the conclusion of a group of scholars but the first-hand testimony of a prophet of God."

Although I had not asked for these visitors,[6] I soon found myself fascinated by what the elder had to say. His conclusions about God were exactly what I had always visualized. I had been raised with the belief that the Father, Son, and Holy Ghost were all the same being much as water, vapor, and ice are forms of the $H_2O$ molecule. The Trinitarian dogma led me to wonder if the one universal God was helplessly lying in a manger when Jesus was born. Who answered prayers at that time—Mary's toddler? When the missionary showed me the Mormon view—the Father, Son, and Holy Spirit are three separate personalities—I couldn't help but feel the

God I had prayed to on Mt. Rubidoux was the same God that Mormons were worshipping. If their God was the true one, then man did indeed create Christianity's traditional God.

However, I certainly wasn't ready to believe that Joseph Smith, Jr. was one of God's prophets. Rational people in our day and age just don't go around telling others that they have seen and talked with God. Furthermore, Joseph Smith was a teenage American farmboy with the generic name of Smith, of all things. And *Junior*?

# 3
# Christ's
# New Testament Church

A week later Elders Green and Johnson returned. Mother was outside working in the garden when they came. She and Daddy had told me earlier that they weren't interested in listening to the Mormons, so just the three of us sat at the dining room table and got reacquainted. It was good to be in their friendly presence.

"I'm glad you returned. I thought you might not come back during the heat of the day. You must be ringing wet after pedaling bicycles in your suits and ties."

Elder Green smiled. "We're used to it."

As usual Elder Johnson sat in silence. He smiled, but was perhaps a little timid about expressing himself since he was a "greenie"—a missionary new to the field.

"Last week I didn't really want to discuss religion with you." I told them. "But after your discussion about the godhead, I couldn't wait for you to return. Not that I believe that Joseph Smith was a prophet, you understand. But your lesson about God really made sense."

As they did during the previous lesson, the elders asked if we could offer a word of prayer. This time they asked me to say it. "No. I'm sorry," I replied, red faced. "I've never prayed in public." After assuring me that I didn't have to pray if I didn't want to, Elder Johnson offered the prayer again.

Taking out his familiar pencil and a pad of paper, Elder Johnson drew instructive pictures while writing scriptural references for me as Elder Green taught the lesson. After reviewing what he had taught during his first lesson, the elder began teaching another concept—one that the Catholic priest had also taught me. Though it was a plausible notion, it was not taught to me during my Protestant nurturing. The elder explained that the Savior had founded a definite religious organization—the Church of Jesus Christ.

Elder Green pointed out, while Elder Johnson drew a picture of a church building on his pad, that Jesus was not a rabbi who decided to put together his own religion because he did not like some of the things going on in the old one. He wasn't there to reshuffle the established religious organizations and come up with a new one from the pieces. He was the Son of God and was sent by his Father to establish his kingdom on earth. In doing so, Jesus explained to his apostles that "No one puts a piece of unshrunk cloth on an old garment, for the patch tears . . . and a worse tear is made" (Matthew 9:16-17; RSV). His doctrine and his priesthood authority had come from his Father, not from the seminaries.

## Revelation

When they were near Caesarea Philippi, Jesus asked his apostles—a title given to his twelve special prophets—who the people thought he was. It was generally believed that he might be John the Baptist, Elijah, Jeremiah, or one of the other prophets who had come back to life. Jesus then asked the twelve who they thought he was.

Peter knew. Without hesitation he answered, "Thou art the Christ, the Son of the living God." By revelation from God, Peter knew that Jesus was the Christ, the long anticipated Messiah: "Blessed art thou Simon Bar-jona [Peter]," Jesus said, "for flesh and blood hath not revealed it unto thee, but my Father which is in heaven." Jesus then taught his apostles that he would build his church upon "this rock" of *revelation,* "and the gates of hell shall not prevail against" the principle of revelation (Matthew 16:13-18). Elder Johnson wrote "Revelation" and "Matthew 16:13-18" above his church drawing.

That was interesting. I had heard a different interpretation. "A Catholic priest taught me that that particular scripture referred to Christ's Church being founded upon Peter" I said. "The gates of hell had not prevailed against the Church because the popes had continued Peter's leadership."

## Priesthood

Elder Green nodded his head as if to acknowledge the Catholic view. He didn't seem bothered by my comment and made no attempt to refute it.

He simply proceeded to explain the LDS concept of priesthood. After their Lord's ascension, the apostles became the mortal administrators of his kingdom. As prophets they were to preach "the gospel to every creature." In addition, the keys of the priesthood were bestowed upon Christ's chief apostle, Peter: "I will give unto thee the *keys* of the kingdom of heaven: and whatsoever thou shalt bind on earth shall be bound in heaven: and whatsoever thou shalt loose on earth shall be loosed in heaven" (Matt. 16:19). Whatever ordinance or inspired action Peter performed by the authority of the priesthood was preserved in the annals of the angels.

Opening his Bible to the book of Ephesians, Elder Green showed me more about the structure of Christ's Church and its priesthood leaders. Paul was writing to converts at Ephesus and welcoming them into the new Church: "Now . . . ye are no more strangers and foreigners, but fellow-citizens with the saints, and of the household of God; and are built upon the foundation of the apostles and prophets, Jesus Christ himself being the chief corner stone" (Eph. 2:19-20). Elder Johnson drew a foundation with a cornerstone under his building and wrote the words "apostles and prophets," "Christ," and "Eph. 2:19-20" in the appropriate places.

## All Things Common

The religion Jesus taught was not a Sabbath day-only faith, according to Elder Green. His kingdom was a community built upon the principle of love. It was the most nearly perfect social mechanism in the world containing "the machinery for an economic system that would take the brood of fears out of the heart of man—the fear of want through sickness, old age, unemployment, and poverty."[1] When a certain rich man came to Jesus and asked, "Good Master, what good thing shall I do, that I may have eternal life?" he was told to keep the commandments. When the young man said that he had done so "from my youth up. What lack I yet?" he was then taught that if he wished to be "perfect" he must "sell that thou hast, and give to the poor" (Matt. 19:13-26).

Everyone willingly sacrificed all that he or she had to the kingdom. Redistribution of their donated material goods was then made among the saints by trusted servants who knew the needs of each individual. "The multitude of them that believed were of one heart and of one soul: neither said any of them that ought of the things which he possessed was his own;

but they had all things common . . . Neither was there any among them that lacked: for as many as were possessors of lands or houses sold them, and brought the prices of the things that were sold, and laid them down at the apostles' feet: and distribution was made unto every man according as he had need" (Acts 2:44; 4:32-37).

## Laws and Ordinances

Christ's kingdom was not complicated. The King's rules and laws—his commandments—were easily grasped by even the least educated. If there were questions, the apostles were consulted.

Candidates for citizenship showed their sincerity by being immersed in water—the outward acceptance of Christ and the ordinance for entrance into the kingdom of God—by those holding the priesthood (John 3:5; Matt. 3:13-16). They were buried and reborn symbolically within God's kingdom. Hands of the priesthood were then laid upon their heads for reception of the Holy Spirit, also known as the Holy Ghost (Acts 8:14-17).

During the baptismal ordinance, the new member made a sincere covenant with God to obey the King's laws—to keep his commandments. In return for obeying the commandments, the peaceful influence of the Holy Spirit was promised to the convert. At least once each week—"upon the first day of the week"—the saints "came together to break bread," and to renew their baptismal covenants (Acts 20:7). Elder Johnson wrote the words "commandments," and "baptism" next to his church building.

## The Temple of God

Most early Christians were of Jewish lineage. Before their conversions, their lives were centered around the temple. After baptism, the temple remained their focal point. The saints continued "daily with one accord in the temple, and breaking bread . . . with gladness and singleness of heart, praising God, and having favour with all people" (Acts 2:46-47).

"The idea of Christ founding a Church had made sense when the Catholic priest taught it to me," I told the elders. "I wondered at that time why such a view had not been taught to me during my previous church experiences. All I ever heard was that the Bible was sufficient for salvation. Yet, those ministers who told me the Bible was all that was necessary were smart men. They had graduated from religious seminaries and must know a lot more about the Bible than you two untrained missionaries."

"Jesus was only one person; he was not divided," Elder Green explained as he pointed to Elder Johnson's drawing. "If he were here today he would not teach a diversity of religious ways. From the mount he had taught that there was only one narrow way 'which leadeth unto life' (Matt. 7:14). His apostles were placed in charge of the one organization that taught that narrow way."

"If Christ's Church really was the way you've described, I wonder where such a Church is today. None that I'm familiar with fit your description."

Our discussion could have gone on much longer, but the Elders were already late for another appointment. They soon left, but not before talking me into doing something I wouldn't have volunteered to do in a million years.

# 4
# Why Prophets?

When I answered the door the following week, there stood Elder Johnson and a giant of a man with a big grin on his face. Elder Johnson introduced him. Holding his hat in one hand, Elder Porter politely extended the other for me to shake.

"What happened to Elder Green?" I asked.

"He was transferred to San Bernardino last weekend," Elder Johnson replied.

"You must be six-and-a-half feet tall, Elder Porter," I guessed as the three of us strolled over to the dining room table. "I'm six-foot two and it looks like I'm staring you in the Adam's apple."

"Pretty close; six-foot-seven is about right," he politely corrected me.

As we sat at the table Elder Porter and I got more acquainted. "So, you're from Boise, Idaho? I'm surprised at the number of places you missionaries call home. Elder Green's the only one of the three of you who's from Utah. I used to think that all Mormons lived in Utah until I found out that Heidi is one. Now I'm meeting elders who come from Idaho and Florida."

"Most missionaries are probably from Utah," Elder Johnson said.

"But we're trying to change that," Elder Porter chimed in.

I laughed nervously with Elder Porter, but Elder Johnson looked mortified, as though his companion had blown their cover. I tried to quickly change the subject. It wasn't like I didn't know they wanted me to join their church. I wasn't planning on converting to Mormonism, but what I had heard so far fascinated me. Whether or not it was true, it seemed to make sense.

At the end of the previous lesson, Elder Green had talked me into offering a short prayer. And it *was* short. He had told me that all I had to do was address God by saying "Our Father," then thank him for whatever I wished, ask for whatever came to mind, then close in the name of Jesus Christ. So I said something like, "Our Father, I thank you for the lesson that Elder Green gave me about his Church, please help me to remember it, in the name of Jesus Christ. Amen." They said I gave a good prayer, but my face became warmer than the thermometer in the kitchen. I never wanted to do that again.

This time I drew out the conversation as much as possible then ducked my head when I could see that the missionaries were thinking about an opening prayer. I didn't want them to call on me. But Elder Johnson did. Again I declined, saying, "Maybe at the end of your lesson."

Elder Porter was the new senior companion. Elder Johnson shyly reviewed the lesson Elder Green had given me about the early Church of Jesus Christ, then he asked if I had any questions.

"I do have one. Did you say that the twelve apostles were also considered prophets like the Old Testament prophets?"

The elders assured me that the Lord had prophets both in the Old and New Testament times. "The twelve prophets that he called apostles became the mortal administrators of Christ's Church after he ascended into heaven," Elder Porter said.

"And you also told me during your first lesson that you believed that Joseph Smith was a prophet. Right?"

Again Elder Johnson nodded.

"Ever since I was a boy and had read the Bible stories that Mother left lying around for my sister and me to read, I have wondered why God had no more prophets. Why were they on earth only during Bible times? Whenever I have asked Protestant teachers and ministers why prophets are no longer here, they have all agreed that there is no further need for them. You elders, though, tell me that Joseph Smith was a prophet. If authorities on religion—they who have devoted their lives to the study of the Bible—say prophets are no longer needed, why should I believe you instead of them?"

To answer my question Elder Porter began with a fascinating discussion about the Bible, though it was not nearly as detailed as it follows below. He explained that other Christians often challenge Mormons with the question, "We have the Bible; why do we need a prophet?"

## A Bible! A Bible! We Have *the* Bible!

Most Christians are taught that all which God will ever reveal is in the Bible. In a comparative study of the beliefs of ten major Christian denominations, only one—The Church of Jesus Christ of Latter-day Saints —believes that God may bring forth further scripture. The other nine believe that the Bible is God's final word. Typical are such statements as: The Bible "contains all of God's teachings for our salvation;" it "is the only rule for faith and practice;" and it "contains all of God's revelations to man."[1]

Devout Israelites, who had the Hebrew Bible, could have asked the same question about Jesus: "We have the scriptures; why do we need another prophet?" In fact, Jewish leaders did use nearly the same argument when they said that they had Abraham as their father and the law of Moses as their guide; therefore, they didn't need another prophet. They said they didn't need John the Baptist or Jesus (Luke 3:8; John 7:45-53; 8:5-7; 37-40; 19:6-7).

Many today believe that every jot and tittle in the Bible was dictated by the very lips of God. Therefore, prophets are no longer needed. However, even though the Bible in its entirety is the word of God, scholars such as William H. Brownlee of the Divinity School of Duke University conclude that "we cannot assume that ancient scribes never miscopied" scriptures. "The [Dead Sea Scrolls] disprove any theory that the traditional Hebrew text is perfect or that the King James Version which is based upon it is perfect. They provide many examples of scribal errors in ancient times. There are hundreds of such errors in the complete Isaiah Scroll from the Second Century BC."[2]

The New Testament alone has numerous inconsistencies which disprove that every word in the Bible was perfectly preserved from earliest times. For instance:

1. Matthew spoke of a prophecy by Jeremiah regarding the thirty pieces of silver received by Judas Iscariot as payment for his betrayal of Christ (Matt. 27:9). Our present Bibles have no such prophecy by Jeremiah, but there is one by Zechariah (Zech. 11:12).

2. In the book of Matthew the mother of James and John asked Jesus if her two sons could be honored in his kingdom by being seated at his right and left hands (Matt. 20:20-21). Mark reports, however, that James and John—not their mother—requested the honor (Mark 10:35-37).

3. According to Matthew, after healing Peter's wife's mother, Jesus "healed *all* that were sick" that were brought to him (Matt. 8:16). But Mark

reports that he merely "healed *many*" of those brought to him (Mark 1:34).

4. Matthew says that Jesus's disciples were surprised that a cursed fig tree withered away immediately (Matt. 21:19-20). In Mark, the disciples didn't notice until the next morning that the tree was dead (Mark 11:14, 20-21).

5. The book of Acts has preserved two inconsistent accounts of the conversion of Paul. In the first, those who were with Saul (Paul) *heard* Christ's voice. In the second, "they that were with [Saul] . . . *heard not* the voice of him that spake" (Acts 9:3-7; 22:7-9).

6. Some believe that it is impossible to see God because John wrote, "No man hath seen God at any time." However, Moses plainly recorded that seventy-four men "*saw* the God of Israel" (Exodus 24:10-11).

7. The inspired Luke reports that the *eleven* apostles who remained after Judas Iscariot died were together when Jesus first stood in their midst after his resurrection. But the equally inspired John reports that "Thomas . . . was not with them," making *ten* apostles who were there (Luke 24:33; John 20:19-24).

Many of the earliest scriptures are not found within today's Bibles. Matthew referred to an unpreserved prophecy about Jesus living in Nazareth "that it might be fulfilled which was spoken by the prophets, He shall be called a Nazarene" (Matt. 2:23). Paul wrote of another epistle to the Corinthians (1 Cor. 5:9), possibly an earlier one to the Ephesians (Eph. 3:3), and a letter from the Laodiceans that was in the hands of the Colossians (Col. 4:16). Jude refers to Enoch's prophecy that forewarns of the Lord's coming "with ten thousand of his saints, to execute judgment upon all" (Jude 1:14-15). Did the apostles whose writings are not in the New Testament write? Many believe they did. Origen, an early Christian who lived in the Second and Third Centuries AD, refers to The Gospel of the Twelve Apostles as scripture.[3] Paul referred to teachings of Jesus that were known by the elders at Ephesus but are not found in today's Bibles: "Remember the words of the Lord Jesus, how he said, 'It is more blessed to give than to receive'" (Acts 20:35). What else did Jesus say that is missing from modern Bibles? For forty days he remained with the apostles after his resurrection. What did he teach them then? Certainly, anything he had to say would be important. In addition to these references, the Bible refers to seventeen other books of scripture which have become lost.[4]

"As important as the Bible is to all Christian religions including Latter-day Saints, what prophet has ever announced that the Bible is all that is needed? And, which Bible?" Elder Porter quizzed me.

"I don't know. No one's ever told me."

## Evolution of the Bible

Attempts have been made to clarify the most popular English Bible of today's Protestant world—the King James Version. Italicized words in the KJV indicate efforts to come as closely as possible to what the original authors may have intended. When it was first put together, only 43 words were italicized. Recent editions have hundreds of such words.

In the Third Century BC the Hebrew scriptures (essentially the Old Testament) were translated into Greek for Greek-speaking Jews. That translation is known as the "Septuagint." The earliest Christians had no New Testament. They used the Septuagint. By the Fourth Century AD the New Testament books and letters had been copied and passed around from group to group. It wasn't until the Fourth and Fifth Centuries that the Old and New Testaments were compiled together on scrolls and in codex (book) form. Even then, since there was no prophet to guide the compilers, there was disagreement as to which writings should be included in the canon of scripture. Hebrews, James, II Peter, III John, Jude and Revelation were left out of some earlier Bibles.[5] For more than four centuries, then, early Christians had virtually no "Bible" except the Old Testament.

In the Fourth and Fifth Centuries, Jerome translated the Old and New Testaments into Latin. That edition became known as the *Vulgate*. For roughly 900 years, it was the only Bible used by Christians.

In 1382, John Wycliffe finished his monumental English translation from the Vulgate. Johannes Gutenberg and his associates then printed the *Mazarin Bible* in Latin—the first large book to come off the printing press. Martin Luther extracted the Apocrypha from within the Old Testament and placed it between the two Testaments in his German translation of 1534. It did not include 1 and 2 Esdras (4 Ezra), which he felt contained "absolutely nothing which one could not find more easily in Aesop."[6] Luther also wanted to throw out the book of James. To him it was an "epistle of straw."

*William Tyndale's Bible* of 1525 or 1526 was the first English translation since Wycliffe's. Hiding in Germany from his English king, Tyndale had copies of his New Testament smuggled into England in barrels, cases, bales of cloth, and sacks of flour. He was betrayed, imprisoned, strangled, and burned at the stake by decree of the king of England. His work was completed by Miles Coverdale, who excluded the Apocrypha's *Prayer of Manasseh.*

John Rogers' *Matthew's Bible* of 1537, the first English Bible to be licensed by the king of England, reintroduced the Prayer of Manasseh. The *Great Bible,* also known as the *Chained Bible*—chained to the pulpit so no one would steal it—was authorized by Henry VIII and prepared by Coverdale in 1539-1541. People stood in line for hours to read it! The *Geneva Bible* (often referred to as the *Breeches Bible* because in this version Adam and Eve sewed fig leaves into "breeches") was completed in Switzerland by exiled English scholars in 1560. It was used by William Shakespeare, John Bunyan, and the Plymouth Rock Pilgrims. The *Bishops' Bible* was finished in 1568 by fifteen English theologians, eight of whom were bishops.

English scholars, exiled in Douai, France, translated the Vulgate into English for the Roman Catholic Church. It has come to be known as the *Douai (*also *Douay) Bible.*

King James I, in 1603, appointed 54 scholars (reduced to 47 by 1607 when the translation began) to revise the Bible so that it would have the approval of the many religious parties in England. The *King James Version,* known also as *The Authorized Version,* was completed in 1611 but was revised five times between 1611 and 1769.

When complaints were made by Protestants during the nineteenth century, that certain Catholic beliefs could be justified by using the Apocrypha, printers began producing the Bible without it. Various Bibles followed until in 1940, Edgar Goodspeed combined the Apocrypha with his earlier Bible to form *The Complete Bible: An American Translation.* The *Revised Standard Version* was completed in 1952 without the Apocrypha included. Since then, additional renderings have appeared from time to time.

Which Bible, then, should be consulted if "it" is the final word of God?

# Interpretations

Besides multiple editions, translations, and revisions of the Bible, there is a whole spectrum of interpretations. Pentecostals speak in tongues, but members of most other churches do not. Infants in Baptist families are not baptized as they are in many other religions. Eastern Orthodox priests baptize each person by immersion (or by sprinkling in extreme circumstances) three times—once each for the Father, Son and Holy Ghost.[7] Roman Catholics baptize once by sprinkling. Nazarenes and others feel that baptism is nice but unnecessary because Jesus told the thief on the cross (who presumably was not baptized) that he would be with him in Paradise. Most Congregationalists do not accept the virgin birth. Disciples of Christ reject the doctrine of original sin. Because pianos and organs are not mentioned in the Bible, many branches of the Church of Christ do not use them. The Episcopal Church rejects the authority of the Pope, but preserves other "ancient Catholic creeds." Saluting the flag is regarded by Jehovah's Witnesses as image worship, and Christmas is pagan to them. Sin, to a Lutheran theologian, is not wrongdoing; but rather wrongdoing is the result of a sinful personality. Methodists encourage each individual to interpret the Bible for him or herself "under the guidance of the Holy Spirit." Presbyterians do not believe in the literal resurrection of the body because Paul wrote: "It is sown a natural body, it is raised a spiritual body. There is a natural body, and there is a spiritual body" (I Cor. 15:44). Friends ("Quakers") replaced the usual names of the months and days of the week with numbers "because of their pagan origins." According to Seventh-day Adventists there is no life after death until the second coming of Christ; before then the dead are "asleep." Although they love the person and the message of Jesus, Unitarians do not believe that he is the Messiah.[8]

It is nearly impossible to refer to the Bible to find definite, unerring, doctrinal answers without consulting the prophets. But where are they in modern Christianity?

Never did Jesus or any other Bible prophet say there would be no more scriptures. Nor did he recommend that the Septuagint be thrown out because the New Testament, which was written after his death, would take its place. On the contrary, he implied on numerous occasions that the Hebrew scriptures were essential to living righteously (Matthew 4:4).[9] They, as well as the New Testament, were composed for the benefit of believers who ought to be devoted students of them.

# The Need for Prophets

There is no place within the scriptures that teaches that God will cease using prophets. In fact, the prophet Amos promised: "Surely the Lord God will do nothing, but he revealeth his secret unto his servants the prophets" (Amos 3:7).

The Savior was known as a prophet and referred to himself as such (John 6:14; Matt. 13:57). To his twelve he said, "He that receiveth you receiveth me, and he that receiveth me receiveth him that sent me. He that receiveth a prophet [an apostle] in the name of a prophet [Christ] shall receive a prophet's reward" (Matthew 10:40-41).

In a letter to a former ministerial colleague, Orson Spencer, who was a Latter-day Saint at the time of his writing, wrote: "You and I have been taught that the church can be perfected without prophets; but where is the first scripture to support this view? I was confounded and made dumb, when asked [by a Mormon missionary] why I taught another gospel than what Paul did—why I taught that revelation was ended, when Paul did not—or why I taught that prophets were not needed, when no inspired [Bible] teacher ever taught such a doctrine."[10]

After their Lord left, the prophets were taught by divine revelation. Peter was shown in a vision that the gospel must be taught to gentiles. Also, while fasting and praying, "certain prophets and teachers" at Antioch were instructed by the Holy Ghost: "Separate me Barnabas and Saul for the work whereunto I have called them" (Acts 13:1-5). As with the ancient prophets in Christ's Church, Joseph Smith received divine revelation for every doctrinal statement that he made. Revelatory thoughts were the bedrock of both his and their teachings.

Since Jesus taught that his early Church members needed continual communication with living prophets, the missionaries concluded, it follows that we also need the same source of guidance today. Therefore, there is an important need for a prophet—someone like Joseph Smith.

"That may be," I agreed, "but why wouldn't God pick a theologian who is already trained in Bible interpretation? Someone who is looked up to by the vast majority of Christians? Ministers devote themselves to years of study in order to understand the scriptures and pass on what they have learned to their congregations. Why would he choose a mere boy for his prophet? Especially one who had little formal education and who described himself as 'obscure' and 'of no consequence in the world?'"

Elder Porter responded with a question of his own: "From which of the hundreds of Christian factions would God choose his trained theologian? The very fact that so many denominations exist is proof that they do not agree on interpretations of the Bible and the "narrow way" that Jesus talked about. The Roman Catholic Church has told the world for centuries that the Pope has inherited the seat of Peter, the chief apostle during Jesus's ministry. Catholics don't go so far as to say that the pope is a prophet, but they do believe he represents the Lord Jesus Christ at the head of his one true church. Not many Protestants are converting over to Catholicism because of such a belief. How many Catholics would convert to Protestantism if Billy Graham told the world that God had chosen him to be a prophet and that all Protestant churches should unite and become one? How many Episcopalians, Seventh-day Adventists, Jehovah's Witnesses, Methodists or Presbyterians would swing over to Billy Graham's denomination if he announced that he was a prophet? God evidently wanted to train his prophet himself. He wanted to use someone who was young and fresh—someone who was not steeped in the philosophies of men."

When the lesson drew to a close, Elder Porter invited me to offer the closing prayer. Again I tried weaseling out of it, but who wanted to argue with a bespectacled Goliath?

After my stumbling, mumbling attempt, the elders patted me on the shoulder and said, "Good job, Bill. See? Praying in public isn't hard."

That's what *they* thought.

# 5
# Fruits of a Prophet

When Elders Johnson and Porter returned we sat at the table chit-chatting, trying to enjoy the swamp cooler's breeze as it whooshed by us. The kitchen thermometer read 100° when I retrieved the goodies for us to munch on during the discussion.

Mother made sure she was out of the house when the elders came. She never talked about it to me, but I later learned that she was very worried about her only son taking religion lessons from those Mormons! Having been raised in rural Missouri during the early part of this century, she had been told all she wanted to know about Utah Mormons and their many wives.[1]

On the dining room table I had placed a bunch of bananas, three drinking glasses and butter knives, a cold bottle of milk, and a jar of crunchy-style peanut butter. Elder Porter's nose wrinkled up when I spread the tip of my banana with peanut butter and downed it. A loud "Yuk!" escaped his lips.

"Try it, Elder," I invited. "You'll like it."

"You've never eaten bananas and peanut butter?" Elder Johnson asked in delighted surprise. "Our whole family loves bananas-lettuce-pickles-and-peanut butter sandwiches. Mmm. Delicious," he said as he washed his down with a gulp of milk. "We call them peanana sandwiches."

"Double Yuk! You'll never get me to try it," Elder Porter groaned.

"Now Elder. You sound like me when you ask me to believe that Joseph Smith was a prophet. At least I'm listening to you. You ought to listen to your companion and give peananas a try," I challenged.

"OK. But I won't like it." Elder Porter daubed a micro-portion of peanut butter on the end of his fruit and tasted it. Screwing up his face at first, a smile immediately replaced his frown. "Say, that *is* good. But you'll never get me to eat it with lettuce and pickles."

"Apples and peanut butter are good, too," Elder Johnson smiled.

I had to join Elder Porter in moaning at that suggestion.

After finishing his second peanana Elder Porter expertly moved us on into a prayer and a review of the previous lesson about prophets. "You'll never get me to believe that God called an unseminaried farmboy to be his latter-day spokesman," I told the elders as I leaned back with my arms crossed. "Can you prove that Joseph Smith was a prophet?"

Unmoved, Elder Porter said, "Bill. Just a few minutes ago you heard me say nearly the same thing about peananas. But watching you two made me want to taste it and see for myself. I found out from listening to your experience and doing what you did that peananas are delicious.

"Now, here we are donating two years of our lives away from our families, school and girlfriends. Why? Because we are happy with the restored gospel of Jesus Christ and its prophet, Joseph Smith. We wish to share that happiness with others. Have you seen that joy in our eyes, Bill?"

"You're pretty slick, Elder. Ok, I'll try harder to see for myself. I'll try tasting your restored gospel. But, knowing skeptical me, it won't be easy."

"You're like 'Doubting Thomas' must have been when the other apostles told him they had seen the risen Christ. He had to see for himself. I hope you will continue trying to see, Bill."

After kindly calling me to repentance, this young bear of a man opened up his scriptures and began the discussion.

"Prior to his death and resurrection Jesus taught his disciples about a narrow way that his followers must stay on to be with him forever." Opening his Bible to the book of Matthew, Elder Porter asked me to read.

"Strait is the gate, and *narrow is the way,* which leadeth unto life, and few there be that find it" (Matthew 7:14).

"Jesus also warned his disciples about false prophets who would attempt to entice them along a destructive way: 'Wide is the gate and broad is the way that leadeth to destruction, and many there be which go in thereat,'" Elder Porter read (Matthew 7:13).

"I've always been taught that 'It doesn't matter to which church you belong as long as you believe' or, 'All roads lead to Rome' or, 'As long as we live a good life, we'll make it.' Now you're trying to tell me that such an attitude is wrong?"

"A narrow way of life—not a broad way—was taught by the Lord," Elder Johnson repeated.

"How can a person know what that 'narrow way' is?" I asked somewhat insincerely.

"Jesus explained that he and the other true prophets would lead them," Elder Porter answered. Continuing on in Matthew he read: "'He that receiveth you receiveth me, and he that receiveth me receiveth him that sent me. He that receiveth a prophet [the apostles] in the name of a prophet [Jesus Christ] shall receive a prophet's reward' (Matt. 10:40-41). Jesus further taught that, 'Every good tree [a true prophet] bringeth forth good fruit; but a corrupt tree [a false prophet] bringeth forth evil fruit . . . By their fruits ye shall know them" (Matt. 7:13-20).

"Many theological trees produce seemingly good fruit," I argued. "I can't taste the fruit like we're tasting these peananas. So how can I know if a fruitful tree is Christ's good tree and is, therefore, producing his good fruit? How can I tell if Joseph Smith was a true prophet on Christ's narrow, sure pathway? If what you say is true, my eternal destiny may depend upon my judgment."

# Prayer

Elder Porter took the pad and wrote the word "ASK." "Jesus taught his disciples to 'Ask, and it shall be given you; Seek, and ye shall find; Knock, and it shall be opened unto you: For every one that Asketh receiveth; and he that Seeketh findeth; and to him that Knocketh it shall be opened' (Matt. 7:7-8). To know whether or not Joseph Smith was God's oracle, those who care need to do what Jesus suggested—prayerfully ask as they examine his 'fruit.'"

"I've *been* asking," I answered. "The reason I became religious in the first place is because I prayed for the truth to come into my life. But nothing has happened. I'll keep on praying though. . .

"I think what I need is more information. How am I supposed to test the fruits of Joseph Smith if I don't even know what they are? It seems to me that one of the fruits of a true prophet ought to be his character. What can you tell me about Joseph Smith's character that would convince me that he was a true prophet of God?"

## To Err is Human

Elder Porter thought for a moment. "Some believe that a man must be perfect (whatever that means) in order for him to be selected by God to be his spokesman. Every Bible prophet except one was blemished. 'All have sinned and come short of the glory of God' (Romans 3:23). And, like all others, they sometimes had to repent. However, God still called them to his service."

He explained that everywhere we find those who delight in smearing others. The Pharisees and Sadducees enjoyed trying to find ways to prove that Jesus was preaching against the prophets as well as disobeying their precepts. Because he was undermining their "orthodox" teachings, they influenced a crowd of their followers to demand the crucifixion of Christ.

He told me that much has been written about Joseph Smith's character. Many who knew him have written estimably about him. Others have slandered him unmercifully. Joseph frankly admitted that he was not perfect. And, like Peter and Paul and all the rest, he was a prophet in spite of his weaknesses.

(I later learned that one LDS convert, formerly a Protestant minister, said that "accepting Joseph Smith as a prophet [was his] chief struggle" because Joseph was not perfect. Then he realized that if someone today were to announce that God had given him gold plates containing scripture, "'the entire power structure of the community would turn against him. Joseph Smith was bound to get bad press." He was setting a standard for Joseph Smith "that was not a biblical standard. Only Jesus Christ was perfect.")[2]

"Getting to know Joseph Smith then boils down to whose writings we believe?" I asked. "Whose information do we consider to be factual? Are we honestly interested in knowing the truth, or only libelous tales? Is that what you're suggesting?"

"Yes," Elder Porter said as he took out a handkerchief and wiped a trickle of perspiration from his glasses. "If you ask the right questions and examine his fruits, you will have a clearer picture of his true character."

## Selected Fruits of Joseph Smith

Many fruits associated with Joseph Smith can be examined, Elder Porter continued to explain. No single fruit by itself, except the Book of

Mormon, necessarily shows that Joseph Smith was a prophet. But when they are all considered together, Joseph Smith's claim to being a prophet cannot easily be dismissed. Consider such fruits as Joseph's teachings about God and Jesus Christ, the priesthood of God, what Joseph had to say about divine revelation, the gathering of Israel, Joseph's predictions, the fulfillment of Bible prophecies through Joseph Smith, the doctrine taught by him, temples, his concern for the poor and needy, miracles with which he was associated, the persecution of Joseph Smith and others who were near and dear to him, the kinds of disciples found in the LDS Church, the Book of Mormon and witnesses of the Book of Mormon plates.

"Just a darned minute!" I interrupted. "That's the second or third time you've mentioned the Book of Mormon. What *is* the Book of Mormon? A catechism of Mormon beliefs?"

Elder Porter turned to his companion with an incredulous expression as if questioning why he and Elder Green hadn't already taught me about the Book of Mormon. Elder Johnson silently shrugged his shoulders, as if to say, "Don't blame me!"

Elder Porter then turned to me and apologetically explained that the Book of Mormon is an ancient book, written on gold plates, of an early people who lived somewhere in the Western Hemisphere. He explained that because Joseph Smith translated the Book of Mormon it is the most important fruit to investigate. "Those people were visited by Jesus Christ shortly after his resurrection in Jerusalem," he explained. "The Book of Mormon bears detailed witness of that historical event. Joseph referred to the book as the 'keystone of our religion.' If it is a true account of an ancient people, then Joseph Smith is a true prophet of God, and more importantly to a skeptic like you, that Jesus is truly the Messiah."

"How do you know the Book of Mormon is true?" I asked incredulously.

"Again, Jesus said to prayerfully ask as Joseph's fruits are examined. The only way a person can know if it is true is to read the Book of Mormon sincerely and prayerfully. In addition, witnesses are often provided by the Lord to bear testimony of the truth. Jesus called twelve men to be special witnesses of his ministry and resurrection. Twelve others, including Joseph, were also called as witnesses to swear that they saw the original golden plates of the Book of Mormon. Did the early twelve actually see their Lord's resurrected body? Did the twelve latter-day witnesses truly see engraved gold records? Those are important questions. If the Book of Mormon—the keystone of our religion—is true, then Joseph Smith was indeed a prophet, and what we are teaching you is true."

"It will take me a while to grasp that one," I laughed. "Your tale about the Book of Mormon sounds pretty much like science fiction to me." But it did sound interesting since I was a devoted science fiction fan.

"You have already told me about some of Joseph's other fruits, like his concept of God," I reminded the elders. "You say that not one of the fruits by itself, with the exception of the Book of Mormon, can prove that Joseph Smith was a true prophet of God. That's probably true. But if the Book of Mormon is fictional, then Joseph Smith is a false prophet. There would be no need to even consider his other fruits."

The elders looked like they wanted to answer, but I felt that we had reached a good closing point in the discussion. They reluctantly stopped the discussion, set up another appointment and left.

I could tell they were disappointed that they hadn't accomplished what they had set out to do. That only bothered me a little bit. After all, I rationalized, they were only guests in my home, so I should decide what I did and did not want to discuss.

# 6
# When Reasoning
# Replaced Revelation

Elder Porter loved to tell Mormon jokes before we began our discussions. As we sat at the table talking, this time without anything to munch on, he politely asked if I'd like to hear one.

"Sure, if it's clean."

Smiling he said, "My girlfriend, Becky, wrote this in her last letter: A woman accidentally dialed a Mormon bishop when she was calling the record store to order a new album. Not realizing her mistake, she asked, 'Do you have *A Winning Smile That Moves Me?*'"

"'I sure do,' answered the bishop. 'But I also have a wife and seven kids.'"

"'Is that a new record?'" she asked.

"'Well, not exactly, but it's way above average.'"

Elder Johnson said through his laughter, "You ought to hear him back in our apartment. And last week I almost had an accident on my bicycle he had me laughing so hard."

After some more conversation and a prayer, I decided to bring up my questions before they could begin with another topic. "All week I've thought about what you told me about the need for prophets and how to discern one by examining his fruits. But I just can't bring myself to accepting Joseph Smith as a true prophet. My Protestant upbringing continues to commit me to view Protestant ministers as authorities to look to for answers about religion. But I would like to know why Christ's prophets aren't found among today's Protestant and Catholic leaders."

Drawing another picture of a church building sitting on a foundation of apostles and prophets with Jesus Christ forming the cornerstone, Elder Johnson wrote below it: "Church of Jesus Christ." Opening his Bible to Ephesians 2:20 Elder Porter once more showed me that the Church of Jesus Christ was "built upon the foundation of the apostles and prophets, Jesus Christ himself being the chief corner stone." He then went on to teach me about what LDS members call the great apostasy—the decline of earliest Christianity after the martyrdom of the apostles. According to him, corruption had crept into the Church of Christ so that today, no branch of Christianity has come down through the ages untainted. None is the unblemished Church of Jesus Christ that he founded when he walked the earth.

Because the elders were so young and had no degrees in history, I did not believe most of their conclusions. But after later reading a number of articles and books about the evolution of the Catholic and Protestant religions, I came to realize that an apostasy from Christ's early Church had indeed occurred.[1]

Elder Porter continued explaining that the apostles did not lead the Church of Jesus Christ for long. Dark times were already upon them even during their mortal ministries. Shortly after its founding, the Church came to an end because of the martyrdoms of the apostles and the consequent contamination that came into it in the absence of their prophetic leadership.

At this point Elder Johnson erased the foundation of apostles and prophets and asked, "What will happen to any building if the foundation crumbles?"

"It won't last very long, that's for sure."

"Exactly. When the apostles were no longer leading Christ's Church, inspired leadership ceased. The membership of the Church was left on its own making it possible for more and more heresy to spread amongst them."

He explained that decay was not unexpected nor was it unique in Israelite history. Even during Jesus's ministry, Israel was in the midst of apostasy. More than 400 years had passed since the last true prophet—Malachi—had spoken. Throughout the intervening centuries, a group of ecclesiastical rulers known as the Sanhedrin had evolved and had assumed—as much as their Roman conquerors would allow—political and religious control over the people. Their philosophy became mingled with the scriptures in the absence of prophets.

## Bible Predictions of General Apostasy

Elder Porter then began a discussion of how the primitive Church of Jesus Christ fell into apostasy, although he did not use as much detail as follows. The Bible tells of future apostasy. "The days come, saith the Lord

God, that I will send *a famine* in the land, not a famine of bread, nor a thirst for water, but *of hearing the words of the Lord;* and they shall wander from sea to sea, and from the north even to the east, they shall run to and fro to seek the word of the Lord, and shall not find it" (Amos 8:11-12).

"How do you know that Amos isn't referring to the apostasy between Malachi and Jesus?" I asked.

"He could be. But New Testament prophets also foretold an apostasy," Elder Johnson said.

Paul warned the saints that *"of your own selves* shall men arise . . . to *draw away disciples"* (Acts 20:30). He later reported that his companion, Demas, had forsaken him (2 Tim. 4:10). In an epistle to the Corinthians, he said that he had heard of *divisions among* them (I Cor. 11:18). Correcting the saints who mistakenly believed that the second coming of Christ was imminent, Paul said: "Let no man deceive you by any means: for that day shall not come, except *there come a falling away first"* (2 Thess. 2:1-3). Judaizers—a faction of Christian Jews—wanted to retain parts of the Law of Moses. Paul accused them of *"quickly deserting"* Christ's teachings and *turning to* a different gospel (Gal. 1:6, RSV) He then counseled, "Though we, or an angel from heaven, preach any other gospel unto you than that which we have preached unto you, let him be accursed" (Gal. 1:7).

Peter cautioned: *"There shall be false teachers among you,* who privily shall bring in damnable heresies . . . And *many shall follow their pernicious ways"* (2 Peter 2:1-3).

John wrote of mounting corruptions: *"It is the last hour . . .* so *now* many antichrists *have come;* therefore we know that *it is* the last hour" (1 John 2:18-19).

Jude alerted the saints in Syria and Arabia that in the Church *"there are* certain men crept in unawares . . . ungodly men, *turning the grace of our God into lasciviousness,* and denying the only Lord God, and our Lord Jesus Christ . . . The apostles . . . told you there should be mockers . . . who should walk after their own ungodly lusts. *These be they"* (Jude 4, 17-19).

## Heresy in the Early Christian Church

During my later reading I learned that a group known as Gnostics believed that they had secret "knowledge" from Jesus. According to them, spirit is perfect and matter is imperfect, therefore matter is evil. God, the perfectly good spirit, can have nothing to do with evil matter. Since man is a creature of matter, God and man can have no direct relationship. Intermediary deities known as aeons could talk with God, since they were imperfect spirits. Paul warned Timothy to "avoid the godless chatter and contradictions of what is falsely called *knowledge*" (1 Tim. 6:20-21, RSV).

Similarly, Docetists—a branch of Gnostics—believed that Christ's resurrected body was an illusion. It only *seemed* that he had flesh because man's material eyes, which are evil, can only discern error.[2]

Hegesippus, who lived in the first part of the second century wrote: "Thebuthis made a beginning, secretly to corrupt [the Church] on account of his not being made bishop [of Jerusalem]. He was one of those seven sects among the Jewish people. Of these also [were] . . . the . . . Simonians . . . the Cleobians . . . the Dositheans . . . the Gortheonians . . Masbotheans . . . Hence also the Meandrians, the Marcionists, and Carpocratians and Valentinians, and Basilidians, and the Saturnillians, *every one introducing his own peculiar opinions,* one differing from the other. From these sprung the false Christs and the *false prophets and false apostles, who divided the unity of the Church* by the introduction of *corrupt doctrines* against God and against His Christ."[3]

## Changes Within the Church

Following the martyrdoms and deaths of the apostles, a professional clergy evolved. Distinctions of rank arose. Bishops of congregations in wealthier cities assumed authority over poorer ones. Those in branches claiming apostolic ties such as Jerusalem, Ephesus, Corinth, Rome and Antioch had even higher status. Only those with wealth or education were ordained.

About a hundred years after Hegesippus, the concerned Cyprian who was bishop of Carthage recorded: "The pastors and the deacons each forgot their duty. Many bishops gave themselves up to secular pursuits . . . They traveled through distant provinces in quest of pleasure and gain . . . [and]

were insatiable in their thirst of money: They possessed estates by fraud and multiplied usury."[4]

With no inspired prophets, scripture writing ceased. Disagreements about which of the hundreds of circulating documents were enlightened were rampant. For example, Marcion, a Gnostic, taught that the Old Testament was not Christian. He felt that it should be left out of the canon and only the Gospel of Luke and ten epistles of Paul retained.[5]

Eastern converts brought into the church ideas of the esteemed Hellenic thinkers. As the Hebrew scribes did with the Old Testament prophets' inspired thoughts, teachings of the "unlearned and ignorant" apostles (Acts 4:13) were replaced with the "educated" logic of the philosophers. In the popular minds, no fisherman, tax collector or tent maker could come close in scholastic attainment and reasoning abilities to scholars such as Plato and Aristotle.

With no prophetic voices, philosophical thought brought unscriptural changes in doctrine and unwarranted additions into Christianity such as pomp and splendor, adoration of images, the concept of the depravity of man with its accompanying doctrine of "original sin," baptism of infants and adults by sprinkling and pouring, the doctrine of Real Presence (transubstantiation), asceticism, celibacy, monasticism, the sign of the cross, icons, relics, genuflecting, rosaries, canonization, deathbed repentance, purgatory, stockpiling of good works, indulgences, holy water, veneration of Mary and other saints, the Immaculate Conception, Mary's perpetual virginity, the infallibility of the popes, church control of the state, buying and selling church offices, predestination, prophets no longer needed, the cessation of revelation, a closed Bible, the unimportance of the physical body, justification by faith alone, and authoritative tradition.

For the greater part of two thousand years the philosophies of men have had corruptive influence on the Lord's truth. An LDS convert says that "eight distinct doctrines" brought about by philosophy constantly bothered him while he was an ordained Catholic priest: celibacy, transubstantiation, the infallibility of the pope, the immaculate conception, mediatrix of all graces (Mary is a mediator along with Christ), Mary a co-redeemer with Christ, the priest being called "father," and the power of priests to forgive sins.[6]

Forgotten were the Bible's true teachings about God's identity, his relationship to mankind, premortality, life's purpose, eternal progression, the law of divine justice, free agency, the sacredness and importance of a physical body, the Christian identity and kinship with Israel, covenant making, the Abrahamic covenant, unending family bonds, Melchizedek and Aaronic priesthoods, ongoing revelation, living prophets, the temple and its ordinances, conversational prayer, faith and works, scripture writing, the law of consecration, the gifts of the Spirit, the laying on of hands, the gathering of Israel, universal resurrection, baptism by immersion for the remission of sins by priesthood authority, voluntary tithing, vicarious work for the deceased, and other important truths.

## The Identity of God is Lost

Theologians continually grappled with the concept of God. Who was he? What was he like? Neo-Platonic thought, with apostate Hebrew conclusions, advocated that only one God was possible. Yet how could Jesus be God when he worshipped another?

Two learned Alexandrians—Arius and Athanasius—acridly disagreed about the nature and number of God. Their disagreement led to a profound split within Christianity which in turn led to the description of God upon which most Christian churches of today base their beliefs.

The popular Arius believed that the Son is inferior to his father because the Father had no beginning, while Jesus was created and therefore had a beginning. The even more admired Athanasius proclaimed that the Father and Son are equal. Jesus was never created because he was co-eternal with the Father.

Non-Christians were amused. The heathen clearly knew who their gods . were. To them, it was hilarious that Christians who claimed to have the true religion were arguing among themselves about the god they worshipped.

Alarmed because Christianity could not pray to a definite deity for the welfare of his empire, Constantine, the Roman emperor and chief priest over all the religions of the state (Pontifex Maximus), ordered Christian leaders to settle the question once and for all time. In 325 AD he gathered Christian churchmen into what has come to be known as the Council of Nicea. Only 318 of approximately 2,000 bishops attended. The emperor, a pagan, presided.

For two months the priests bickered. Under the emperor's impatient thumb, a formula was agreed upon—the Nicene Creed. It was a compromise and few were completely satisfied. But the "Nicean Compromise" has become the basis for Christianity's various credos about Deity. The original creed stated:

> We believe in one God, Father Almighty, maker of all things visible and invisible; and in one Lord Jesus Christ the Son of God, begotten of the Father, only-begotten, that is from the substance ['immaterial essence'] of the Father, God from God, Light from Light, true God from true God, begotten, not made, of one substance with the Father, through whom all things were made, both the things in heaven and the things on earth; who for us men and our salvation came down and was made flesh, was made man, suffered, and rose again on the third day, ascended into heaven, and cometh to judge the quick and the dead; and in the Holy Spirit. But those who say 'There was once when he was not,' and 'Before his generation he was not,' and 'He was made out of nothing;' or pretend that the Son of God is of another subsistence or substance, or created or alterable, the Catholic [universal] church anathematizes.[7]

At the Council of Nicea, Christianity officially divorced itself from the God of the Bible. Logic became Christianity's god. Reasoning replaced revelation.

# Church and State

Constantine took the Christian church under his protective wing as he did the other religions of the empire. One important decree he announced, which favored the growth of the church, was that Christians living in cities (not the country folk) could have their Sabbath—Sunday—as a day of worship. This meant a day of rest from work. Many city pagans joined the church so they too could have a day off each week. Christianity eventually became popular and was adopted by the state as its official religion. With official state recognition, competition for church offices intensified. The office of bishop evolved into a higher status symbol than that of a general.

# The Papacy

At one time, various bishops were referred to as "popes"—a title found nowhere in holy writ. The Roman branch, because of its location at the seat of the empire and its supposed link to Peter, emerged as the dominant one. Its bishop became the only one retaining the title of Pope. Wherever the church was established, popes claimed the right to direct the affairs of nations. If an emperor failed to court favor with the pontiff (pope), he could be excommunicated.

Among the more than two hundred and sixty men listed as successors to Peter, many have been sincere and excellent churchmen. Leo the Great (440-464 AD) is often mentioned as one. The popes within the last century or so have also earned fine reputations. However, corrupt popes are scattered generously throughout historic Christianity.

In 1309, confusion over who was pope almost eliminated that office. The French king, Philip the Fair, succeeded in getting the pope to move the church's headquarters to Avignon, France, which antagonized the Italian cardinals. An Italian pope was elected by them, which meant there were now two pontiffs. A council was called in Pisa, Italy, to solve the problem by selecting a new pope. The rivals each expected to emerge as the new leader. When yet another pope was elected, the first two refused to resign, so that there were then three. This situation continued until 1414, when Martin V in Rome finally emerged as the only claimant to Peter's supposed papal seat.

## Persecution by Christians

As the early centuries passed, the persecuted became the persecutors. Christians, who had rightly complained about Roman persecutions, began killing, torturing and banishing non-believers in the name of Christ.

Beginning in 1095 and continuing well into the thirteenth century, Christians were urged to unite in crusades, where even armies of children participated, to reclaim Jerusalem from the Moslems—another example of philosophy usurping revelation.

Christian depravity reached a sickening climax during the various Inquisitions. Their purpose was to "save the souls" of unwed mothers, homosexuals, apostates, heretics, Jews, witches, warlocks, alchemists and anyone else not favored by the ecclesiastical elite. Being suspected of having even a forbidden thought was cause enough for the rack or the stake. Anyone could be accused by anyone else as long as two adult males swore that the accusation was true.

Even the renowned were sometimes indicted. Galileo Galilei, the eminent astronomer and physicist, came under the Inquisition's scrutiny for reasoning that Nicolaus Copernicus was correct—that the earth revolves around the sun and is not at the center of the universe. Galileo was found to be at odds with church dogma and was forced to say that he no longer believed Copernicus's heliocentric conclusions. Sentenced to confinement in his villa in Florence, Italy, he was watched constantly for the remainder of his life. Copernicus's writings were then placed on the church's *Index* of prohibited books, where they remained for two centuries.

The general Christian populace, ignorant of actual Bible teachings because of their illiteracy or because they had no access to a Bible, gleefully enjoyed the agony of "sinners" as they were burned at the stake or tortured to rid Christianity of the sinner's supposed corruptive influence. All the people knew about original Christianity was what their church leaders taught. The leaders themselves were not necessarily at fault in urging such horrible scenes because they had also been taught by their leaders that such hideousness was the will of God.

As Amos predicted, the dank days came during the Dark Ages when there was indeed a terrible "famine of . . . hearing the words of the Lord." If there were any who ran "to and fro to seek the word of the Lord" it was they, who could for centuries literally "wander from sea to sea, and from the north even to the east" and would "not find it" (Amos 8:11-12).

"Some of the things you've told me I've already read about in history classes," I informed the elders. "But frankly, you young men do not bring with you the air of authority that a clergyman would bring into our home. Even the Pope would seem more authoritative to me.

"Those churchmen would, no doubt, have a different viewpoint," I continued. "They might admit, for instance, that the original Church of Christ, if he actually founded one, was no longer on earth. They might say that the Christian churches of today are trying to bring Christ's Church back—to overhaul their systems of worship so that eventually the original Church will again be available. I have also been told that Christ intended that the various factions of his Church be here so people can choose the one which they are more comfortable in. The Pope would say that the original Church has been on earth since the time of Christ and that religious tradition is equal to the scriptures in determining which religion is true."

"That's true," Elder Porter admitted. "But as the Lord said, the only way you can know the truth about anything as important as religion is to study and pray."

"I know something about the crusades and the inquisitions," I went on, "and honestly it is beyond me how those who claimed to be following in the footsteps of Jesus and safeguarding his religion could equate such depravity with the Lord's teachings about love even of one's enemies. But such hideous mutilation and butchery of human beings is not carried on today. Christianity has changed its ways and its leaders are clearly trying to do the best that they know how."

"True. Fine religious leaders are found in all religions. Which one has a true prophet, though?"

"That's what I'd like to know," I responded. "Where are the prophets today? Why hasn't God raised up prophets like he did in Bible times?"

"He has."

"Of course, you say that he has. But I can't accept Joseph Smith as a prophet. However, you're partially right in your reasoning: If Christ's Church became corrupt, Jesus surely would not leave mankind that way forever. He would have provided some way for his Church and prophets to be brought back. But I believe it would be through some already existing Christian church."

# 7
# The Restoration of Revelation

Since the hour had grown late, the missionaries had postponed their answer to my challenge about Jesus providing a way for bringing his Church back through already established Protestant or Catholic churches. Instead of making an appointment for the next week, as they usually did, they agreed to return the following day.

From the time I invited the elders in, that next day I could tell there was something different about Elder Johnson. He seemed more relaxed and for once took an active part in the conversations we always had before talking about religion. After we prayed, Elder Johnson was the first to speak. "I've thought about a story that my grandfather used to tell that might help yesterday's lesson:"

There was once a village potter who worked very hard at his trade. Though his other pottery was excellent, his vases became particularly valuable because of their beauty in design and in symmetry. Whenever he was asked why his vases were so wonderfully decorated and had few blemishes in them he replied that he had not yet made the perfect vase—he always kept trying for perfection.

After many years of loving toil, the gray-headed potter at long last cried tears of joy when he uncovered a vase from the hot ashes of his fire. There it was! A perfect vase! No stains blemished its form. No hairline cracks scarred its surface. No dents or waves marred its lips and body. Perfectly symmetrical, it sparkled with the beautiful colors and care of a true craftsman. 'This vase will never be sold,' he told his wife. 'It will be mounted in a locked glass case and placed outside each day for all who walk by to admire.'

One day the potter forgot to lock his case. It just so happened that a stranger came to the potter's shop that day to purchase one of his famous vases. The potter was busy at his wheel in the back room and did not see nor hear him enter. As he waited, the stranger's eye caught sight of the beautiful vase inside the unlocked case. He opened the glass door to lift it out. Holding the vase up to admire it, he turned it around and around in his fingers.

Just then the potter came out of his workshop to the front of the building where he sold his goods. 'Ah. You like my vase do you?' he asked as he got ready to take it from the stranger before it accidentally slipped from his grasp.

Startled, the stranger jerked and dropped the beautiful vase, breaking it into many pieces. "Oh no!" he exclaimed. "I am so sorry! Here, allow me to pick up the pieces and glue them together."

Kneeling among the fragments, the potter cried out through streaming tears, 'It's no use! It's no use! It was a perfect vase! It had no cracks nor blemishes whatsoever! If you glued it back together, flaws will remain. There is no way this vase that I worked so many years to create can be patched together perfectly. I will need to start again and produce a new vase from scratch."

"Now let's say the potter is Jesus Christ, the stranger is a kind theologian, and the vase is Christ's perfect Church," Elder Johnson proposed. "The analogy is imperfect, of course, because the potter produced the perfect vase through trial and error. But you get the idea, Bill. Why couldn't the stranger put the vase back together into its state of perfection even though he was sorry and wanted to do so with all of his heart?"

"Because cracks and chips would remain. The potter was the only one who could make a new one," I responded. "But theologians have the Bible. They can study it and learn what Jesus wanted his Church to be like and then bring it back."

"That's what they've been doing for centuries and it has created more and more denominations and factions within Christianity. And what about prophets and apostles—the foundation of Christ's Church?"

"The theologians could call them from among other Christians," I weakly replied, realizing I was losing an argument to a brand-new missionary.

"The Bible tells us that Christ's apostles were chosen and called by him—not by the religious leaders of their day. 'Ye have not chosen me, but I have chosen you, and ordained you,' Jesus told his apostles (John 15:16). Unless a church that was pieced together by Christian theologians sits on a foundation of Christ's personally-selected apostles and prophets, it will once more fall apart."

Elder Porter then took over and taught me about what he called the "restoration" of Christ's gospel. He stated that although the various modern Christian religious leaders are generally good men and women, none can assume the authority to restore Christ's Church along his or her denominational lines. Nor would they have the knowledge of what to bring back unless they were taught by divine revelation. Only Christ could bring back his Church uncorrupted by the philosophies of men that continue in modern Christianity. It would be done the way Amos predicted when he said that God would do nothing except through his personally selected prophets. Since no modern Christian church will claim to have apostles and prophets, God would have to provide such a person outside of traditional Christianity. Roger Williams believed that. The founder of Rhode Island and leader in the fight for religious freedom during the 17th century, he resigned as minister of his church because he realized that there was at that time "no regularly constituted church of Christ on earth . . . nor can there be until new apostles are sent by the great head of the Church."[1]

## Bible Predictions About a Restoration

The restoration of Christ's Church was predicted in the Bible. "In the second year of the reign of Nebuchadnezzar," Daniel interpreted a special dream of the king's. It foretold "what shall be in the latter days." The king had seen "a great image" which represented kingdoms that would come after his. "In the days of these kings," Daniel prophesied, "shall the God of heaven set up a kingdom, which shall never be destroyed" (Dan. 2:1-48).

The Lord said through his prophet, Malachi: "I will send you Elijah the prophet before the coming of the great and dreadful day of the Lord. And he shall turn the heart of the fathers to the children, and the heart of the children to their fathers, lest I come and smite the earth with a curse" (Malachi 4:5-6).

After Jesus's ascension, Peter taught about the restoration about which he had learned from Jesus on the Mount of Transfiguration as recorded in Matthew 17:1-13. He told a crowd who had witnessed a miraculous healing that "times of refreshing shall come from . . . the Lord; and he shall send Jesus Christ . . . whom the heaven must receive until the times of restitution [restoration] of all things" (Acts 3:12-21).

In order for something to be restored, it must first disappear. The fulness of Christ's gospel was, evidently, not going to continue. After its disappearance, it would be brought back, according to Jesus (Matt. 11:11-14; 17:1-13).

John, who was present with Peter when Jesus taught them about the restoration, wrote of "an angel" coming from heaven "having the everlasting gospel to preach . . . [unto] every people" (Revelation 14:6-7). If the complete gospel had remained down through the ages, there would be no need for John's prophecy about a future angel coming from heaven "having the everlasting gospel."

Paul spoke of an era when Jesus would "gather together in one all things in Christ" which would occur during "the dispensation of the fulness of times" (Eph. 1:10).

# Age of Religious Enlightenment

Peter's prophesy about "times of refreshing" were just that—times. It was spread out over many years. Torture and execution in the name of Christ continued well into the 17th and 18th centuries, as is evidenced in the Salem witch trials, but that didn't interfere with the enlightened plans of the truly courageous. As the depravity of the Christian church became more obvious, and as outcries were made by those brave enough to cry out, the Lord helped certain individuals introduce important ideas for change. Rudiments of refreshing religious freedom began to emerge from the smothering political and ecclesiastical blanket of medieval despotism.

## Martin Luther

Certainly one of those most responsible for permanent refreshment was Martin Luther. An Augustinian monk, Luther dared to nail to the door of the All Saints' Church in Wittenberg his "Ninety-Five Theses" that challenged the sale of indulgences, which were another result of philosophy taking the place of divine revelation. Although he did not wish to found a new church, Luther's blatant questioning of papal edicts led to much of Europe eventually breaking away from the church of Rome.

For his public proclamation that the Bible, and not the pope, was infallible, Luther was condemned by the pontiff as a heretic in a document known as a papal bull. Luther burned the bull and, in 1521, was excommunicated. The Catholic Emperor Charles V ordered him to appear before the

Imperial Diet at Worms so he could formally retract his statements. Although Luther journeyed to Worms, he would not recant. The emperor refused him permission to preach.

Finding protectors among the princes of Germany, Luther hid in the Wartburg castle. It was there that he translated the New Testament into German. While in hiding, he began organizing his own church, defying the emperor and the pope.

Though much of what Luther taught reflects the philosophies of his medieval upbringing, he was remarkable in his courage as he waded into his own formidable church. Ironically, though he believed "freewill is but an idle word," Luther was instrumental in bringing about the eventual freedom of religious thought enjoyed by much of the world today.

## Ulrich Zwingli

In 1519, Ulrich Zwingli of Zurich, Switzerland, also a Catholic priest, began preaching his views. Zwingli's ideas spread throughout Switzerland and southern Germany. Needing all the help they could receive, friends of Protestantism brought him and Luther together hoping for a union between the two. Although compromises were made in some of their ideas, neither would give in on their interpretation of the Lord's Supper. Whereas Zwingli felt partaking of the bread and wine was merely symbolic, Luther believed Christ's body and blood were actually present in the emblems. Luther also taught that a Christian could do anything not specifically forbidden by the scriptures; Zwingli preached that they could do only those things which were expressly stated in the Bible. A consolidation between the two failed.

## John Calvin

Born in France, John Calvin became known for his teachings about the utter depravity of man and of predestination.[2] In Geneva, Calvin founded a theological institute where Protestant leaders from throughout Europe heard him teach. They took his conclusions to their home states where Presbyterianism, Puritanism, Congregationalism and the Reformed churches of Switzerland, Holland, and Germany eventually took root.

These and other courageous reformers risked their eternal souls as well as their mortal lives in voicing their opinions. In their minds, if they were wrong they would burn forever in hell. If they were caught—and many were—they were burned at the stake.

## Counter Reformation

Because of continued dissent from within and because of the Protestant Reformation, the Roman church began a Counter Reformation in an effort to cleanse itself. In so doing Rome hoped to bring the Protestant factions back into the mother church.

## Protestantism

As the years went by, churches branched off from one another when disgruntled members felt that some teachings were non-Biblical or that they had discovered doctrine in the Bible that was not being taught. Today, hundreds of Christian denominations exist under the three general headings of Roman Catholic, Eastern Orthodox, and Protestant.

## A New Birth of Freedom

"Times of refreshing" neared fruition when concepts for a unique kind of government matured. The Magna Charta, the Mayflower Compact, and Roger Williams and William Penn's free religious societies paved the way for a written guarantee that certain basic rights could be enjoyed by all—not merely the wealthy and powerful.

In the late 18th century, an inspired constitution granting citizens almost unheard of rights and freedoms was composed and signed by some of the most knowledgeable and wise men to ever come together into one body. A new "nation conceived in liberty and dedicated to the proposition that all men are created equal" was founded. Though not all, such as children, women and slaves, were then free to vote, the United States of America emerged from a revolutionary concept of representative government based on rule by the people. Its Bill of Rights granted freedom of religion, speech, the press, and assembly, among others.

It was an enlightened idea, and an enlightening ideal that would create a world climate of religious tolerance and freedom. Refreshing preparation for the ushering in of "the dispensation of the fulness of times" was completed. The world was now prepared for angels of God to "restore all things."

# Birth of a Prophet

On December 23, 1805, fourteen short years after religious freedom was granted in the United States of America, a prophet of God was born—

the first since the martyrdom of the apostles. Born during winter solstice when the effulgent sun begins expanding its radiance northward, Joseph Smith came into the world to help the Lord spread his spiritual illumination. Once more the God of heaven would begin flooding mankind with his everlasting light.

Another fourteen brief years passed. In answer to humble prayer, Joseph was visited by the Father and the Son in a grove of trees. From the lips of the Holy One of Israel, he learned that he was a chosen messenger who was to prepare mankind for the "harvest" when Christ would "gather the wheat" and separate it from "the tares" that would be burned at his second coming (Matt. 13:24-30).

On April 6, 1830, Jesus Christ organized his kingdom one last time before his second coming. The Church of Jesus Christ of Latter-day Saints was established through His servant, Joseph Smith. "Strangers and foreigners" are once again invited to become "fellowcitizens with the saints" within the "household of God" which is built upon the foundation of [living] apostles and prophets [with] Jesus Christ . . . being the chief corner stone" (Ephesians 2:19-20). As in Christ's earliest Church, all who become saints are automatically adopted into the house of Israel and are, therefore, the children of Abraham.

Foreordained in the heavens, Joseph was born to help ministering angels having the everlasting gospel restore all things within the indestructible latter-day kingdom of Nebuchadnezzar's dream during this the dispensation of the fulness of times when Christ shall make a sudden appearance at his temple.[3]

Although I didn't like to admit it, after the elders explained the restoration of the true gospel of Jesus Christ through a prophet, it made more sense than the attempts at gradual rejuvenation through ecumenical councils that were taking place in Christianity. All that seemed to do, it now seemed to me, was spread more of men's philosophies throughout the various Christian churches, because Christian leaders believed that inspired prophets were no longer needed.

True Christianity could not, I was beginning to decide, spring from a base that included the horrors of the inquisitions and crusades. None of the Christian churches that participated in such agonies during those times could be the true Church of Jesus Christ, I decided. Neither could any church be the true Church if they sympathized with such methods to gain converts. Therefore, those particular churches were almost eliminated in my quest for truth.

But, I still couldn't help wondering whether Jesus actually founded a formal church organization. Catholics (including the Eastern Orthodox), Mormons, and a few Protestant groups believed he did, but most Protestant leaders generally agreed that he did not. And, was Jesus truly the Messiah? If he was, was Joseph Smith his prophet of the restoration?

"Joseph Smith was untrained in theology, but so were most Bible prophets," I observed aloud. "God had no requirement for his prophets to be schooled in the rabbinical seminaries. As you elders said the other day, perhaps Joseph Smith was used instead of seminary graduates because he was less likely to have been tainted by the philosophies of men. Joseph could have been God's clean slate through whom he worked to bring back his Church with its original precepts and ordinances. But there is a major difference between 'could have been' and 'actually was.'"

"The restoration of the gospel of Jesus Christ was very similar to Jesus's founding of his Church when he was here personally," Elder Porter pointed out. "He came to earth after centuries of apostasy as did Joseph Smith. Jesus was not a graduate from a school of rabbis; neither did Joseph Smith graduate from a Christian seminary. Jesus organized his Church from scratch—not from pieces of the existing apostate religion that was there to greet him when he came to earth. He said that 'No man putteth a piece of new cloth unto an old garment, for that which is put in to fill it up taketh from the garment, and the rent [tear] is made worse (Matt. 9:16).' Similarly when Jesus restored his Church through his latter-day prophet, he began again with a fresh and unprejudiced mind."

"Every Sunday we have services at 10:00 and 2:00. Why don't you come and meet the members and see for yourself what the Church is like?" Elder Johnson suggested. "We have an excellent Sunday School teacher who will try to answer any questions you ask."

# 8
# A Visit to a "Mormon" Church

A month or so after the missionaries first came to our door, I nervously ventured a visit to the only "Mormon" church in town. The elders had informed me where it was.

It's a scary thing to go to another church by yourself—especially one that I'd heard only negative things about most of my life. I hadn't seen Heidi Kopp since she sent the missionaries over. She was a pretty girl who was normal in every way, but I didn't know anyone else in the LDS Church. Though the elders and Heidi were like everyone else I knew, for some reason I expected to meet fanatical zealots swooping down on me with demands to become one of them. Idle talk about people rolling and dancing in the aisles in some churches caused me almost to expect that kind of exhibition from Mormons.

## First Impressions

As I did when I decided to pray on Mt. Rubidoux, I drove by the church a couple of times before I finally made up my mind to park the car and go in. Walking up the steps that morning was a nice looking family consisting of a father and mother and three little girls whose mother obviously had made identical flowered dresses for each of them. When I strolled up the sidewalk and paused for a few moments in front of the church, I was impressed by the exterior of the building. It was a beautiful design, but not ornate. The name "Mormon" was nowhere to be found. Instead, a very simple sign greeted the visitor: "The Church of Jesus Christ of Latter-day Saints." Although a steeple adorned the building, there was no cross. Jesus Christ was supposed to be the founder of their Church; so why wasn't a cross decorating it?[1]

Others were entering the building as I approached. Inside, Heidi and the elders greeted me. People were quietly visiting in cushioned pews while others were bustling about, engrossed in their various responsibilities. None of the women wore pioneer bonnets or floor-length gowns as I supposed they would, nor were the men wearing overalls stuffed in scuffed clodhoppers.

Elders Porter and Johnson introduced me to several members. Their friendliness was wonderful and kind as we shook hands and got acquainted. Guiding me through the hallways and classrooms, the missionaries steered me to a basketball court and a stage. I was told that the "cultural hall" was used for social activities such as basketball, volleyball, plays, dances, concerts, dinners, and wedding receptions.

Certain customs seemed unique. Sunday School was held in the morning; Sacrament meeting was in the afternoon.[2] No dominant figure monopolized the pulpit. Someone welcomed everyone, another led the singing, and still somebody else gave the invocation. The opening prayer was a simple conversation with God—not an over-praising to what seemed to me must be egotistical God which I had heard elsewhere. After the prayer, the congregation startled me by chorusing a quiet "Amen." Even though this block of hours was only for Sunday School lessons, the Sacrament (which I'd also known as the Lord's Supper or Communion) was passed among the members. It was also quite different than what I'd experienced in other churches. Neatly dressed teenage boys blessed and passed bread and water instead of wine or grape juice throughout the congregation.

Children nervously delivered talks along with adults. The talks were inspiring, but they were not professionally delivered. I also learned that Mormons were not always as strait-laced from the pulpit as I supposed they would be. One of the speakers began his short sermon by telling us about the time when he and his wife were driving home from a Sacrament meeting where he had spoken. Noticing a tiny cut on his jaw, his wife asked him what had happened. He explained that he had cut himself shaving that morning because he was concentrating so much on preparing his talk. Smiling, she teased, "You should have concentrated on your face and cut your talk."

The congregational singing was less impassioned than in the Church of the Nazarene which I had been attending with our next door neighbors. In the Nazarene Church they have fun, rocking with the rhythm. I would have thought members of a church that claims the famous Tabernacle Choir would enjoy group singing, too. They did, but not like the Nazarenes.

I was surprised that collection plates were never passed. I wondered how the ministers, organists, musicians and secretaries were paid. The missionaries later explained that officers, teachers and clerks serve voluntarily in the LDS Church.[3]

The most impressive thing I discovered that first day was the caliber of the Latter-day Saints I met. I was surprised and happy to become acquainted with low-keyed, friendly housewives, teachers, secretaries, two school principals, Kaiser Steel mill employees, custodians, a mechanic, a storekeeper, a nurse, law enforcement officers, carpenters, and youth of all sorts—even a mortician and his family.[4]

## The Book of Mormon

In a Sunday School class that morning I was treated to an expanded discussion of the strange work known as the Book of Mormon.[5] Wayne Bell, the teacher, taught us that the Book of Mormon is another set of scriptures similar to the Bible. Just as the New Testament added to the witness of the Old, the Book of Mormon strengthens the witness of the Bible and is another witness of Jesus Christ.

The Book of Mormon explains that around 600 BC, Lehi, a Hebrew prophet, led two families of Israelites away from the impending destruction of Jerusalem. Lehi was warned to flee into the wilderness and then on to the Western Hemisphere, where he and his descendants kept sacred records. Their writings, preserved on gold plates, tell about the descent from the heavens of Jesus Christ when he visited Lehi's posterity shortly after his resurrection. Jesus stayed with them for a brief while, taught them his gospel, and left after promising to return.

Quetzalcoatl! The nearly forgotten story from my childhood returned to my mind. Could Jesus have been the legendary Quetzalcoatl? Both were bearded white men who descended from the sky. Both taught their disciples how to live a good life. Both promised to return. What a wonderful coincidence! However, I quickly rationalized that the two couldn't possibly be the same event, for I had already decided that the Book of Mormon simply can't be true.

"Why not?" something whispered in my mind.

Brother Bell asked us to read John 10:16. I had to use the Table of Contents to find it since I wasn't familiar enough with the layout of the Bible to automatically turn to the reference. Jesus told his apostles, "Other sheep I have, which are not of this fold: them also I must bring, and they shall hear my voice; and there shall be one fold, and one shepherd" (John 10:16).

Our teacher explained that Jesus's "other sheep" were Israelites not living in his Palestinian "fold." Jesus knew their whereabouts, but his Judean followers did not. The other sheep would hear his voice when he personally taught them. After his ascension, Jesus came to the Americas. His teachings were recorded by his prophets who were already there.

"Why couldn't the other sheep have been gentiles?" someone in the class asked. I wanted to ask the same question, but in those days I was too shy to inquire in front of others. I was surprised how easily he handled it.

Brother Bell pointed out that Jesus never referred to gentiles as his "sheep." He was the shepherd of Israel's flock. Never during his mortality did he visit groups of gentiles. After Jesus left, his prophets taught the gentile nations.

He continued, noting that when Jesus departed from the land, his disciples in the Western Hemisphere lived in peace for nearly 200 years:

> And it came to pass . . . the people were all converted unto the Lord . . . and there were no contentions and disputations among them, and every man did deal justly one with another. And they had all things common among them; therefore there were not rich and poor, bond and free, but they were all made free, and partakers of the heavenly gift. . . . And the Lord did prosper them . . . because of the love of God which did dwell in the hearts of the people. . . . Surely there could not be a happier people among all the people who had been created by the hand of God."
>
> (4 Nephi 1:2-16)

There was the same reference to the members of Christ's Church having all things in common that is found within the New Testament. It was a brilliant idea for Joseph Smith to include such a wonderful concept in his book, I thought. That way it reads more like the Bible.

Brother Bell showed how the people eventually slid back into their wayward behavior. As they gradually forgot God, horrible wars of extermination were waged. Nearly four hundred years after Christ's visit, one of the last prophets, Mormon, was commanded to abridge the precious records onto gold plates so that they might be preserved for a later generation. The condensed volume he created bears his name—the Book of Mormon.

## An Angel and His Book of Gold

Mormon's son, Moroni, inherited the metallic plates and then engraved additional information on them. He concealed the record in a hill near Palmyra, New York, where they remained until he revealed them to Joseph Smith fourteen centuries later.

For the three years after Joseph spoke with the Father and the Son in the grove of trees, he continued to help his father on the family farm. When he could, he hired himself out to help pay the bills. Those who ought to have been his friends ridiculed him, but he continued to affirm that he had seen a vision.

At the age of seventeen, Joseph brought upon himself added abuse by letting it be known that he had been visited by an angel. Near the night of the autumnal equinox (September 21, 1823), he offered a special prayer for forgiveness of his sins and follies, and also for a manifestation that he might know of his standing before God:

> While I was thus in the act of calling upon God, I discovered a light appearing in my room, which continued to increase until the room was lighter than at noonday, when immediately a personage appeared at my bedside, standing in the air, for his feet did not touch the floor. The angel wore a loose robe of most exquisite whiteness. It was a whiteness beyond anything earthly I had ever seen . . . His hands were naked, and his arms also, a little above the wrist; so, also, were his feet naked, as were his legs, a little above the ankles. His head and neck were also bare.
>
> . . . Not only was his robe exceedingly white, but his whole person was glorious beyond description, and his countenance truly like lightning. The room was exceedingly light, but not so very bright as immediately around his person. When I first looked upon him, I was afraid; but the fear soon left me.
>
> He called me by name, and said unto me that he was a messenger sent from the presence of God to me, and that his name was Moroni; that God had a work for me to do; and that my name should be had for good and

evil among all nations, kindreds, and tongues, or that it should be both good and evil spoken of among all people.

He said there was a book deposited, written upon gold plates, giving an account of the former inhabitants of this continent . . . He also said that the fulness of the everlasting Gospel was contained in it, as delivered by the Savior to the ancient inhabitants. Also that there were two stones in silver bows—and these stones, fastened to a breastplate, constituted what is called the Urim and Thummim . . . God had prepared them for the purpose of translating the book.

. . . Again, he told me, that when I got those plates . . . I should not show them to any person; neither the breastplate with the Urim and Thummim; only to those to whom I should be commanded to show them; if I did I should be destroyed. While he was conversing with me about the plates, the vision was opened to my mind that I could see the place where the plates were deposited, and that so clearly and distinctly that I knew the place again when I visited it.

After this communication, I saw the light in the room begin to gather immediately around the person of him who had been speaking . . . and it continued to do so until the room was again left dark, except just around him; when instantly I saw . . . a conduit open right up into heaven, and he ascended till he entirely disappeared, and the room was left as it had been before this heavenly light had made its appearance.

I lay musing on the singularity of the scene, and marveling greatly at what had been told to me by this extraordinary messenger; when in the midst of my meditation, I suddenly discovered that my room was again beginning to get lighted, and in an instant, as it were, the same heavenly messenger was again by my bedside.

(Joseph Smith History 1:30-45)

Moroni repeated what he had previously told Joseph. He also informed him "of great judgments which were coming upon the earth, with great desolations by famine, sword, and pestilence." Again he left the same way he had come. "Sleep had fled from my eyes and I lay overwhelmed in astonishment . . . But what was my surprise when again I beheld the same messenger at my bedside."

Moroni again repeated what he had taught Joseph during the other two visits. This time he added a caution that Satan would tempt him to sell the gold because of the poverty of his family. He "must have no other object in view in getting the plates but to glorify God, and must not be influenced by any other motive than that of building his kingdom; otherwise [he] could not get them." Moroni once again "ascended into heaven . . . and I was again left to ponder on the strangeness of what I had just experienced; when almost immediately . . . the cock crowed, and I found that day was approaching, so that our interviews must have occupied the whole of that night."

Joseph went out to the fields to work with his father, but he had lost his stamina. He was totally exhausted. His father told him to go get some rest. On the way home he fell, unconscious.

After regaining his senses, Joseph heard a voice. Looking up, he saw the same messenger standing in the air, surrounded by light. Moroni repeated his instructions of the night before. He then told Joseph to share with his father the spiritual manifestations he had received. Unlike the minister whom Joseph tried to talk with three years earlier, his father believed him, realizing "it was of God." He told his son to go and do as the angel commanded.

Not far from Joseph's home rose the hill about which Moroni had spoken. Joseph knew exactly where to find the records. Near the top of the hill, under a stone of considerable size, lay the plates:

> Having removed the earth, I obtained a lever, which I got fixed under the edge of the stone, and with a little exertion raised it up. I looked in, and there indeed did I behold the plates, the Urim and Thummim, and the breastplate, as stated by the messenger. The box in which they lay was formed by laying stones together in some kind of cement. In the bottom of the box were laid two stones crossways of the box, and on these stones lay the plates and the other things with them."
>
> I made an attempt to take them out, but was forbidden by the messenger, and was again informed that the time for bringing them forth had not yet arrived, neither would it, until four years from that time; but he told me that I should come to that place precisely in one year from that time, and that he would there meet with me, and that I should continue to do so until the time should come for obtaining the plates.
>
> (Joseph Smith History 1:51-53)

Hearing of Joseph's experience reminded me of a poem I had read of Abou Ben Adham's fictitious angel and his book of gold.[6] The angel Moroni's appearance in Joseph's bedroom sounded much like Ben Adham's angel who also appeared in his bedroom. Moroni told Joseph where gold plates were; Ben Adham's angel held a book of gold in his hands. How could an intelligent man like Brother Bell believe in engraved metal plates that were revealed by an angel coming down through a ceiling in a beam of light?

(I later learned, however, that engraving information on metal—gold, silver, copper, bronze and lead—was once common practice, presumably for preservation purposes.[7] Gold and silver plates of Emperor Darius I of Persia, which were buried in 518 BC—shortly after the departure of Lehi to the Western Hemisphere—have been unearthed. Other metallic tablets have been found in Java, Thailand, India, Pakistan, Iran, Portugal, Spain, Italy, Greece, Egypt, Iraq, Lebanon, Palestine, Mexico, Ecuador and Peru.[8]

(Stone boxes were also used by the ancients. The plates of Darius were found lying in a stone box. Beautifully carved boxes of stone for housing valuables have also been discovered in Mesoamerica.[9]

(The truly fascinating part is that, in Joseph Smith's day, no one in the entire world knew about ancient engravings on metal. Every known engraved metallic artifact that has the semblance of a book has been unearthed since Joseph Smith's death. Moroni's gold plates were the first such inscriptions about which anyone in modern times had ever heard. How did Joseph know that the ancients used such metallic writing material?)

Brother Bell continued quoting Joseph Smith: "Accordingly, as I had been commanded, I went at the end of each year, and at each time I found the same messenger there, and received instruction and intelligence from him at each of our interviews, respecting what the Lord was going to do, and how and in what manner his kingdom was to be conducted in the last days" (Joseph Smith History 2:54).

Joseph's brother, William, wrote of him:

> With the moral training he had received from strictly pious and religious parents, [he] could not have conceived the idea in his mind of palming off a fabulous story, such as seeing angels . . . There was not a single member of the family . . . but what had implicit confidence in the statements made by [him]. Father and mother believed him; why should not the children? I suppose if he had told crooked stories about other things, we might have doubted his word about the plates, but Joseph was a truthful boy. That father and mother . . . suffered persecution for that belief shows that he was truthful.[10]

For four more years young Joseph endured the jeering of others with nothing to show for his faith. But he also received more sacred education than anyone else in nearly two thousand years. Like a modern Moses receiving the tablets of stone, Joseph was permitted to remove the gold tablets from their concealed container. He then translated them into English by the gift and power of God. Taunting by mockers continued. Forced by unbelievers to move from Manchester to Harmony, Pennsylvania, then to Fayette, New York, Joseph finished the translation of the 520-page record in June of 1829. Diaries of those involved reveal that the total process of translating took only sixty-five to ninety working days, a truly astounding phenomenon.[11]

When someone in the class asked where the records are now—again, a question that I had also wanted to ask—Brother Bell explained. Throughout the centuries before Joseph Smith's time, the plates had been concealed so thieves could not steal them for their gold content. Because over half of them are sealed and are yet to be translated, they were again hidden by Moroni for protection.

Original Bible records, including the stone tablets which contained the Ten Commandments, are not available either, Brother Bell pointed out. All we have are copies of the earliest writings. Even the Dead Sea scrolls, some of which date to 200 years before Christ, are duplicates of earlier works. If the primary sources were obtainable for the Bible and the Book of Mormon, most of us would be unable to read them; their translation would still need to be entrusted to others. Which translation would be correct? So, we'd be back to where we are today—continuing to rely on our faith in the translators.

Throughout Christendom the Book of Mormon caused quite a stir. Another set of scriptures had invaded Bible territory! To admit the possibility of any other holy writ than "Jesus' Bible" would be scandalous. Known as the "Gold Bible" or the "Mormon Bible," newspapermen wrote slanted editorials about it. Those who believed it were nicknamed "Mormonites" (later "Mormons") by nonbelievers. Mobs harassed them. Accused of "stirring up" the area with his false ideas, a string of arrests of Joseph Smith began.

Even today many believe the unschooled Joseph Smith was an ingenious novelist who lied when he claimed the first book he ever wrote was ancient. If so, he is a fraud without parallel. Who else in the history of the world has ever undertaken such an elaborate scheme? Augustine, Mohammed, Confucius, Buddha, Mary Baker Eddy, Ellen White were good people, but none claimed their writings came from an ancient source.

Though errors have been found—spelling and typographical mainly—the Book of Mormon was translated from its original language into English only once. It was, therefore, received by Joseph Smith without the kind of errors and omissions which are found in every modern Bible. Soon after completing the translation of the Book of Mormon, young Joseph boldly asserted for the entire world to read that "the Book of Mormon is the most correct of any book on earth, and the keystone of our religion, and a man would get nearer to God by abiding by its precepts, than by any other book."[12]

The Book of Mormon, called by the LDS Church "Another Testament of Jesus Christ," was given to mankind for "the convincing of the Jew and Gentile that Jesus is the Christ, the eternal God, manifesting himself unto all nations."[13] Millions of Jews and gentiles have been converted to Christ after prayerfully reading that book.

Years after Brother Bell's lesson I read about a rabbi in the Sephardic Orthodox Jewish religion—the sixteenth generation of his family to be so ordained—who was one of those Jews. Having earned doctorates in divinity, psychology and linguistics, and having been a professor at the Hebrew University at Jerusalem and the Universities of Mississippi, New Mexico, California, Denver, and at Marquette, he was well qualified to make a scholarly comparison between the Book of Mormon and various Bible translations. After making a thorough comparison he testified that "study [of the Book of Mormon] will not only confirm your belief in your Heavenly Father and His son, Jesus Christ, but it will guide you to obey His commandments and covenants."[14]

Either the Book of Mormon came from God's early American prophets, or it was cleverly concocted by Joseph Smith. There can be no middle ground. Jesus taught that by their fruits we can know the prophets. The Book of Mormon is the most important fruit of Joseph's prophetic produce. *If the Book of Mormon is a true and accurate narrative of ancient people, then Joseph Smith must be a prophet of God.*

## Growth of the Church

Mormon missionaries were sent to tell the world about God's greatest miracle since the resurrection of Jesus Christ—the coming forth of the Book of Mormon. All they asked was that it be sincerely read as Christian missionaries would want the Bible to be read by their proselytes.

In spite of the negative publicity and an area-wide boycott of "Joe's Bible," people dared to ally themselves to the book and to the prophet who had translated it. They believed. During its first two decades the new Church grew from the original six men needed to make it official in New York, to an astounding 51,000.

More recent reports show that between 1950 and 1975, nearly 1,400,000 converts were baptized; 1976-1984 saw another 1,900,000 become members; and in only five years from 1985 to 1990—an additional 1,500,000 joined the church (an average of nearly 6,000 each week!).[15] By 1995, more than 9 million living souls worldwide called themselves Latter-day Saints, with other millions having passed on since the Church's inception. Demographic projections show that at present rates of growth, by the year 2080 the membership of The Church of Jesus Christ of Latter-day Saints will exceed 265 million![16]

I left the church with mixed emotions that morning. It was satisfying to realize that Mormons were not the uneducated fanatics I had previously imagined them to be. They seemed to be good people—the kind of people that would be a part of the faith established by a prophet of God. I believed that if Christ had a Church it would be a school of heavenly ethics. The offices of apostles, prophets, evangelists, pastors and teachers would be hollow if they weren't involved in the "perfecting of the saints" as Paul mentioned (Ephesians 4:11). Other religions produce fine people; God's Church should do as much and more.

But I also left realizing that I had been given something profound, something that was utterly unique in Christian thought. No other religion to my knowledge claimed such a book as the Book of Mormon. No other faith tells about an angel—a wingless one at that—beaming down through the ceiling in a column of light to tell a seventeen-year-old boy where he can find ancient plates of gold.[17] Obviously, if the Book of Mormon is true there was such an angel and Joseph Smith was a prophet of God. But who can tell if the Book of Mormon is true?

Because the Book of Mormon story, with its angel named "Moroni" (instead of Gabriel, Michael, or Raphael), was so different from anything found in other religions or anything I had ever heard before, I didn't dare believe it. Neither did I want to risk telling my non-Mormon friends that I harbored even a wisp of a thought that what the Mormons taught might be true. What would they think of me? I hoped none saw me around the Mormon church that day.

# 9
# Expert Opinions

Within a month after attending my first Mormon meeting, I confided in Dr. Grant, a professor at U.C. Riverside to whom I felt close. As a Sociology professor and a white member of the National Association for the Advancement of Colored People (NAACP), he often called our attention to the oppression of various groups of oppressed people. I told him about my experiences with the Mormons and asked if he had any insight on the matter.

"I don't know much about the Mormon faith, but I have read the Book of Mormon," he told me, "and I think it is ridiculous. I don't see how anyone can believe it, in spite of what Dr. Broadbent believes."[1]

I felt a twinge of disappointment, for I looked up to Dr. Grant very much. I almost felt that any judgment he would make on anything in the world would be good enough for me. If he believed the Book of Mormon to be "ridiculous" then it must be.

However, his reference to Dr. Broadbent struck at my previous bias about ignorant Mormons. An educated faculty member of the prestigious University of California—a dean—believes the Book of Mormon! How can that be unless there is something to the book?[2]

I left Dr. Grant's office somewhat puzzled. Determined to find out what other authorities thought about the Mormon theology I sought out ministers of three of the largest churches in Riverside plus another in Fontana, who was my mother's pastor. The products of extensive training in the finest seminaries, these men obviously were experts about all religions and could steer me straight, if anyone could. Though they differed in their opinions about what Christ taught, I only wanted to find out at that time why they weren't Mormons if the LDS religion is true. I could investigate why they differed from one another later.[3]

The learned clergymen, planted behind oaken desks in front of shelves stacked with hundreds of impressive volumes, presented thoughtful images of solemn, scholarly wisdom. Though far more educated than I, they each patiently listened to my story and to my query: "If what the Mormons say is true, why aren't you a Mormon?"

The three Riversiders sincerely tried to help. None ridiculed the Latter-day Saints, nor did they laugh at me for my inquiries. The Fontanan, however, razzed me. "How can you be so simple-minded as to listen to Mormons?" he asked. "Their leader, Brigham Young, was a sex maniac." He refused to waste his time answering questions about what he called the Mormon cult. (When he referred to Brigham Young as a "sex maniac," I wondered how he felt about David and his many wives.) Disregarding the fact that Christianity originated as a cult, all four referred to Mormonism as a cult. It therefore could not be part of the larger group of Christian churches that had represented Christ for so many centuries. Consequently, its claims could not possibly be true, they concluded.

The thoughtful, caring manner in which the three Riversiders presented their perceptions of LDS theology boosted my previous prejudices about Mormons to a new high. Wrath and indignation swept over me. Those young missionary lads I had been talking with simply didn't know what the older, more experienced, seminarians understood about Jesus and the Bible. Mere boys, they had no training in theology. What degrees could they display that proved that they deserved to be called "missionaries?"

## No New Scripture

The three basic points the churchmen made were that the Bible is closed; that a Presbyterian preacher, Solomon Spaulding, had written a novel which Joseph Smith turned into the Book of Mormon; and that the Book of Mormon was largely plagiarized from the Bible.

Turning to the book of Revelation at the end of the Bible, the ministers read John's admonition, which according to them, refers to the entire Bible: "If any man shall add unto these things, God shall add unto him the plagues that are written in this book. And if any man shall take away from the words of the book of this prophecy, God shall take away his part out of the book of life, and out of the holy city, and from the things which are written in this book" (Rev. 22:18-19). The clergymen reasoned that since the Bible is the only word of God, and the Book of Mormon has been added to it, the Book of Mormon cannot also be God's word.

According to the ministers, a Presbyterian preacher named Solomon Spaulding had given his book to a Pittsburgh printer who was his employer, and had tried unsuccessfully to get it published.[4] Later, in Kirtland, Ohio, the renowned minister, Sidney Rigdon, had become disgruntled with Alexander Campbell, the founder of the Disciples Church, and had left his church. Rigdon had stolen Spaulding's manuscript from the printer when he lived in Pittsburgh, and had taken it to Ohio. After leaving Campbell's movement, he took the book to Joseph Smith in New York. Including parts of the Bible in it to make their book appear theologically authentic, the two schemers then had it published as the Book of Mormon.

The third point the ministers wanted to impress me with was that large portions of the Book of Mormon were plagiarized from the Bible. They said that page after page of Isaiah is reproduced verbatim in the Book of Mormon along with Christ's Sermon on the Mount.

Outraged, I decided to tell the missionaries to not return. How could I have been so naive as to harbor even a trace of a thought that Joseph Smith might have been a prophet? How could those two kids dare call themselves "elders?" The young missionaries couldn't possibly measure up to the combined wisdom of the older intellectuals. Not even Brother Bell was trained in theology. He was merely the manager of a supermarket. Why had I let the Mormons plant doubts about orthodox Christianity, the religion of my parents and grandparents, into my mind? No more would they be allowed to corner me with their scripturemanship.

Still, I thought, why were the dignified divines so diversified in their theological discipleship? Why did they claim to believe in the same Bible and in the same God, yet teach a variety of doctrines? If a person sincerely wanted to join a Christian church because it taught Bible truth, he would have a difficult time sorting out which denomination truly represented the Savior. Christ had taught a single faith—not many. If he were to return in our time he would again teach us to enter in at the strait gate because "narrow is the way, which leadeth unto life." But what is that strait gate and narrow way?

When I had joined the Methodist and Fontana Community churches, I did so because of the friendly people and because I had a desire to return to some semblance of my childhood upbringing, not because I believed the doctrine taught by those two factions was the complete set of precepts taught by Jesus.

Now I was determined to find the truth. Hopefully it would be found within Christianity so it wouldn't take so long to discover. But when I began to think about the diversity of denominations, each one calling itself Christian, I became dizzied by the impossibility of the task.

## The Missionaries Reply

When the missionaries returned, my triple-barreled shotgun was primed and ready to explode. The three ministers and Dr. Grant had me well prepared to come out fighting. I would let the Mormons have it first with the Bible's warning, then I would unload my gun's remaining two barrels with an attack about Joseph Smith and Sidney Rigdon plagiarizing Solomon Spaulding's novel and the Bible when they wrote the Book of Mormon. After that I would show them to the door and tell them to never return. One of Christianity's factions would be eliminated from my search for truth. I'd just have to start over again with the Nazarenes or some other group.

Answering the doorbell, I let the missionaries in. I could hardly wait to shoot. "Hi, guys." I said in a syrupy tone. "Come in. I've got some news for you."

## Revelation 22:18-19

After we were seated around the table I squeezed the trigger and let the first shell fly. "I've been visiting some ministers and guess what? You fellows don't know what you're talking about. All this bunk about angels and gold plates is just a bunch of hogwash. Look here," I bristled, feeling proud that I could find Revelation 22:18-19. "Here at the end of the Bible it says you can't add anything to the Good Book! Your Church has added the Book of Mormon! If the Bible's true, then the Book of Mormon can't be true. And if that's so, Joseph Smith wasn't a prophet!"

Smiling, Elder Porter returned friendly fire. "It's our custom to open a discussion with prayer. Is that all right, Bill?"

"Sure. But you offer it. I'm not feeling very friendly right now."

Having heard my accusations before, Elder Porter aimed straight. After a prayer he said, "If he wishes to, the God of heaven certainly can raise up a prophet and direct him to write more scripture. Since all scriptures originated with him, who would dare tell God that he cannot write more?

"Detractors of Mormon thought believe that this particular passage in John's Revelation refers to the entire Christian Bible. But John wrote his Revelation hundreds of years before there was a Christian Bible. Plus, several books in the New Testament were written after John wrote the book of Revelation. The 'book' referred to is John's book, the book of *Revelation.* The Greek word *biblia,* from which *Bible* was derived, means "collection" or "library of books." Back in John's day there was no single bound Bible containing all of the books that are in our Bibles of today. There are 66 of those books in the King James version of the Bible, with John's being only one.

"John's Revelation also warns about taking words away. If taking away refers to the Christian Bible, to which one does it refer? The earliest, the *Latin Vulgate,* includes an Apocrypha of fourteen books; the Catholic *Douay* has eleven, and Protestant Bibles do not generally have any. Could John be warning Protestant canoneers who have taken away the Apocrypha that their part will be taken "out of the book of life, and out of the holy city?" Or are Catholic theologians who took away three of the *Vulgate's* books to compose the *Douay* Bible being told that they will be locked out of the holy city with their Protestant cousins?"

I sat helpless as the elder diverted my blast with his armored defense. But I wasn't finished yet. I still had two more shells in my gun. I pulled the second trigger and let them have it about Rigdon and Smith using Spaulding's story in their scheme. "The ministers told me that a man by the name of Sidney Rigdon stole a novel written by a Solomon Spaulding which he and Joseph Smith used to write the Book of Mormon. If that's true, your Book of Mormon certainly can't be from the ancients."

## Spaulding's Manuscript

According to Elder Porter, and from what I have since read, Solomon Spaulding's story is nothing like the Book of Mormon. His effort is, among other things, a romance about an Indian prince and a princess from two neighboring kingdoms who fell in love, causing a war between the two empires.[5]

Further, Sidney Rigdon had joined the LDS Church *after* the Book of Mormon was published in the spring of 1830. Parley P. Pratt was the first to introduce it to him that fall. It was not until then that Rigdon had left the Campbellite movement in Ohio, not prior to the Book of Mormon's publication as the ministers had led me to believe. Pratt, himself, hadn't heard of the book until after it was published.

Around 1833, a man by the name of Doctor (his name—not a title) Philastus Hurlburt was excommunicated from the LDS Church "for attempting to seduce a young female." He was rebaptized after repenting, but was excommunicated again for the same reason. Seeking revenge, he set out to "expose" Mormonism by writing the book, *Mormonism Unvailed* [sic]. At the same time he was also making inflammatory speeches against the Church.[6]

While speaking in Pennsylvania, Hurlburt became acquainted with a family by the name of Jackson, who told him that Spaulding had written a novel containing strange names.[7] Theorizing that that book could have been the source of the Book of Mormon, Hurlburt contacted Spaulding's widow, Mrs. Davieson. She gave him a copy of her husband's novel and also informed him that Solomon had lived in Pittsburgh from 1812 to 1814.[8] Hurlburt never published Spaulding's story though, because he discovered that the copy he had was nothing like the Book of Mormon. He then proposed that Spaulding must have written another book.

Realizing that the uneducated Joseph Smith could not have written the complex Book of Mormon himself, Hurlburt reasoned that a more learned man must have been involved. After Sidney Rigdon joined the Church, Hurlburt had his man. He fabricated a story saying that since Rigdon was raised in Pennsylvania, he had had ample opportunity to copy Spaulding's mysterious other novel. He then must have taken it with him when he moved to Ohio, contacted Joseph Smith in New York, and then he must have written the Book of Mormon using Joseph's name as the "translator." Hurlburt preached his theory to anyone who would listen. Because he had once been a Mormon, some believed him.

But according to his mother, Sidney had not been in Pittsburgh from 1812 to 1814, when Spaulding was there. It was not until 1821 to 1826 that he lived there. Interestingly, the printing office where Spaulding worked was no longer in existence in 1821. One of the owners, a Mr. Lambdin, died in 1825, and so could not be contacted by subsequent investigators. Mr. Patterson, the other owner, had "no recollection of any such manuscript."[9]

When Hurlburt threatened to assassinate Joseph Smith, his reputation, already shady because of his alleged romances with other women, became worse. Advised to sell his book, it was then published with E. D. Howe as its supposed author. Since the book's real author was well known, *Mormonism Unvailed* died quietly almost.

Editors of religion then took up the theme. According to them, the "Mormon Bible" was authored by "knaves" and believed by the "superstitious." Unsubstantiated "facts" were printed: "Sidney Rigdon was connected in the printing office of Mr. Patterson . . . [and] this is a fact well known in that region, as Rigdon himself has frequently stated."[10] The *Boston Recorder* printed a letter supposedly written by Spaulding's widow, Mrs. Davieson, saying the Book of Mormon was plagiarized from her husband's book.

Mrs. Davieson, however, denied that she had ever written such a letter. She had never even seen the letter until she "saw it in the *Boston Recorder.*"[11]

Parley Pratt wrote that "about the 15th of October, 1830," he, with Oliver Cowdery and Peter Whitmer began a missionary journey which took them through Ohio. While there they visited Sidney Rigdon who *"for the first time* . . . beheld the Book of Mormon." Only after "much persuasion" did he agree to read it. Only after "a great struggle of mind" did he fully embrace it. When he was "finally convinced of the truth, he called together . . . his friends, neighbours, and brethren, and then addressed them, very affectionately for . . . two hours," during which time both he and his "congregation were melted into tears." The following morning, he and his wife, Phebe, were baptized by Oliver Cowdery.

According to Pratt, in December, 1830, Rigdon visited Joseph Smith

> in New York, *for the first time,* and from that time . . . rumour began to circulate that he . . . was the author of the Book of Mormon. The Spaulding story never was dreamed of until several years afterwards, when it appeared in *Mormonism Unvailed* [and] was converted, by the ignorant and impudent religious editors . . . into something said to be positively certain, and not to be disputed.[12]

Between 1839-1840, two non-Mormons, L. L. Rice and his partner, purchased the *Painesville Telegraph* with its types, press, and a large collection of books and manuscripts. Approximately forty-five years later, Rice accidentally discovered Spaulding's *Manuscript Found* in the collection. He wrote:

> It is certain that this Manuscript is not the origin of the Mormon Bible . . . There is no identity of names, of persons, or places; and there is no similarity of style . . . It is unlikely that any one who wrote so elaborate a work as the Mormon Bible, would spend his time in getting up so shallow a story as this . . . From all I have seen and learned . . . this is the *only* writing of Spaulding.[13]

President J. H. Fairchild of Oberlin College, Ohio, where the manuscript is presently housed, also concluded that

> the theory of the origin of the Book of Mormon in the traditional manuscript of Solomon Spaulding, will probably have to be relinquished . . . Mr. Rice, myself, and others, compared *[Manuscript Found]* with the Book of Mormon, and could detect no resemblance . . . There seems to be no name or incident common to the two. The solemn style of the Book of Mormon, in imitation of the English Scriptures, does not appear in the manuscript.[14]

Other eminent scholars not affiliated with the LDS Church have seen through the Spaulding theory. Marcus Bach concluded after reading the Book of Mormon:

> These auxiliary scriptures . . . surpassed in magnitude and content my most extravagant expectations. The style was Biblical, the references to Holy Writ were voluminous, the ancient story was tremendously involved. It was not the kind of book a man would read for pastime or write for profit. It was solemn and ponderous and heavy as the plates on which it was inscribed. No Vermont schoolboy wrote this, and no Presbyterian preacher tinkered with these pages.[15]

Charles J. Finger judged that the Book of Mormon is a

> literary masterpiece; how an unschooled lad could have had the imagination, the patience, the perseverance to write a volume of nearly six hundred . . . pages; in imitation of the biblical style; teaching a faith for which men died; for which hundreds of thousands faced hardships; accepted as truth by [millions of] people today . . . The book does not make exciting reading by any means, but I . . . cannot cease to wonder at the broad sweep of canvas which Smith filled with his tale.[16]

In spite of the missionary's smothering cannonade, I persisted in my prejudices. I would finish them off with my remaining shell. There was no way they could defend themselves against this accusation: "Another thing I was told by those I hold in the highest esteem is that Smith used the Bible in his hoax. It's obvious that the Book of Mormon is written in King James English like the Bible. It even sounds like the Bible when you read it. Many KJV scriptures are included between the Book of Mormon's covers so it must have been plagiarized from the Bible," I concluded with a scowl. I was becoming very uncomfortable with the way this young man could so easily and so logically dismiss what the four more learned men had taught me.

## Bible Passages in the Book of Mormon

In reply, Elder Porter explained that Joseph may have been commanded to translate the book into King James English because it was the kind of writing Bible reading people were used to in that part of the world during the early 19th century. It would be more palatable to them—and to many of us—to read a book of scripture written the same way as the Bible than if it were written in colloquial English. "Can you imagine the hoots had the Book of Mormon been translated into frontier language?" he laughed.

Lehi's family brought brass plates to the New World which contained the portion of the Old Testament that was written before 600 BC. That section contains the book of Isaiah which itself may or may not have been an exact translation of the original Isaiah text. Small parts of the Book of Mormon use quotations from the brass plates' Isaiah because of their prophetic importance. The Isaiah passages would naturally be similar to the King James Version of Isaiah.

However, I later learned, of the 433 Isaiah verses found within the Book of Mormon, more than half are different from the KJV. John Tvedtnes, who made a thorough comparison of Book of Mormon Isaiah passages with other versions of Isaiah within the KJV, the Masoretic Text from which the Old Testament of the KJV was translated, the two Isaiah scrolls found with the Dead Sea Scrolls, the Septuagint, the Vulgate, The Targumim (an Aramaic translation), and the Peshitta (Syriac), concluded, "It is inconceivable that Joseph Smith could have made so many correct changes in the Isaiah text and placed them in a fraudulent book. He could have made himself a much better reputation in the scholarly community by writing a philological treatise on the subject of the Isaiah text."[17]

One example can be found in 2 Nephi 12:16 (compare Isaiah 2:16) which says: "And upon all the ships of the sea, and upon all the ships of Tarshish, and upon all pleasant pictures." The Septuagint has the phrase "ships of the sea" but not "ships of Tarshish"; the Hebrew and the King James' versions have "ships of Tarshish" but not "ships of the sea"; the Book of Mormon has preserved both.[18] Joseph Smith did not have access to the Septuagint. Even if he had he could not have read it. If he created the Book of Mormon, how did he dream up the "ships of the sea" phrase in that very verse?

Another interesting passage—2 Nephi 20:29—contains the place-name, "Ramath." The KJV of Isaiah 10:29 spells the name, "Ramah," which is a later Hebrew form of Ramath.[19] The question, of course, is how did Joseph Smith know that fact? If he had plagiarized Isaiah, he would certainly have used "Ramah."

In front of 1 Nephi 21:1 is a preface written by Isaiah. There is no preface to the corresponding verse of Isaiah 49:1. The Book of Mormon preface is a chiasmus—an early Hebrew poetic form—which very few scholars in Joseph Smith's day knew anything about:[20] (See page 178 for a definition of Chiasmus).

> **a** *Hearken,*
>> **b** *o ye house of Israel,*
>>> **c** *all ye that are broken off* and *are driven out*
>>>> **d** because of the wickedness of the pastors of my people;
>>> **c** yea, all *ye that are broken off,* that *are scattered abroad,*
>> **b** who are of my people, *O house of Israel.*
> **a** *Listen*[21]

Why would Joseph Smith write a preface in front of that portion of Isaiah, and how did he know how to arrange it into a chiasmus? If the greatest Hebrew linguists in his day knew little about such a device, Joseph Smith certainly could not have written a chiasmus on his own.

H. Clay Gorton has made a detailed comparison between chiasma in the Book of Mormon Isaiah passages and chiasma in various Bibles including the King James Version. He found that five of the ten chiasma that are in both books are essentially the same, but the other five in the Book of Mormon have completed the chiasma structure, compared to degraded chiasma in the KJV:

In the ten chiasma that are common to the Isaiah chapters in the BM and KJV, there are found no embellishments or enhancements in the Bible version. However, textual deletions from KJV have seriously degraded the chiastic structure of four of the chiasma and entirely eliminated a fifth chiasmus . . . If Joseph Smith had been an imposter and had copied the Isaiah chapters from the Bible, it is inconceivable that he could have made additions to the text that would have filled in the missing elements in five of the ten chiasma that are common to the two texts.

On the other hand, the fact that five of the ten common chiasma appear in the KJV in a degraded form clearly demonstrates that the [later] KJV is an altered form of the [earlier] Brass Plates Isaiah that had been copied by Nephi and then translated by Joseph Smith.[22]

The Brass Plates Version of the Old Testament from which the Book of Mormon writers quote is dated at approximately 600 BC and earlier. The KJV was taken from much later translations. Since the ten chiasma studied by Gorton in the Book of Mormon are still intact, and five of the corresponding ten in the KJV are degraded and do not have the entire chiasmic structure, then two different sources must have been used by Joseph Smith and the King James translators. Clearly, Joseph Smith did not copy the King James Isaiahs into the Book of Mormon.

When Jesus appeared at his temple in the western world, he preached the same hillside sermon that Matthew recorded. After delivering his sermon at the temple, Jesus informed the Nephites that what he had taught them was previously taught in his mortal ministry: "Ye have heard *the things which I taught before I ascended* to my Father" (3 Nephi 15:1). Therefore, Jesus knew that similarities would be preserved between the two addresses.

However, what has been called history's greatest sermon looms even greater and more understandable in the differences seen in the Book of Mormon's rendition. Certain points that scholars have long questioned about the Sermon on the Mount are cleared up in the Book of Mormon— points of contention that Joseph would have known nothing about.

For instance, in the Beatitudes part of the sermon, Matthew wrote: "Blessed are the poor in spirit: for theirs is the kingdom of heaven," and, "Blessed are they that mourn: for they shall be comforted" (Matt. 5:3-4). Why should they who are poor in spirit and they who mourn be more blessed than they who are not poor in spirit and who do not mourn? The conjunction "and" that begins each temple beatitude refers back to the first beatitude where Jesus says those who *"come unto me"* will be blessed. Therefore, they who are poor in spirit and who mourn and *come unto Christ* are blessed because they will be comforted and they will enter into the kingdom of heaven (3 Nephi 12:3).

It is interesting to note also that Jesus invited the people to "come unto me" six times within the first chapter of his Book of Mormon sermon but not once in the corresponding chapter of his Sermon on the Mount (3 Nephi 12:3, 19, 20, 23 [twice], 24). Either he saw no need to use the phrase in Palestine, it has not been preserved in the book of Matthew, or Joseph Smith was brilliant enough to scoop Matthew and include it in the Book of Mormon.

In Matthew's version of the Beatitudes, Jesus says, "Blessed are they which do hunger and thirst after righteousness: for they shall be filled" (Matt. 5:6). Filled with what? Jesus's temple sermon reads that they who hunger and thirst after righteousness will be *"filled with the Holy Ghost"* if they come unto Christ (3 Nephi 12:6).

Nephi has not preserved the reference about God sending "rain on the just and on the unjust" found in Matthew 5:45. Such a beautifully profound and wise phrase would never have been left out of the Book of Mormon if Matthew's representation was plagiarized.

Similarly, a plagiarizer would never have dared to omit two complete sentences of Matthew's very popular version of the Lord's Prayer (Matthew 6:9-13). The Book of Mormon's rendering of that prayer is: "Our Father who art in heaven, hallowed be thy name. Thy will be done on earth as it is in heaven. And forgive us our debts, as we forgive our debtors. And lead us not into temptation, but deliver us from evil, for thine is the kingdom, and the power, and the glory forever. Amen" (3 Nephi 13:9-13).[23]

Many other obvious, as well as subtle, differences are found between the two sermons.

Jesus also quoted part of Malachi's prophecy, within the Book of Mormon, about his own second coming. Malachi had made his predictions after Lehi left Jerusalem. Because Malachi's book was not in the much earlier Brass Plates, Jesus commanded his Nephite disciples to *"write the words which the Father had given unto Malachi"* (3 Nephi 24:1). The Lord then dictated only the portions he wanted preserved.

Whoever composed the sermon at the temple in Bountiful, the Isaiah passages, and the prophecies of Malachi within the Book of Mormon, obviously used the King James Bible wording for portions of those three books. But was the KJV used for plagiarizing or for translating? Using another text is not unusual among translators. Whenever such texts can be used they often are. Those who translated most of the various editions of the Bible used previously printed Bibles to aid them. From what the Lord told Oliver Cowdery, it appears that the process of translating was exhausting (D & C 8:10-11, 9:7-8). In view of that fact, who can blame Joseph for relying on the wording from another source, especially if the Lord commanded him to do so?

So now what was I to do or to think? The well-read dignitaries of Christendom—the Riverside ministers—had many years of schooling and experience in religion, while the much younger elders had comparatively little. Men and women of the cloth were perceived as experts in religion by everyone else that I knew who had any regard for religion at all. Because of the lofty place they enjoy in our culture, I decided that the ministers' conclusions far outweighed those of the immature, inexperienced, and undegreed Latter-day Saint youth. If the ministers said the Book of Mormon was plagiarized, then it was, even if that didn't make sense in view of what the missionaries showed me.

But underneath my irrational conclusion, the questions continued to quietly harry me: Who was right, the ministers or the Mormons? Was Joseph Smith a prophet or wasn't he? Did he translate an ancient record or did he not?

Though still partial to my prejudices about the elevated pedestal enjoyed by the Christian clergy, I decided to let the elders continue to teach me. Though I leaned toward the ministers' and Dr. Grant's attacks against Mormonism and believed that the LDS Church could not be the true Church, the Mormon missionaries defended themselves well against my blasts. They had won those battles, but the war was not yet over.

# 10
# Clerical Converts

"Come in, elders," I said as I opened the door. "I've been looking forward to meeting with you again." We strolled over to the dining room table where I had a peace offering prepared. "Do you like Rocky Road or Neapolitan or both?"

"We were afraid that you might not want us to come after last week's confrontation," Elder Johnson said as he dipped his dipper and filled his dish.

"I'm looking for the truth. The only way I know how to do it is to question everything. I apologize if I came on too strong. I really thought I had you cornered when I came at you with those three accusations."

As we sat enjoying our cool ice cream, I commented, "You know, of course, that I talked with three ministers about your religion and they told me what they thought they knew about it. I really look up to clergy people as the cream of the crop when it comes to religion. It suddenly dawned on me a few days ago that Sidney Rigdon was a preacher. He had converted to Mormonism. He gave up his livelihood and turned himself over to the despised Mormon cult."

"His entire family was converted too, I think," Elder Porter interrupted as he dipped out some more Rocky Road.

"He was humble enough to submit himself to a man who was more than ten years his junior and who was far less educated. The Book of Mormon is what converted him to the restored gospel and its prophet. Were there others?"

Elder Porter looked at his companion. "Were there, Elder?"

"I don't know. I've never thought about it before."

"If there were others, that would give more credence to your story," I informed them. "One such convert might be a fluke; but a flock would be even better."

Together with members of the Fontana ward, the missionaries eventually came up with a small collection of stories of former male and female preachers who became Mormons during the time of Joseph Smith. I wished I could have talked personally with each of them about the LDS

Church, but reading the stories about their conversions helped me realize that even the theologically trained—they whom I held in such high esteem —could be persuaded that Joseph's experiences might have actually occurred and that the Book of Mormon might truly rank as a companion volume with the Bible.

# Early Ecclesiastical Converts

## Ezra Booth

A Disciples of Christ history reports that Ezra Booth, a Methodist preacher, his wife, Mr. and Mrs. Johnson, and others were visiting Joseph Smith in Kirtland, in 1831. Mrs. Johnson had been afflicted for some time with a lame arm, and was not able to lift her hand to her head.

> During the conversation someone said, 'Here is Mrs. Johnson with a lame arm; has God given any power to men now on the earth to cure her?' A few moments later, when the conversation had turned in another direction, Smith rose, and walking across the room taking Mrs. Johnson by the hand, said in the most solemn and impressive manner: 'Woman, in the name of the Lord Jesus Christ I command thee to be whole.' and immediately left the room.
>
> Mrs. Johnson at once lifted [her arm] with ease, and on her return home the next day she was able to do her washing without difficulty or pain.[1]

The Booths and the Johnsons were so impressed that they were all baptized.

## John Greene

John P. Greene, also a Methodist preacher, and his wife, Rhoda, were given a copy of the Book of Mormon by Samuel Smith, Joseph's brother. At first, Greene refused to read the book, calling it a "nonsensical fable." But when his believing wife later pleaded with him to read it prayerfully, he relented and was converted. That same copy became instrumental in the conversions of Brigham Young, his brothers Phineas and Joseph (also itinerant Methodist ministers), and their sister, Fanny.[2]

## Jane Johnston

For four years during the early nineteenth century, Jane Johnston preached the Methodist doctrine in Northern Ireland for her father, Reverend Daniel Johnston, who had unexpectedly died.

After marrying William Black, Jr., the family moved to England where they were invited to a meeting in a crowded cellar. It was there that they heard the message of the restoration and were converted.[3]

## Parley Pratt

Born April 12, 1807, in Burlington, New York, Parley P. Pratt was a Disciples of Christ minister in Mentor, Ohio before his conversion to the restored gospel.

In 1830, feeling "called upon by the Holy Ghost to forsake" his fifty-acre Ohio farm "for the gospel's sake," Parley and his wife, Thankful, journeyed eastward with only $10 between them. In Rochester, Parley told his wife that he had to "stop awhile." He did not know why, but "it was plainly manifest by the Spirit." He told Thankful to go on and visit their friends. He had "work to do . . . and what it is, or how long it will take," he did not know.

Parley had breakfast with a Mr. Wells who then accompanied him through the neighborhood to visit the people. One person he visited was an old Baptist deacon by the name of Hamlin, who told Wells and Pratt about a "strange book in his possession which had been just published." The next morning Parley began reading the Book of Mormon. All day he read. "As I read," he recorded, "the spirit of the Lord was upon me, and I knew the book was true, as plainly as a man comprehends and knows that he exists."[4]

## Sidney Rigdon

Sidney Rigdon was ordained in 1821 as minister of the First Baptist Church in Pittsburgh.[5] Two-and-a-half years later he resigned because of what he felt were inconsistencies between his religion and the Bible. While working as a tanner, he, with Walter Scott and Alexander Campbell, founded the "Disciples" church (Campbellites) and moved to Mentor, Ohio.

While traveling through Mentor, Parley Pratt and other LDS missionaries spoke to Rigdon's congregation and gave them copies of the Book of Mormon. Two weeks later Rigdon finished reading his copy. He was so impressed "by a revelation from Jesus Christ" that he told his wife, Phebe, about it. She too had been "diligently investigating the subject" and was converted. The Rigdons, with about twenty others, were baptized November 14, 1830—seven months after The Church of Jesus Christ of Latter-day Saints was organized.[6]

## Orson Spencer

Orson Spencer, a Baptist minister, earned a master's degree in Hamilton, New York. Because of his speaking brilliance, Spencer was invited by George Briggs, Governor of Massachusetts, to take charge of the church where the governor resided.

Spencer accepted the teachings of the restored gospel during the Nauvoo period. There he served as a chancellor of the University of Nauvoo. Before embracing the new doctrines, he and his well-educated wife, Catharine, "counted the cost, laid their hearts on the altar and made the sacrifice! How few realize what it involved to become a 'Mormon' in those early days! Home, friends, occupation, popularity, all that makes life pleasant, were gone. Almost overnight they were strangers to their own kindred."

While living in Nauvoo, Spencer composed a book-length response to a letter of inquiry from Reverend William Crowel in Boston.

His observations about the Book of Mormon and Joseph Smith are especially enlightening. He wrote that he "diligently read the Book of Mormon" along with anti-Mormon comments from newspapers and private letters from friends of Solomon Spaulding. After reading the Book of Mormon he had a "strong conviction that its pages were graced with the pen of inspiration" and that "no enemy of truth or godliness would ever take the least interest in publishing the contents of such a book." Spencer then asked those of his "friends of pure religion" in the eastern states that they "read the Book of Mormon with the same unprejudiced, prayerful, and teachable spirit that they would recommend unbelievers in the Bible to read those sacred records."

In response to why he sacrificed his "respectable standing in the ministry to adhere" to such an "odious and revolting" a person as Joseph Smith and his followers, Spencer pointed out that "even Jesus Christ had many objectionable points of character" to the orthodox religious leaders of his day who did not know him. Similarly, orthodox ministers in Joseph's day found fault with him, a man they didn't bother to get to know personally. The orthodox in both Jesus's and Joseph's day had already judged them guilty of being impostors, so why stoop so low as to find out for themselves what kind of men they truly were? He went on:

. . . I shall speak of [Joseph's] character from an intimate acquaintance of more than one year, and from an intimate acquaintance with those who have been with him many years. I firmly avow, in the presence of God, that I believe Mr. Joseph Smith to be an upright man, that seeks the glory of god in such a manner as is well pleasing to the Most High God. He is kind and obliging; pitiful and courteous; as far from dissimulation as any man; frank and loquacious to all men, friends *or* foes. His friends are as ardently attached to him as his enemies are violently opposed. Free toleration is given to all opposing religions, but wherever he is accredited as a Prophet of the living God, there you will perceive his influence must be great. That lurking fear and suspicion that he may become a dictator or despot, gradually give place to confidence and fondness, as believers become acquainted with him.

In doctrine, Mr. Smith is eminently scriptural. I have never known him to deny or deprecate a single truth of the Old and New Testaments, but I have always known him to explain and defend them in a masterly manner. At his touch the ancient prophets spring into life, and the beauty and power of their revelations are made to commend themselves with thrilling interest to all that hear.[7]

It must have been quite a picture, I thought, to see these former clergymen and women—especially the more learned Orson Spencer— sitting at the feet of Joseph, eagerly absorbing wisdom from one who in most cases was much younger and far less educated. To them it didn't matter about his name, his age, or his lack of letters. For the first time since the days of the apostles, a prophet of God, schooled by the angels, stood in their presence.

Orson Spencer's description of the Book of Mormon, the Latter-day Saints with whom he was living, and particularly of Joseph Smith's character was especially important to me. Here was a man with a master's degree in theology who was so thoroughly convinced of the truthfulness of the restored gospel and its prophet, Joseph Smith, including the belief that the Book of Mormon was divinely bestowed to the world, that he was willing to give up his prestigious pulpit at the head of the Massachusetts governor's congregation to take his family west and join with the despised Mormons in Nauvoo, Illinois. To read Spencer's description of Joseph Smith was almost like listening to his story in person. I couldn't help but wish he had been one of the Riverside ministers with whom I had talked.

But because his words were from so long ago, it was easier to dismiss them. If he could have been resurrected and personally stood in my presence and told me the same things that I read, perhaps then I would have been more willing to lean toward the Mormon missionaries' point of view. "Doubting Thomas" and I were of the same ilk.

## More Recent Ecclesiastical Converts

From that discussion on, I have continually collected article after fascinating article about scores of men and women close to the cloth who formerly believed that the LDS Church was a cult to be shunned. After study and prayer and with a great deal of personal anguish, each one has humbly admitted that that "cult" is the same Church which Jesus Christ established when he walked the earth.[8]

Included in my collection are the captivating conversion stories from all over the world of nuns, priests, missionaries, monks, a rabbi, Jehovah's Witnesses, a Shinto priest, various Protestant pastors, two military chaplains (one Catholic, one Protestant), a "Mormon Basher" assigned by his church to "straighten out" those who might be showing an interest in the LDS religion, a religion editor, and high school and college theology teachers.

While all of the conversion stories are interesting, a few of the most fascinating include:

• a minister who joined the LDS Church and then gave his skeptical father, also a Protestant pastor, a copy of the Book of Mormon. Both of his parents read it and were converted.[9]

• a paraplegic preacher whose miraculous healing after his baptism into the LDS Church led to the conversion of his skeptical wife, who was a minister of music.[10]

• a Catholic priest who became a Latter-day Saint after discussing the restored gospel with another converted priest and his wife, herself a former nun.[11]

• a clergyman who "had always thought of Mormons as ridiculous—even stupid." After meeting an FBI agent and a navy commander who were Latter-day Saints, he suddenly realized that Mormons were not the "dummies" he had thought they were.[12]

• the grandson of a Hindu temple priest who became a Protestant minister and was then converted to the LDS religion by a spiritual experience he had while reading anti-Mormon literature.[13]

• a pastor who found, in a heap of ashes, a mysterious book of scripture similar to the Bible. Its cover and identifying pages were torn off and ruined, making the book unidentifiable to him for many years. Realizing the book was from God, he used it along with the Bible in his weekly sermons until he was defrocked by his superiors for doing so.[14]

• various other ministers who knowingly used the Book of Mormon along with the Bible to prepare their weekly sermons.[15]

• two teen-age converts to Mormonism who helped their minister fathers, along with their mothers, receive testimonies about the restored gospel.[16]

• a nun who sang in an LDS ward choir while still wearing her habit.[17]

• a minister who was working on his second doctorate when he discovered the truth at a humble LDS "open house."[18]

• a Catholic missionary who worked among African natives as he lived with them in their mud huts.[19]

• a Mother Superior who was also secretary for three popes.[20]

• a nun whose brother was disowned by his family because he became a Mormon. Eleven years later the nun's mother, sister and her sister's husband, as well as a sister-in law, all joined the Church. Wondering what was happening to her family, the nun read LDS literature and became a Latter-day Saint.[21]

• a monk who was involved in the operation and administration of "60 missionaries, 12 parishes, a trade school, a hospital, and about 215 primary schools" in Uganda, East Africa.[22]

• a minister who moved to Utah to save the "demon-possessed Mormons."[23]

How is it possible, I have quietly wondered, that anyone could believe the unschooled Joseph Smith wrote a work of fiction on his very first attempt, that got so many religious leaders to believe that it was truly from an ancient source? There is no precedent for such an accomplishment of which I am aware.

And, where is there another belief that has attracted—and continues to attract—such a worldwide congregation, who were trained for the professional ministry? Laypersons by the millions have left one religion to join another. But to have scores of trained men and women of the cloth freely convert to a single faith shunned by "mainstream" Christianity is quite a testimony in itself of the credibility of that faith.

# 11
# Who Are We?

When the three of us had finished our third helping of ice cream we got down to why the missionaries were there that afternoon. They had come prepared to teach me about God's plan for his children. When they told me that, I could sense deep within me that they had brought with them something of major significance.

Many concepts of God's plan were new and nearly unbelievable to me. But as I pondered the divine design I came to realize that it satisfactorily answered many—but not all—of the questions that had continually plagued me.

At the time, I didn't know whether the answers I received from the missionaries and from various LDS books I later read were factual, but they were more thorough and seemed to be more authoritative than any others I had ever heard or read. If what the missionaries were teaching me was true, God's plan of happiness—his plan of salvation—reliably answered questions about which philosophers have only speculated: where did we come from? Why are we here? And, most important to me, what happens to us after we die? According to the missionaries, the answers to these awesome mysteries were not derived from debate or philosophy. They flowed from the Fountain of All Truth. They were arrived at by revelation from God.

## Our Premortal Existence

"To understand the plan," Elder Porter began, "We need to recognize that we—our majestic spirits—lived elsewhere before birth. We dwelled in the presence of our Heavenly Father and 'many of the noble and great ones' (Abraham 3:22-23). We are our Father's children and Jehovah is our elder brother."

### Bible References

The idea of having previously lived isn't strange to Bible believers. Jesus arrived from elsewhere: "In the beginning was the Word [Jehovah], and the Word was *with* God [the Father]. . . . And *the Word* [Jesus] *was made flesh, and dwelt among us* (John 1:3, 14).[1]

During mortality, Jesus was reared in Joseph's and Mary's family. However, another family in another world also claimed him. They named him Jehovah—he who was worshipped by the Hebrews of old. "Yehosua" or "Yeshua" is Hebrew for "Jehovah" which translates to the English, "Joshua." "Jesus" is Greek for "Joshua." "Jesus," then, is the equivalent of "Jehovah."[2]

His virgin mother was the pure vessel chosen to bring Jehovah into the world. Joseph and Mary were given the sacred responsibility of nurturing him, but Joseph was actually Jesus's stepfather, not his biological sire. Gabriel, an angel of God, announced to Mary, "The Holy Ghost shall come upon thee, and the power of the Highest [the Father] shall overshadow thee; therefore . . . that holy thing which shall be born of thee shall be called the Son of God" (Luke 1:35). Jesus is the only person to be sired by an immortal father through a mortal mother.[3]

In a Capernaum synagogue Jesus intimated that he had lived in other places than on earth: "What . . . if ye shall see the Son of man ascend up where he was before?" He also informed his disciples that he "came forth from the Father." In his "intercessory" prayer, Jesus prayed, "O Father, glorify thou me with thine own self with the glory which I had with thee before the world was" (John 6:62; 16:28; 17:5).

Though he was a majestically magnificent adult spirit—the omniscient God of Israel who created our world—Jesus did not enter mortality with a fully grown body. Like all others, he came as a helpless infant, totally dependent upon caring adults.

After his birth, the Holy One enjoyed an ordinary childhood, but he became an extraordinary adult who "waxed strong in spirit . . . and increased in wisdom and stature, and in favour with God and man" (Luke 2:40, 52). The infant from another realm became our Savior.

Elsewhere the Lord has spoken of an existence before earth. He asked Job, "Where wast thou when I laid the foundations of the earth . . . when the morning stars sang together, and all the sons of God shouted for joy?" (Job 38:4, 7). God clearly shows that Job and we (the "morning stars" and his "sons") were with him when the earth was created.

Jehovah informed Jeremiah, "Before I formed thee in the belly I knew thee; and before thou camest forth out of the womb I sanctified thee, and

I ordained thee a prophet unto the nations" (Jer. 1:5). Paul told the Ephesians that the "God and Father of our Lord Jesus Christ . . . hath blessed us with all spiritual blessings in heavenly places . . . [and] hath chosen us . . . before the foundation of the world" (Eph. 1:3-4).

## Other References

The notion of premortality is not unique to Latter-day Saints, I have since learned. Sir Oliver Lodge wrote, "We . . . are ignorant of whatever experience our larger selves may have gone through in the past—yet when we wake out of this present materialized condition, we may . . . realize . . . the wide range of knowledge which that larger entity must have accumulated."[4]

Marcel Proust, the eminent French novelist, believed "Everything in our life happens as though we entered upon it with a load of obligations contracted in a previous existence . . . founded on kindness, scruples, sacrifice, a world entirely different from this one, a world whence we emerge to be born on this earth, before returning thither."[5]

# The Purpose of Earth Life

## Agency

Everyone brings into the world the important gift of choice referred to by Latter-day Saints as "agency." We are not predestined to do God's will. "Men are free . . . to choose liberty and eternal life, through the great Mediator of all men, or to choose captivity and death, according to the captivity and power of the devil" (2 Nephi 2:27). Even Jesus overcame temptations by choosing to obey the commandments. "Though he were a Son, yet learned he obedience by the things which he suffered" (Heb. 5:8).

## Know God and Become Like Him

Jesus said, "This is life eternal that they might know thee the only true God, and Jesus Christ whom thou has sent" (John 17:3). He also commanded us to become "perfect, even as [our] Father which is in heaven is perfect" (Matt. 5:48). Since it is life eternal to know God and to become perfect like he is, we need to know our relationship to him and what he is like.

Besides being vastly superior to us mentally and spiritually, our Father is also remarkable physically. Housing his regal spirit is an exalted, perfect body.

Today, Jesus also lives within a perfect body. When the apostles were gathered together after Jesus's resurrection, "Jesus . . . stood in the midst of them, and saith unto them, 'Peace be unto you.' But they were terrified and affrighted, and supposed that they had seen a spirit. He said unto them '. . . Behold my hands and my feet, that it is I myself: handle me, and see; for a spirit hath not flesh and bones, as ye see me have'" (Luke 24:36-39). While his disciples were watching their master's ascension, angels told them that "Jesus . . . shall so come in like manner as ye have seen him go into heaven" (Acts 1:11).

"I have been told that God is a spirit. If Jesus was also the Father, as I have been taught, then how could God have a body now?" I asked, bewildered. "If, as I have previously been informed, the Father is a spirit without a body and Jesus was resurrected with a body, I guess that would mean that the Father now has a body. So how could he be a spirit? It's very confusing."

"Before he was born as Jesus, Jehovah was a spirit without a body," Elder Johnson reminded me. "But Jesus was subsequently resurrected with a perfect body much like his Father's. As you have shown, they who believe that God is a spirit without a body also teach that the Father, Son, and Holy Ghost are the same being. If Jesus is the only God, and if he was resurrected with an immortal body, he—God—must have that body today. If not, what was the point of being resurrected? If Jesus no longer has a body what became of it?"

## Our Test of Integrity

As we matured for untold eons along a path of eternal progression in God's celestial world, there came a point when we could not progress to become like our Father unless we lived outside of his immediate presence for a period. A council was convened. We were there. Father explained that since it was his "work and glory to bring to pass the immortality and eternal life of man," he must prove us to see if eternal life—his life—was what we truly wished. Could we be trusted as he is trusted? Would we be as honest with our brothers and sisters outside of our Father's presence as we were in his presence? How loyal to him and his life of righteousness would we prove to be?

An earth would be created upon which we would dwell to see if we would "do all things whatsoever the Lord . . . shall command" (Moses 1:39; Abraham 3:22-26). If we proved that we wished God's life to also be our life—if we "overcometh"—we would "inherit all things" (Rev. 21:7). It wouldn't be easy, but it would be worth it.

## Penalties for Sin

Along with the reward of eternal life, the plan of salvation includes penalties for disobedience. "Justice [cannot] be destroyed; if so, God would cease to be God" (Alma 42:13). One penalty based on justice alone is everlasting physical death—the loss of our physical bodies. Another penalty is spiritual death—being banned eternally from God's presence.

# The Need for a Messiah

Father realized that all would break his laws from time to time—that we would sin. Because he is a God of mercy as well as of justice, he provided a way for us to return to him. If his first-born son would serve the ends of justice by living sinlessly and freely allow himself to be punished for the sins of all others—to atone for them—that sacrifice would be acceptable in the place of our continual individual suffering.

The Chosen One would become our Savior, for he would save us from physical and spiritual death. All would be unconditionally resurrected, thus escaping physical death. However, we must do our part to escape spiritual death. We must genuinely repent and live righteously, accepting Jesus Christ and keeping his commandments as best as we are able. If we do not, we will forever be banished from God's presence. "The plan of mercy could not be brought about except an atonement should be made" (Alma 42:15).

When Jehovah graciously consented to be our Messiah, we gratefully "sang together, and . . . shouted for joy" (Job 7:7).

## Obtain a Body

Before conception, we had no flesh. Another reason for coming to earth, then, was to briefly obtain a body so that we could eventually become as perfect as our Father, physically as well as spiritually. During mortality, that body would be used for a short time to demonstrate how we would use it in the eternities. At death, it would be temporarily cast aside while we continued our probationary status elsewhere. Finally, everyone will have his or her body returned forever in what is known as the resurrection. For those who proved by the way they lived that they would remain true and faithful throughout eternity, their bodies would become glorified like Father's. Contrary to what some philosophers have taught—that the body is an impediment to the spirit—a perfected body gives greater dimension to the spirit.

## The Veil of Forgetfulness

To ensure that we were given a valid test, a veil was placed across our minds so we could not recall our former lives. We would be required to walk by faith, for if we could remember, many would be obedient to the commandments of God out of fear rather than out of a desire for righteousness. Virtue for virtue's sake would need to be demonstrated.

## Covenants and Ordinances

The plan of happiness includes sacred covenants and ordinances. Baptism is one. "All . . . who humble themselves before God, and desire to be baptized" make a solemn covenant that they "are willing to take upon themselves the name of Jesus Christ, having a determination to serve Him to the end, and truly manifest by their works that they have received of the Spirit of Christ unto the remission of their sins" (D & C 20:37). Other important ordinances are the laying on of hands for the gift of the Holy Ghost, partaking of the sacrament in remembrance of Christ's sacrifice of his body (which is a renewal of our baptismal covenant), and temple ordinances in which further covenants with God are made.

## Guides Along the Way

Our Father would not completely abandon us. Along the pathway back to him, trail guides will aid us if we will allow them to. Our conscience, prayer, the Holy Ghost, prophets, parents, scriptures, commandments, ordinances, covenants, wise men and women, teachers, inspired stories, movies, music and plays, friends, angels and spirits are a few. Joseph Smith taught, "If there is anything virtuous, lovely, or of good report or praiseworthy, we seek after these things."[6]

# War in Heaven

Another of God's sons—Lucifer—came up with what he thought was a better idea. Unwilling to work out his own salvation, he proposed that our agency be eliminated. We would be sent into the world, be given a body, then be compelled to do what was necessary in order to return to

Father's celestial world. We would become like robots. Everyone would then inherit all that Father has; no one would become lost.

Under Lucifer's plan, however, there was no way to gain all that Father has. With the destruction of agency, there would be no growth, no ability to become like our Father. Satan wanted to have all that Father has to himself with endless numbers of obedient but helpless servants below him. No Messiah would be needed. Lucifer wanted all the glory and honor for himself. He would become our God.

Many agreed with Lucifer. He and his followers rebelled because his plan was not accepted. They alienated themselves from the presence of God. They chose eternal exile and a bodiless existence. For their unrepentant hostility, Lucifer and one-third of Father's children denied themselves bodies and the opportunity to progress. Never will they know the cuddle of a child. Never will they enjoy the fond embraces of loved ones. Isaiah exclaimed, "How art thou fallen from heaven, O Lucifer, son of the morning! how art thou cut down to the ground, which didst weaken the nations! For thou hast said in thine heart, 'I will ascend into heaven, I will exalt my throne above the stars of God . . . I will be like the most High" (Isaiah 14:12-14).

"There was war in heaven: Michael [Adam's premortal name] and his angels [us] fought against the dragon [Lucifer]; and the dragon fought and his angels [the rebels], and prevailed not; neither was their place found any more in heaven. And . . . Satan, which deceiveth the whole world . . . was cast out into the earth, and his angels were cast out with him" (Rev. 12:7-9).

Here they live, still trying to win converts to their legions. Temptations are their ammunition; selfishness is our weakness. Though Satan cannot force us to do his will, we must be alert. "How great the inequality of man is because of sin and transgression, and the power of the devil, which comes by the cunning plans which he hath devised to ensnare the hearts of men" (Alma 28:13).

"I have often wondered how and why Satan was created, if there is such a creature," I remarked to the missionaries. "It is unthinkable to me that if there is a God who is all that is good and holy, he would cause evil to be a part of our existence or that he would deliberately produce a being such as the devil whose only function is to induce evil."

# Here We Are

Under Father's direction, Jehovah created our world. Weather and climate systems were established. Food, water, and all the basics that are needed to sustain life were put in place.

## Adam and Eve

The elders explained that Adam and Eve were selected to begin the long train of humanity that would follow them into mortality.

"Hold the phone, Elders!" I exclaimed. "Do you really believe that Adam and Eve were the first humans? What about such fossil finds as Pithecanthropus erectus ["erect ape man"] or the Australopithecus group of Africa who were supposedly antecedents to Homo sapiens? Weren't Adam and Eve related to them?"

"Like us," Elder Porter answered, "Adam and Eve lived with our Father during premortality. They and we are literal children of God. They were created in his image and likeness. 'As the horse, the ox, the sheep, and every living creature, including man, propagates its own species and perpetuates its own kind, so does God perpetuate his.'[7] Whoever or whatever these fossil creatures were, if they lived before Adam and Eve, they were not related to them."

Adam's body was created first. After his creation "the Lord God said, 'It is not good that the man should be alone; I will make him an helper'" (Gen. 2:18, RSV). He then made Eve. Theirs was the first marriage; they were made for each other. The couple lived in a beautiful paradise in Eden where they could dwell as long as they wished. Their bodies were "unmortal;" they did not need to suffer death.[8] Because the veil blocked their memories, they came into the garden with an absence of knowledge and no memory of their former lives. Very nearly like innocent, naive children, they lived in adult bodies.

Two commands were given them: they were to have children and they were not to eat the fruit that would give them knowledge of good and evil. Without knowledge of good, they probably knew not how to bear children. Though he was able to instruct them, God apparently chose not to; their agency would not be violated. Father left them alone to see what they would do, for that is the purpose of this life.

Eventually Eve succumbed to the enticements of Lucifer. By eating the fruit of the tree of knowledge of good and evil she disobeyed Father; she had to leave the garden and eventually die.

Adam realized that because Eve would be cast out of the garden they would not be together and therefore could not have children. He would need to partake of the fruit so that he could be with Eve. "If Adam had not transgressed he would not have fallen, but he would have remained in the garden . . . [He and Eve] would have had no children; wherefore they would have remained in a state of innocence, having no joy, for they knew no misery; doing no good, for they knew no sin" (2 Nephi 2:22-24).

Both became mortal. Eviction from the presence of God—spiritual death—was the consequence. They and their children were also to die physically because of the change that had taken place in their bodies.

Sufficient time was needed for the pair to repent and to prove that paradise was where they really wished to live again. To keep them from partaking of the healing fruit of the nearby Tree of Life, and thereby lose the probationary period in which they could repent and prepare to meet God, "The Lord God said, 'Behold, the man is become as one of us, to know good and evil: now, lest he put forth his hand, and take also of the tree of life, and eat, and live for ever' . . . he drove out the man [and woman]; and he placed at the east of the garden of Eden Cherubim and a flaming sword which turned every way, to keep the way of the tree of life" (Gen. 3:22-24). Through obedience to the commandments and ordinances they would have to earn the right to enjoy the fruit of that tree; it was now only available by way of the atonement of Jesus the Christ.

In summary, for an unspecified time Adam and Eve chose to obey God by staying away from the forbidden tree. Eve was eventually deceived into tasting the fruit (1 Tim. 2:14). Adam then chose to heed the higher command to multiply by disobeying the lesser one of not eating the forbidden fruit. "Adam fell that men might be, and men are that they might have joy" (2 Nephi 2:25).

"Then Adam and Eve weren't the terrible creatures I have been taught they were if what you say is true," I interjected. "I've never heard such a sensible explanation. Somehow I've understood that they partook of the fruit and committed a sexual sin. Consequently they had to be cast out of the garden which meant we had to suffer along with them. I've been told that if they had not partaken of the fruit we could have been born in the garden and lived with them forever. What is your belief about original sin?"

## Original Sin

"There is no such doctrine as original sin within LDS theology," Elder Porter taught me. "'We believe that men will be punished for their own sins, and not for Adam's transgression.'[9] Though they transgressed a commandment and brought death to their posterity, Adam and Eve were not the dastardly devils that history has portrayed them to be. The only 'crime' they committed was eating a bit of forbidden food. But that transgression turned out for the good of mankind."

I have since come to learn that the doctrine of original sin and its accompanying precept of baptism of infants has caused many former ministers, priests, and nuns to look elsewhere for a religion that did not teach it. Some have become LDS. One such convert said that his former church informs its members "that all men are born under original sin and must be cleansed by baptism at birth or relegated to 'limbo' [and] barred from heaven through no fault of their own." He asks, "How could an all-just, all-loving God hold a tiny infant responsible for something he or she did not do?"[10] Another, looking at his newly born daughter through the maternity room glass, whispered, "You do not know what sin is. If they had lined up all the bishops in the world that day, they couldn't have convinced me that original sin was true."[11]

"According to your belief, is Satan the cause of so much grief and sorrow in the world?" I wondered aloud to the elders. "How can there be a God when we see war, disease, poverty and devastation all around us every day?"

## Adversity

Our test in mortality would not be a true test if everything happened the way we wished it would. Frailty of the mortal bodies inherited from Adam and Eve, the unleashing of the powers of nature, and the foolish and selfish use of agency often cause mankind's tragedy and heartache. Satan's temptations are partly to blame, but he cannot be blamed for everything that seems to go wrong. Adversity is part of God's plan. The prophet Lehi taught his son, Jacob, that "it must needs be, that there is an opposition in all things. If not . . . righteousness could not be brought to pass, neither wickedness, neither holiness nor misery, neither good nor bad" (2 Nephi 2:11). Not only does adversity come from natural causes in our environment, it is sometimes given by God to help us correct our course—to help us repent and return to him.

Viewed from an eternal perspective, *adversity is the fuel of God's refining fire.* How do we handle it? What are our actions and reactions? Do we realize in the midst of grief that "there can be no rainbow without the storm?" Do we "look for the silver lining" in the dark clouds of turmoil? Or do we curse God and lash out? When we ask, "Why me?" do we hear, "Because I love you?" What do we do when adversity crosses the path of another? Are we merciful and comforting? Do we forgive those who hurt us or someone else? Sacred promises have been made that "after much tribulation come the blessings" (D & C 58:4) when "he that overcometh shall inherit all things" (Revelation 21:7). Part of our test is to see how we will handle adversity in our lives and in the lives of those around us.

"I have heard people say when adversity enters their lives that 'It is God's will,' I commented. "Is it God's will if a baby is killed when some drunk crashes into the car its parents were driving?"

"It was God's will and ours that we be placed on earth to be tested," Elder Porter reminded me. "We chose to come here, therefore we chose to suffer adversity. Although God does intervene in human affairs, he generally allows the consequences of agency to follow their natural course. God does not cause bad things to happen, he allows them to happen. And why shouldn't he? How would we ever learn to be righteous if we were continually shielded from the effects of our actions? How would we learn the lessons taught by adversity if we were never exposed to it?"

I hadn't looked at things that way before. Then again, many of the strongest people I knew had overcome a lot of adversity in their lives. Likewise, many of the weakest people I knew had been so sheltered that they did not know how to handle even minor setbacks. What Elder Porter told me was starting to make sense.

"God knew we would suffer grief and pain during our lives," Elder Porter continued. "He knew we would be spiritually damaged by the unrighteousness of ourselves and others. But he prepared the way for us to overcome the effect of grief and sin."

# The Atonement of Christ

As the Babe of Bethlehem, Jehovah, came forth; the Messiah was born. Though he was born a man with the same frailties and weaknesses as other men, an important difference in Jesus's nature set him apart from the rest of us. He could die because of traits passed on through his mortal mother, but he could also choose to never die because of power over death inherited from his immortal Father.

Jesus lived an untainted life and therefore had no personal sins for which to be punished. The Lamb without blemish was ready to be sacrificed for our sins and become our resurrected Shepherd.

The atoning sacrifice had to be freely accomplished. Forcing a man to die for others would be unjust and, therefore, could not appease the law of justice. With his inherent power of life over death, Jesus was at liberty to voluntarily give himself. No mortal could end his life without his permission. "I lay down my life that I might take it again. No man taketh it from me, but I lay it down of myself. I have power to lay it down, and I have power to take it again" (John 10:17-18).

The garden of Gethsemane was the sacred site of the most difficult part of the atoning process. Within that peaceful olive orchard, Jesus freely assumed our sins and suffered for them. He took upon himself all our pain and hardship. He fully understood the ordeal that he had to endure. His anguish would be so unbearable that only He, God, could withstand it. "God himself atoneth for the sins of the world to bring about the plan of mercy, to appease the demands of justice, that God might be a perfect, just God, and a merciful God also" (Alma 42:15). He understands all our grief and weakness because he has suffered all of it. He fully understands the effects of sin because he has paid the price for the sins of all mankind.

So awful was his suffering that he entreated his Father, "If it be possible, let this cup pass from me: nevertheless not as I will, but as thou wilt." As he prayed, he "began to be sore amazed, and to be very heavy" in sorrow. Three times he pleaded with his father. During the third offering "there appeared an angel unto him from heaven, strengthening him." Still, "being in agony he prayed more earnestly [and] sweat . . . great drops of blood" (Luke 22:44).

When his impassioned suffering ended, Jesus came forth, meekly allowing his persecutors to seize him, to illegally try him, to give him over to the Romans to be tortured, and to have cruel spikes sledge-hammered into his hands and feet, fixing him to the ghastly cross. Hanging by the nails, with no place to perch on that merciless "tree," the mortal—yet immortal—Messiah had the power to linger on or to mercifully give his life for those he loved.

The Messiah's death was the second part of the atonement. It was necessary in order for him to be resurrected and bring about a general resurrection for all. Adam's transgression began the process of physical death; to balance the scale of justice, Jesus's death and resurrection began the process of resurrection. "For since by man came death, by man came also the resurrection of the dead. For as in Adam all die, even so in Christ shall all be made alive" (1 Cor. 15:22).

Not only did our Lord's generous sacrifice overcome physical death, it made it possible for us to overcome spiritual death as well. If we choose, we will be allowed back into Father's presence with perfected bodies. Eternal Life—God's life—may be our life. Whereas the resurrection is a free gift to every mortal regardless of how we live, we must merit the privilege of returning to live in the presence of our Father. We must work for our inheritance through obedience to the laws and ordinances of the gospel of Jesus Christ. No one may inherit eternal life on his own merits. All who would not suffer as Jesus suffered and die a spiritual death must come to the Father by way of Jesus Christ. To choose any other path is to be overcome by the effects of mortality rather than overcoming them through the power of him who overcame all. "If ye are not the sheep of the good shepherd . . . the devil is your shepherd, and ye are of his fold" (Alma 5:39).

So, here we are. Our orbiting globe is the designated place to receive a physical body, our reward for having lived righteously before birth. Unable to remember that life, we must walk by faith while we demonstrate to our father our worthiness to return home. Because of the atonement of Christ, "Ye are free to act for yourselves—to choose the way of everlasting death or the way of eternal life" (2 Nephi 10:24).

# Resurrection

All of us eventually will be given new physical bodies—a process that began when the Savior left his tomb: "The hour is coming in the which all that are in the graves shall . . . come forth; they that have done good unto the resurrection of life; and they that have done evil unto the resurrection of damnation" (John 5:28-29).

## Celestial Bodies

Not all will receive the same type of resurrected body: "There are . . . celestial bodies, and bodies terrestrial: but the . . . celestial is one, and the . . . terrestrial is another. There is one glory of the sun, and another glory of the moon, and another glory of the stars: for one star differeth from another star in glory. So also is the resurrection of the dead" (1 Cor. 15:40-42).

If we have proven by obedience to the laws and ordinances of the gospel and by faith in Jesus Christ that we wish to be with our Heavenly Father and Christ forever, we will receive a perfect body—one that is "celestial," like the bodies of Jesus and our Father. The place where the celestialized live is known as the Celestial Kingdom. There we will live eternally with our loved ones. We will forever enjoy familial relationships as we lovingly embrace and mingle with our parents, our grandparents, our eternal companions, our children and grandchildren who have also demonstrated that they wished it that way. "Eye hath not seen, nor ear heard, neither have entered into the heart of man, the things which God hath prepared for them that love him," Paul wrote the Corinthians (I Cor. 2:9). And, Joseph Smith taught that "happiness is the object and design of our existence; and will be the end thereof, if we pursue the path that leads to it; and this path is virtue, uprightness, faithfulness, holiness, and keeping all the commandments of God."[12]

"Pardon me for interrupting again," I said. "But that quote from Joseph Smith is beautiful. It seems to me that only a good man would teach his followers that the road to happiness is living a virtuous life. Did he practice what he preached?"

"Only by prayerfully examining his fruits will you know. That succinct quote is one of his fruits. Another is the plan of happiness that we are bringing you today. Keep it up, Bill. You'll become a Mormon, yet," Elder Porter promised.

Any other time, a comment implying that I would convert to their faith would have bothered me. But for some reason, it did not this time. Perhaps it was because what they were telling me seemed to be true. I was virtually already converted to the ideas they were telling me about; so the thought of joining their church didn't seem to be too far of a stretch.

## Terrestrial Bodies

They who have shown that their hearts are virtuous but have rejected Jesus as their master and would not covenant to live a celestial law, will receive "terrestrial" bodies and will dwell in the Terrestrial Kingdom with those having the same honorable character. Paul compared their resurrection to the moon's glory. Though fine individuals, they will never again enjoy eternal relationships with their families.

## Telestial Bodies

They who desire lasciviousness and other evils will receive the least. Though resurrected, their bodies will be of a telestial nature which Paul compared to the observed differences in star brightness. Their worlds will be the Telestial. Like terrestrial beings, never will they delight in family relationships which they might have enjoyed if they had lived the gospel.

"If our hearts have been hardened . . . against the word . . . then will our state be awful, for then we shall be condemned. For our words will condemn us, yea, all our works will condemn us; we shall not be found spotless; and our thoughts will also condemn us; and in this awful state we shall not dare to look up to our God; and we would fain be glad if we could command the rocks and the mountains to fall upon us to hide us from his presence. But this cannot be; we must come forth and stand before him in his glory, and in his power, and in his might, majesty, and dominion, and acknowledge to our everlasting shame that all his judgments are just . . . and that he is merciful unto the children of men" (Alma 12:13-18).

# 12
# Eternal Family Relationships

"Being judged according to how we live seems more reasonable than faith alone saving us," I interrupted. "As a child I used to think that being a Christian was easy. All I had to do was believe in Christ, and then I could do anything I wanted whether or not it was a sin. When it came time to die, all I had to do was say I believed in Christ and I would immediately be ushered into heaven. Now you elders come along and spoil that scene," I laughed as a sign that I wasn't convinced that we are saved by faith alone either.

"Seriously, I have been shown a scripture that says we are saved through faith and not by works," I challenged. "What about that?"

## Faith and Works

Probably because it had been quoted so many times by antagonists, Elder Porter knew precisely where to find the passage: "'For by grace are ye saved through faith; and that not of yourselves: it is the gift of God: Not of works, lest any man should boast.' (Eph. 2:8-9). It is a typical example of how verses are taken out of context to fit a person's own ideas."

The missionaries then asked me to read the entire chapter. I discovered that when this verse is tied to all of Paul's epistle, his intent is clear: Paul was writing to Gentile converts. They knew nothing about the law of Moses. Since the earliest Christians were mainly Jews, the new Ephesian saints were concerned that they would need to be circumcised and would have to obey other Hebrew laws such as animal sacrifice, obeying strict Sabbath rules and abstaining from certain foods. Paul was trying to set their minds at ease by letting them know that they need not worry about such "works" because Christ had done away with them. Converted Israelites and Gentiles were now "fellowcitizens . . . of the household of God" and need not adhere to older Hebraic customs.

Jesus told his disciples that he "shall reward every man according to his works" (Matt. 16:27). On the mount he said, "Let your light so shine

119

before men, that they may see your good works, and glorify your Father which is in heaven" (Matt. 5:16). In the same sermon he taught: "Not everyone that saith unto me, Lord, Lord, shall enter into the kingdom of heaven; but he that doeth the will of my Father which is in heaven" (Matt. 7:21).

One former minister that I have since read about found that "the 'works' passages far exceeded the 'grace' passages" in the Bible.[1] Two others point out to those in their former congregations who insist that works are unnecessary because "they are saved by their belief in Christ," that "the devils also believe. Are the devils saved then?" When their friends insist that "faith alone is necessary to salvation" they are shown that "James clearly teaches that faith without works is dead (James 2:14-20). As Mormons, we too believe that we are saved by grace, but only after all we can do."[2]

"Out of the blue" James's scriptures that "by works a man is justified, and not by faith only" (James 2:21-26) became "beautifully clear and profoundly meaningful" to a Protestant seminarian who knew of the teachings of the restored gospel.

"Warmth and indescribable happiness and calm came over me" because of what Joseph Smith also taught concerning the relationship of faith and works, "I knew that Joseph Smith was a true prophet."[3]

## Christ's Parables

Nearly all of Christ's parables have to do with how we conduct our lives—how we work out our salvation and demonstrate our faith in his words. Consider only a few: building our house on a rock, the children of the bridechamber, the beam and the mote, the sower, the lost sheep and the ninety and nine, the harsh servant and the debt, the good Samaritan, the foolish rich man, the good shepherd, the wedding feast, the prodigal son, the rich man and Lazarus, the labourers in the vineyard, the wicked husbandman, the ten virgins, the talents, the sheep and the goats.[4]

## Jesus's Sacrifice

Jesus performed the supreme example of service. He told certain Jews that "the works which the Father hath given me to finish, the same works that I do, bear witness of me, that the Father hath sent me" (John 5:36). If the conclusion is carried to its extreme, that all a person need do is believe in Christ, all Jesus would have needed to do was believe in himself and his atonement would have been accomplished. If instead, he had not come into the world and worked at living a perfect life in order to qualify to be our sacrificial lamb, if he had not voluntarily undergone excruciating punishment to pay for our sins, if he had not willingly died and resurrected himself to atone for Adam's transgression, we would not have been saved from an everlasting lingering in the world of spirits. To fulfill the demands of justice, Jesus intentionally underwent all of our pain on our behalf to finish the works that the Father gave him. His caring was so fervent that he performed the greatest work of all. He suffered "temptations, and pain of body, hunger, thirst, and fatigue, even more than man can suffer, except it be unto death; for behold, blood cometh from every pore, so great [was] his anguish for the wickedness and the abominations of his people . . . All these things are done that a righteous judgment might come upon the children of men" (Mosiah 3:7, 10).

"What about those who have never heard of the plan of happiness?" I asked. "Billions of people all over the world and throughout history have died without even hearing the name of Jesus Christ, let alone being informed about his plan of salvation. If all of us need Christ for salvation, how could a just God let so many live and die without knowledge about the purpose of life and what they can inherit if they live righteously? Where is the justice in not informing everyone about life's purpose?"

## Beyond Death

All will eventually hear the gospel of Jesus Christ in this life or after death, the missionaries explained. Though our bodies die, our personalities—our spirits—continue to live somewhere on earth. At the instant of death, the righteous find themselves channeled into a wonderfully curious dimension where most will dwell longer than when they existed in the flesh. Relationships with friends and relatives will continue. There they will come to realize the importance of flesh and bones when they are unable to do many of the things the body enabled them to do. They will look forward to the resurrection so they can regain a body.

"The spirits of all men, as soon as they are departed from this mortal body . . . whether they be good or evil, are taken home to that God who gave them life. And then shall it come to pass, that the spirits of those who are righteous are received into a state of happiness, which is called paradise, a state of rest, a state of peace, where they shall rest from all their trouble and from all care, and sorrow" (Alma 40:11-12).

Those who have lived unrighteously in mortality will continue to so live if that is what they choose. Bad habits and evil thoughts will linger. In that state of darkness, in what is termed a spirit prison, they will live until they repent or are resurrected. "The spirits of the wicked, yea, who . . . have no part nor portion of the Spirit of the Lord; for . . . they chose evil works rather than good . . . shall be cast out into outer darkness; there shall be weeping, and wailing, and gnashing of teeth, and this because of their own iniquity, being led captive by the will of the devil. Now this is the state of the souls of the wicked, yea, in darkness, and a state of awful, fearful looking for the fiery indignation of the wrath of God upon them; thus they remain in this state, as well as the righteous in paradise, until the time of their resurrection" (Alma 40:13-14).

While he hung writhing in agony on the unmerciful cross, one of the malefactors gasped, "Lord, remember me when thou comest into thy kingdom." Jesus answered, "Today shalt thou be with me in paradise" (Luke 23:42-43). Through his anguish, Jesus let the thief know that after they died they would, that same day, be together in paradise, the abode of spirits. While Jesus's body lay entombed between death and resurrection, those whom we call dead were listening to "the voice of the son of God" (John 5:28). One was the crucified thief. Peter informs us that "the gospel [was] preached . . . to them that are dead, that they might be judged according to men in the flesh, but live according to God in the spirit" (1 Peter 3:18-20; 4:6). All who had died were being given an opportunity to come unto Christ.

In the story about the rich man and Lazarus, a "great gulf" separated the two after they died (Luke 16:19-31). That gulf was bridged when the gospel was preached unto the spirits who were like the imprisoned rich man. The Lord's missionaries mingle with the wicked, giving them the opportunity to accept the gospel and live with the righteous until their resurrection. The repentant David sang, "My heart is glad, and my glory rejoiceth: my flesh also shall rest in hope. For thou wilt not leave my soul in hell [prison]" (Psalms 16:9-10).

Eventually every soul will hear the great plan of salvation either in this life or the next. They must then choose. Is it God's plan and is it for them? Is it *the* way of eternal life, not merely *a* way of life? Is it the Lord's *narrow* way? If they live the gospel to the end, they will inherit eternal life. All that God has will also be theirs.

## Baptism for Those Who Have Died

An important part of the plan is the ordinance of baptism. Jesus taught, "Except a man be born of water and of the Spirit, he cannot enter into the kingdom of God" (John 3:5). To his apostles, Jesus said, "Go . . . and teach all nations baptizing them in the name of the Father, and of the Son, and of the Holy Ghost" (Matt. 28.19-20). Jesus set the example when he himself was baptized "to fulfil all righteousness" (Matt. 3:15).

Most "have died without baptism," a former minister pointed out. "Was there no hope for their salvation? Apparently my previous church had no answer."[5]

God has established a way for those who have died, and who have not been baptized with priesthood authority, to receive this critical ordinance. Jesus performed his atoning ordinance as a proxy for others. We may either accept or reject his effort. Similarly, Latter-day Saints are baptized in their sacred temples on behalf of others who have departed from this world. He or she for whom the work has been done has the freedom in the spirit world to either accept or reject the baptismal ordinance performed on their behalf.

Paul mentioned the early practice of proxy baptism when he argued with a heretical faction of Corinthian Saints who did not believe in the resurrection: ". . . What shall they do which are baptized for the dead, if the dead rise not at all? why are they then baptized for the dead?" (1 Cor. 15:29). What purpose was there in performing the ordinance of baptism for the dead if the dead are not going to be resurrected?

Baptism is an ordinance that must be performed with a physical body. Since those who have passed into the spirit world are separated from their physical bodies, it is not possible for their flesh to be buried and symbolically resurrected as new creatures.

"When we die, then, we don't permanently enter heaven or hell?" I double-checked with the elders. The possibility of ending up in hell's fearful fires had been the very reason I had become religious in the first place. "I have always understood that there is only one of two places a person can go after death—heaven or hell. You stay in one or the other forever. If you believe in Jesus, and accept him as your personal Savior, you automatically enter into heaven at death. If not, you go to hell and burn eternally in unquenchable flames. If a person has not yet accepted Jesus, he or she may repent while lying on their deathbeds and will then automatically end up in heaven."

After acknowledging my struggles to understand, Elder Johnson quietly mumbled his opinion about orthodox concepts of life after death. There was no way he could ever worship such a barbarous God. How could our loving Father—a beneficent being like his son—be so sadistically maleficent as to cast his children into a furious fire to be roasted forever?

"I tend to agree with you," I admitted. "Could an Adolph Hitler roll over in his deathbed and groan that he believed in Jesus and then automatically be escorted into heaven? How is that equitable when compared with the life of the wise and virtuous Socrates who taught his students to obey the law regardless of its justness? Practicing what he preached, Socrates willingly obeyed an unjust verdict and drank poison hemlock given to him by the prison officials, even though arrangements had been made for him to escape. Socrates, who lived centuries before Jesus's birth, never heard of the Messiah. Because he had the misfortune of being born at the wrong time in the wrong place, is the "doomed" Socrates forever fanning himself in hell's infernal flames while Hitler is strumming his harp at the feet of Jesus? I think I would rather embrace Socrates in hell than see Hitler in heaven if such a doctrine were true."

## Heaven and Hell

Going on, Elder Porter clarified my observations. Heaven and hell are descriptive terms. The scriptures generally speak of the spirit world when they refer to eternal heaven or hell. The place of spirits—the site—is eternal, but we don't stay there forever.

Where we live after our resurrection and the final judgment is permanent. Joy and gratitude will be our heaven if we are allowed to live forever with our families. Anguish (hell) will plague us as we reflect upon what we could have obtained if the verdict is that we must live elsewhere.

We would always wonder what our loved ones were doing if they inherited a higher sphere of existence than we and we could never see them again. It would be as if someone had told us where the Lost Dutchman gold mine could be found and we ignored their tip. When another person later located it, we would probably live in torment wishing we had seriously listened. On the other hand, if we followed up on their information how would we feel when we discovered it?

# Families Can be Eternal

The most important reward for living righteously is to live with our Father and his family forever. Those who inherit the highest degree of the Celestial glory can realize husband-wife relationships, those who merit the other degrees within the Celestial Kingdom will still live with Heavenly Father (D & C 131:2-4). Joseph Smith taught, "That same sociality which exists amongst us here will exist among us there only it will be coupled with eternal glory which we do not now enjoy."[6]

### The Marriage of Adam and Eve

The first nuptial rite uniting the first family on earth occurred in Eden. Within that sanctified site God joined Adam and Eve together forever. Though built without human hands, the Garden of Eden was the first of God's holy temples. As long as the world's first couple dwelled in that sacred section they would be together forever. Outside of the Garden they continued to be married eternally even though they were to die. Only if one lived unrighteously would they live apart after the judgment.

Since all are descended from that first couple, a similar opportunity is available to us. A man and his wife, with their parents and children, may enjoy everlasting companionship if their family is "sealed" together by an authorized representative of God within a temple of the Lord. The ultimate outcome of such a sealing ordinance is conditioned, of course, upon their living righteously.

"Didn't Jesus teach that there is no marriage after the resurrection?" I asked. "I remember hearing various ministers at weddings that I have attended say the couple was married 'until death do you part' or 'as long as you both shall live.' Doesn't that indicate that the marriage will not last after the death of one of the partners?"

## Jesus Taught Eternal Marriage

Pharisees and Sadducees were continually trying to entrap Jesus into saying or doing something that would give them cause to accuse him of being a false prophet or of trying to incite rebellion against the ruling Romans.

The Pharisees, taking "counsel how they might entangle him in his talk," asked: "Is it lawful for a man to put away his wife for every cause?" It was a question that had long been debated in the Hebrew schools. Part of Jesus's answer was, "Have ye not read, that he which made them at the beginning made them male and female, and said, For this cause shall a man leave father and mother, and shall cleave to his wife: and they twain [two] shall be one flesh? Wherefore they are *no more twain, but one flesh*. What therefore God hath joined together, let not man put asunder" (Matt. 19:3-12; 22:15-33). No more are they to be separate. They are *"one flesh"* even after their resurrections. Divorce at any time is an invention of man, not part of God's plan.

A group of Sadducees, who didn't believe in immortality and resurrection, tried to ensnare Jesus with one of their cunning questions. A hypothetical, extremely exaggerated case in which a man died, leaving his childless widow behind, was presented to him. Moses said the dead man's brother should "marry his wife, and raise up seed unto his brother." The widow's second husband then died before she had any children by him. A third brother married her. The same thing occurred with the next four brothers. Finally the woman died. The smug Sadducees were sure they had their nemesis in a spot from which he could not extricate himself. Seeking no authoritative answer, they asked, "Therefore in the resurrection whose wife shall she be of the seven? for they all had her."

Not really caring to know about the principle of eternal marriage because they didn't believe in life after death, the deceitful Sadducees wanted Jesus to appear to be foolish for preaching the doctrine of the resurrection. Like the Pharisees, they hoped to "entangle him in his talk."

Jesus realized their intent. There could be no question which brother the widow would be with if the resurrection was a reality. She and her first husband obviously belonged together. His brothers knew full well that they had married her for the duration of this life only. The reasons for their marriage to her were to provide for her and to "raise up seed unto [their] brother." There would be no reason for Jesus to refer to the brothers raising "seed" for the first brother if he and his children could not be together after death.

The master scriptorian chastised the Sadducees for "not knowing the scriptures, nor the power of God. For in the resurrection they [the brothers] neither marry [the widow], nor are given in marriage [to her], but are as the angels of God."[7]

The Sadducees' intent was to dupe Jesus into admitting that there is no resurrection. Jesus successfully avoided entangling himself in any theological debates by merely speaking to the specific, improbable story about the brothers. He had no intention of teaching them about eternal marriage, which would only make real sense to someone who believed in the resurrection.

## The House of the Lord

All Old and New Testament prophets who said anything at all about it spoke reverently of the House of the Lord—his temple. Until it was destroyed by the Romans, the temple at Jerusalem was the focal point of both Hebrew and Christian activity. It was God's holy house and was personally visited by him and his angels.

Isaiah and Micah both predicted that a temple would be built "in the top of the mountains [in the] last days." To it "all nations shall flow [and] many people shall . . . say, 'Come ye, and let us go up to the mountain of the Lord, to the house of the God of Jacob; and he will teach us of his ways, and we will walk in his paths'" (Isaiah 2:2; Micah 4:1).

One of the Lord's directives toward the end of Joseph Smith's life was the construction of a new temple. The saints had already built one temple in Kirtland, Ohio, but were forced to abandon it after it had served its purposes. The newer one, in Nauvoo, Illinois, which Joseph's contemporary, John Greenleaf Whittier, called "the most splended . . . architectural monument in the new world," was complete enough for certain ordinances to be performed before Joseph was murdered.[8]

When the saints were compelled to abandon Nauvoo they established their headquarters in Salt Lake City which is situated in the heart of the Rocky Mountains. There, "in the top of the mountains" in these "last days," another temple among many was built. Millions from all over the world annually visit Temple Square to learn about the Lord's ways as revealed through his prophet Joseph Smith. Many commit themselves to "walk in his paths."

**The Tabernacle.** Man-made temples of the Lord have biblical precedence. When Moses was called to lead the children of Israel away from their Egyptian captors, the Lord commanded that a tabernacle be built. More than a tent, the tabernacle was a complex and ornate portable temple. It was Israel's central place of worship. A cloud, representing the presence of God, covered the tabernacle and the glory of the Lord filled it. At night the cloud shined. It determined where and when the Israelites should go during their forty years of wandering. The tabernacle's Holy of Holies and the bright cloud symbolized the divine presence of God whose house it was.

**Temple of Solomon.** At a later time, Jehovah commanded an even more elaborate and permanent temple be built (2 Samuel 7:5). Solomon's Temple, which stood for more than 400 years, "was the approach of a nation to their God. Israelites alone could enter its Inner Sanctuary . . . The temple bound the nation together. It was the religious centre and capital. Its influence permeated the whole nation."[9]

**Temple of Zerubabbel.** Having been held captive in Babylonia for half a century, the Jews returned to find their temple in ruins, destroyed by their captors in 587 BC. The Lord commanded them to rebuild it. Built by Zerubabbel in 515 B.C., it was "about one-third larger than Solomon's . . . [However], It was greatly its inferior in architectural splendor, in ornamentation, and lavish display of gold and precious stones, and the beauty of its textile fabrics."[10]

**Temple of Herod.** Twenty years before the birth of Christ, Herod began refurbishing the old building. Because of his efforts, Zerubabbel's temple became known as the temple of Herod.

**Jesus in the Temple.** When he was an infant, Jesus was brought to the temple by Joseph and Mary "to present him to the Lord" (Luke 2:22-29). As an adult he "found in the temple those that sold oxen and sheep and doves, and the changers of money sitting: and when he had made a scourge of small cords, he drove them all out of the temple," telling them to "make not my Father's house an house of merchandise" (John 2:13-16). After cleansing it Jesus taught in the temple's treasury (John 8:20).

**The Temple After Jesus.** After Jesus's ascension, the apostles were left in charge of the Church. Though now Christians, they and the other converts to Christ continued "daily with one accord in the temple" (Acts 2:46). The peculiar importance and cultural influence of the temple permeated the lives of both kinds of Hebrews—the Christian converts and the Jews. The Lord's holiest of buildings remained their focal point until the Romans leveled it in 70 AD. After its destruction, "temple taxes, as well as voluntary offerings, continued . . . in anticipation of the rebuilding of the Temple."[11]

**Latter-day Temples.** With the restoration of the gospel, the Lord has commanded temples to be built once again. Though the rites performed within modern temples are outwardly different from animal sacrifices offered in Israel's ancient temples under the Law of Moses, they are, nevertheless, holy and eternal and are sanctified by God. In both the older and the newer temples, eternal covenants with the Lord were and are made.

Other Christian religions have their "temples," but The Church of Jesus Christ of Latter-day Saints stands alone within Christianity in safeguarding the tradition of temples as being separate from ordinary church buildings where only properly baptized Israelites may enter. To modern Israelites within The Church of Jesus Christ of Latter-day Saints, the temple is more than a building; it is God's Royal Sanctuary where they stand with him on holy ground. "It is the most holy of any place of worship on the earth. Only the home can compare with the temple in sacredness."[12]

## The Abrahamic Covenant

Abraham understood the concept of eternal family togetherness. When Abraham was ninety-nine years old, the Lord appeared to him and said, "walk before me, and be thou perfect . . . Thou shalt be a father of many nations . . . I will make thee exceeding fruitful . . . I will establish my covenant between me and thee and thy seed after thee . . . for an everlasting covenant, to be a God unto thee, and to thy seed" (Gen. 17:1-8).

Jehovah promised Abraham that if he continued to be obedient ("walk before me, and be thou perfect"), he would have a large posterity ("I will make thee exceeding fruitful"). That Abrahamic covenant was so important that it was repeated to Abraham and was renewed with Isaac and Jacob.[13]

Unless it was possible for Abraham to have a lasting relationship with his great grandchildren's great great grandchildren—an utter impossibility if the covenant was for the remaining seventy-six years of his life—there would be no reason for God to make such a wonderful promise. God intended for Abraham and his descendants to enjoy one another forever.

Baptized members of The Church of Jesus Christ of Latter-day Saints "have put on Christ." They are then "Abraham's seed, and heirs according to the promise" (Galatians 3:27-29).

Through Malachi, God promised that he "will send . . . Elijah the prophet . . . [who] shall turn the heart of the fathers to the children, and the heart of the children to their fathers, lest I come and smite the earth with a curse" (Malachi 4:5-6). What greater curse could God "smite the earth" with than to nullify the Abrahamic covenant so that we with Abraham could not turn our hearts to one another in an eternal family bond?

## The Return of Elijah

On April 3, 1836, within the Kirtland Temple, the ancient prophet Elijah stood before Joseph Smith and Oliver Cowdery and announced: "Behold, the time has fully come, which was spoken of by the mouth of Malachi—testifying that he [Elijah] should be sent, before the great and dreadful day of the Lord come—To turn the hearts of the fathers to the children, and the children to the fathers, lest the whole earth be smitten with a curse—Therefore the keys of this dispensation are committed into your hands" (D & C 110:13-16). Elijah's appearance was also a fulfillment of Jesus's prophecy at the foot of the Mount of Transfiguration when he told Peter, James and John that "Elias [Elijah] truly shall first come and restore all things" (Matt. 17:11).

With the priesthood keys restored by Elijah, every family who wishes to may enter a temple and there be united eternally. If a family has passed on without having been united in an eternal bond, others will perform the ordinance on their behalf.

Couples who were informed at the matrimonial altar that they are husband and wife only "until death do you part" or "as long as you both shall live," may still enter the temple and there be eternally united. The first step is to become a citizen of the kingdom of God by being baptized by proper priesthood authority.

"I have to admit," I told the elders, "the Plan of Salvation is far more comprehensive and makes more sense than any other theological or philosophical explanation about life that I have ever before heard."

In my previous associations with other churches I have understood that if a person had no opportunity to hear of Jesus Christ there was no further chance for them and he or she must go to hell. Or, a vague answer would be given such as, "Somehow in the mercy of God, all will have the opportunity to hear of Christ."

"The Church of Jesus Christ of Latter-day Saints is the only religion of which I am aware that includes all of mankind—even those who have passed on—in its proselytizing efforts" I continued. "Surely the true religion of the universe—if there is one—would have some all-embracing design for getting its message to everyone. The LDS Church is also the only Christian religion that I know about that teaches the concept of eternal family unity. I could be gambling away the possibility of living forever with my family if I reject your Church's doctrine simply because of my prejudices against Mormonism."

Some LDS doctrine did not make that much sense to me, however. "I cannot believe that I have lived before birth, even though Jesus and some prophets apparently did. In fact, I even have a hard time believing there is a God, when he allowed something as awful as the holocaust without stepping in."

"On the other hand, if we don't have hope in a God who has made it possible for us to live again after death, how awful that would be also," suggested Elder Porter. "Paul said it best: 'If in this life only we have hope in Christ, we are of all men most miserable'" (1 Cor. 15:19).

"Your lesson today," I replied, "has gotten me to wondering if the plan of happiness was something that was dreamed up by Joseph Smith. If Joseph created the plan, he certainly was not the ignoramus I had imagined. It's too far-reaching for a simpleton to have authored. It weaves itself so thoroughly throughout the Bible's spiritual fabric that he must have either been a theological and philosophical genius of the first caliber or a prophet. How can I ever know? I feel like throwing in the towel; it's all so overwhelming. Yet it seems so wonderfully true."

# 13
# Predictions and Other Miracles

## Pasadena College

John and Ed Parker, our next-door neighbors, were devout Nazarenes and concerned friends. It was with them that I had attended the Nazarene Church a few times and had gotten to know some of the wonderful people there. A warm, loving lady, Ed knew of my quandary about religion and wanted to help. Being aware also of my desire to become a teacher and knowing that UCR did not have a college of education, she suggested that I consider enrolling at Pasadena College, which was owned by the Nazarene Church.[1]

Feeling that her suggestion might help in my new acclimation to religion in general, I enrolled.[2] Pasadena College was an older campus; some of the buildings looked like they had been built during the early part of this century. It was a lot different in that respect from the much-newer three-year-old campus I had attended in Riverside.

The people at both institutions were equally friendly, except that at PC, swearing and filthy language were not to be heard. None of the PC students drank beer or smoked as they did elsewhere. Nazarenes in those days were also taught not to attend dances or movies, although a few of my friends did. Neither were the girls supposed to wear makeup, but a few fudged.

At PC I was an almost completely different person than I was at UCR. In Riverside I was known as Will instead of Bill. I smoked, chug-a-lugged pitchers of beer with my friends, listened to and told off-color jokes, used the Lord's name in vain, let profanities escape my lips continually, played penny ante poker and did other things which I won't mention because I am too ashamed. I had given up all of those things when I decided to become religious during that late spring, so I felt right at home at Pasadena. Probably because I was so busy with yard work in exchange for a one-room apartment above a garage, working at Vromans' wholesale book warehouse, studying the LDS religion, driving back and forth between Pasadena and Fontana, dating, attending activities and meetings at two churches, plus doing school work, I learned to use my time more wisely and couldn't procrastinate studying like I did at UCR.

Even though the other students were friendly, I did feel somewhat out of place. Perhaps I was. A few years older than most—it had been eight years since I had graduated from high school—I stood out. That didn't really matter. But it seemed that everybody had heard that I was seriously investigating the claims of the Mormons. To many of the Nazarenes, the doctrines of the LDS Church, as they generally misunderstood them, were dreamed up by a kid named "Joe Smith." Nazarenes sincerely believe in Jesus Christ, but most of those that I talked with about the LDS faith had been taught erroneously that Mormons do not believe in the Savior. A few even asked me if Mormons worshipped "Joe Smith."

As in all other Protestant denominations, the Bible is the only set of scriptures to them. Therefore, the Book of Mormon, which most that I knew were proud to say they had never read, was considered heresy and the work of the devil. They were very sincere and good people, but because they often believed what mislead "authorities" taught them, they held Mormons and the LDS Church in contempt. "The Mormon Church isn't Christian, therefore its members need to be saved," seemed to be the attitude of those I knew on the PC campus. I'm sure there were some who were including me in their personal prayers so I wouldn't end up in the confines of hell, which I sincerely appreciate even today.

Everyone was genuinely kind. No one made any nasty remarks about me of which I am aware. From time to time, though, negative comments about "Mormonism" were made which made me feel guilty for even looking into the LDS faith. Except for a few antagonistic references to the Latter-day Saint beliefs during their lectures and their steering me to an "expert on Mormonism," none of my professors talked with me about the LDS religion.

On weekends, I continued my discussions with the missionaries in my parents' Fontana home, seventy-five miles east of Pasadena. I knew no Mormons in Pasadena.

# Predictions of Joseph Smith

It had been three or four weeks since I had last talked with the elders. By the time we next met, Elder Johnson had been transferred to Colton; Elder Thomas, a pianist from St. George, Utah, took his place. Before I enrolled at Pasadena College the missionaries came to our house on week days. Now we got together on Saturday afternoons. As usual, my parents made it a point not to be there when the elders showed up.

After spending some time getting to know Elder Thomas, who promised to play for us when we were finished, we had the usual prayer. Before the elders could say anything more, I informed them, "One of my friends at Pasadena College asked me the other day what predictions Joseph Smith made. If he was really a prophet, he must have prophesied."

It is commonly supposed that a prophet's purpose is to pronounce new predictions, Elder Porter reminded me. If that is true, his short-term forecasts could be easily proven or disproven. His long-term prophecies must be accepted on faith until they either occur or fail to occur. "The great function of [a prophet] is not prediction; it is the proclamation of the will of God, and the announcement of the consequences, if the will of God is not obeyed."[3] While all of the Bible's prophecies about the future were originally composed by specific prophets, many were later requoted or referred to by others who did not come up with predictions of their own. "New truths or unknown events may be revealed [by prophets], or they may . . . confirm and give added witness to truths already revealed and testified to by other prophets."[4]

As with many Bible prophets, Joseph Smith made numerous short-term predictions that have already been fulfilled. One daring prophecy in particular is especially important to consider when it is examined more than a century-and-a-half later. When the Church was less than twelve-years-old, he foretold that the restored gospel would go forth to every country in the world:

> No unhallowed hand can stop the work from progressing; persecutions may rage, mobs may combine, armies may assemble, calumny may defame, but the truth of God will go forth boldly, nobly, and independent till it has penetrated every continent, visited every clime, swept every country,

and sounded in every ear, till the purposes of God shall be accomplished, and the Great Jehovah shall say the work is done.[5]

Today, that prediction is coming true as tens of thousands of unpaid missionaries are being sent to as many nations as will allow them within their borders—many times more than when Joseph Smith lived.

Remarkable long-range forecasts that Joseph Smith made, mostly about the second coming of Christ, are also contained within LDS scriptures. The fact that many of his short-term predictions have actually occurred give more credence to his long-term ones. Of course, Joseph could have been a prophet even if he didn't foretell specific events, but he did. The question is only whether or not they originated with God.

## Fulfilled Prophecy

• When he was only seventeen, Joseph was told by Moroni that his "name should be . . . both good and evil spoken of among all people." Millions upon millions have become Latter-day Saints since the Church's inception. To them, he has a good name. Millions of dollars are being made by authors, publishers, filmmakers and bookstores from the sale of anti-Mormon propaganda within which his name is "evil spoken of."

• Tens of thousands of LDS converts did not formerly believe the Bible. The Book of Mormon led them to it and to Christ. Through Joseph Smith, Nephi predicted that the Book of Mormon "shall establish the truth of [the Bible] ... and shall make known to all kindreds, tongues and people, that the Lamb of God is the Son of the Eternal Father, and the Savior of the world; and that all men must come unto him, or they cannot be saved" (1 Nephi 13:40).

• Before the Book of Mormon was taken out into the world by missionaries, Nephi recorded that "my words shall hiss forth unto the ends of the earth" (2 Nephi 29:2). All over the world, Latter-day Saints and others read Nephi's words daily as they "hiss forth" in the Book of Mormon.

• The next verse foretells what every Latter-day Saint has heard: "And because my words shall hiss forth—many of the Gentiles shall say: 'A Bible! A Bible! We have got a Bible, and there cannot be any more Bible'" (2 Nephi 29:3). A common anti-Mormon excuse for not reading the Book of Mormon is, "We have a Bible, we don't need another book." Those who say they have the Bible and don't need more are fulfilling yet another prediction that came through Joseph Smith.

• When the foreseen gathering of Israel occurs, a prophet must be involved if Amos was right about God doing nothing without first using his prophets.[6] The gathering of all twelve tribes of Israel plus "gentiles" was at the top of Joseph Smith's prophetic agenda. Almost as soon as the LDS Church was organized, missionaries were sent forth to various parts of the United States, Canada and England to find the honest in heart who sincerely wanted to become part of Christ's latter-day Israel.

In 1832, at a time when most did not believe that the Jews would soon return to Palestine, Joseph prophesied to Orson Hyde: "In due time thou shalt go to Jerusalem . . . and by thy hand shall the Most High do a great work, which shall prepare the way and greatly facilitate the gathering of that people."[7]

Eight years later, Hyde was called on a mission to Palestine. The events that occurred after Hyde's dedication of the Holy Land are remarkable. In a letter to Parley Pratt from Alexandria, Egypt, Orson wrote that before daybreak on October 24, 1840 he offered a prayer on the Mount of Olives and there "erected a pile of stones as a witness according to ancient custom." He then did the same at the temple site on Mount Zion.

At the time of Hyde's visit in 1840, there were few Jews in Jerusalem compared with Turks and Armenians. By 1876 the British Consul reported that there were "from fifteen to twenty thousand Jews in Judea." In 1896, the St. Louis *Globe-Democrat* commented that

> the Hebrew population . . . now stands at between sixty and seventy thousand. Whole streets of houses have been built outside the walls on the site of the ancient suburban districts, which for hundreds of years have remained deserted. It is not, however, only in Jerusalem itself that the Jews abound, but throughout Palestine they are buying farms and establishing themselves in a surprisingly rapid manner. In Jerusalem they form at present a larger community than either the Christian or the Mohammedan.[8]

• Thirty years before the American Civil War began, the Lord announced through his prophet: "Ye hear of wars in foreign lands; but, behold, I say unto you, they are nigh, even at your doors, and not many years hence ye shall hear of wars in your own lands" (D & C 45:63). The following year, on Christmas of 1832, the prophet recorded:

Verily, thus saith the Lord concerning the wars that will shortly come to pass, beginning at the rebellion of South Carolina, which will eventually terminate in the death and misery of many souls; and the time will come that war will be poured out upon all nations, beginning at this place. For behold, the Southern States shall be divided against the Northern States, and the Southern States will call on other nations, even the nation of Great Britain, as it is called, and they shall also call upon other nations [France, Holland and Belgium were asked], in order to defend themselves.

(D & C 87:1-3)

In 1843, Joseph again referred to that 1832 prediction: "I prophesy, in the name of the Lord God, that the commencement of the difficulties which will cause much bloodshed previous to the coming of the Son of Man will be in South Carolina. It may probably arise through the slave question. This a voice declared to me, while I was praying earnestly on the subject" (D & C 130:12-13).

Just as the Lord foretold through his prophet, Joseph Smith, the American Civil War began on April 12, 1861, when artillery manned by Southern rebels shelled the federal government's Fort Sumter in the Charleston, South Carolina, harbor. During the same year, the Confederacy sent James Mason and John Slidell to Europe in an attempt to persuade Great Britain and France to help. The European nations refused to intervene in the war except to allow the South to build a few ships in their shipyards.[9]

• Joseph Smith with others unsuccessfully traveled to Washington, D.C. to seek redress for the rapine suffered in Missouri. On November 29, 1839, they presented letters to President Martin Van Buren. "As soon as he had read one . . . he looked upon us with a kind of half frown, and said, 'What can I do? I can do nothing for you! If I do anything, I shall come in contact with the whole state of Missouri.'"[10] Several weeks were vainly spent trying to interest Congressmen in their cause. "[Henry] Clay said, 'You had better go to Oregon,' and [John C.] Calhoun shaking his head solemnly saying, 'It's a nice question—a critical question, but it will not do to agitate it.'"[11]

In his journal, Joseph wrote:

My heart faints within me when I see, by the visions of the Almighty, the end of this nation, if she continues to disregard the cries and petitions of her virtuous citizens. . . . On my way home I did not fail to proclaim the iniquity and insolence of Martin Van Buren, toward myself and an injured people . . . May he never be elected again to any office of trust or power, by which he may abuse the innocent and let the guilty go free.[12]

President Van Buren never was reelected. Though he was the incumbent, Van Buren was defeated by William Henry Harrison in the presidential election of 1840. Harrison received 234 electoral votes to 60 for Van Buren. In 1848 Zachary Taylor was elected, and Van Buren did not receive a single electoral vote.[13]

• During the spring of 1841, Stephen Douglas, Justice of the Illinois Supreme Court, visited Nauvoo. Joseph recorded that Judge Douglas "spoke in high terms" about what he saw in the "enterprise and industry" of the Mormons. Joseph also said that "Judge Douglas has ever proved himself friendly" to the Latter-day Saints.[14]

Two years later, Joseph told him during another visit: "Judge, you will aspire to the presidency of the United States; and if ever you turn your hand against me or the Latter-day Saints, you will feel the weight of the hand of [the] Almighty upon you; and you will live to see and know that I have testified the truth to you; for the conversation of this day will stick to you through life."[15]

On June 23, 1860, long after Joseph's death in 1844, Stephen Douglas was nominated by the Democratic party to run for the office of President. No man in the history of American politics had more reason to hope for success; his Democratic party had received 174 electoral votes compared with 122 for the other two parties combined in the 1856 presidential election. But in the election of 1860, Abraham Lincoln, a Republican, was elected. Lincoln carried 18 states; Breckinridge 11; Bell 3 and Douglas only one!

Why? On June 12, 1857, fourteen years after Joseph made his prophecy, Douglas made a speech in Springfield, Illinois. Most people knew that Douglas was a friend of Joseph Smith and the other Church leaders. He was therefore invited to speak about rumors enemies of the Church had circulated that Mormon leaders were murderers, robbers, and committing high treason against the government of the United States.

In his speech Douglas lied. He said, "Nine-tenths" of Utahns refused to recognize "the government of the United States as the paramount authority in that territory." He also told his listeners, among other things, that Mormons "are bound by horrible oaths . . . to . . . maintain the authority of Brigham Young, and the government of which he is head, as paramount to that of the United States."

Douglas knew from his previous acquaintance with Joseph Smith and the Mormon people that the rumors were untrue. He could have educated the country about the good character of the Mormon people and the oppression they had to endure. "But the demagogue triumphed over the statesman, the politician over the humanitarian; and . . . he turned his hand against [the Mormons] with the result that he did not destroy them but sealed his own doom."[16]

On September 24, 1856, Joseph's prophecy was published in the *Deseret News.* That publication appeared eight months before Douglas's speech and nearly four years before his nomination for president.

In June, 1861, eleven months after being nominated, and when only forty eight years of age, Stephen Douglas died.

Other fulfilled prophecies Joseph made were the future leadership of the Church under Brigham Young, the saints' eventual move to the Rocky Mountains, certain events pertaining to Zion's Camp, a meteor shower, the safe release of those imprisoned in Missouri, his own martyrdom, and many more.

Many prophecies that are yet to be fulfilled were also recorded by Joseph Smith. Most, but not all, pertain to the second coming of Christ and the events surrounding that sacred appearance. Many blend in with already known Bible prophecies as the restoration unfolds into further preparations for the Lord's advent.[17]

As I mused upon these things, I told the elders, "No one else that I'm aware of—even among Bible prophets—has ever foretold the future so many times and with such detailed accuracy. How did Joseph so clearly predict events that have already been fulfilled? What other miracles was Joseph Smith involved with besides his predictions?"

"Well, we've told you about a lot of them already. You know about Joseph's first vision, the angel Moroni, a Urim and Thummim, the healing of Mrs. Johnson's arm, three men seeing an angel holding metallic records and hearing God speak. That ought to be enough, it seems to me," Elder Porter said.

"To me also. But my Nazarene friends have looked at me as if I'm weird whenever I have mentioned those particular miracles. They seem to want proof. Aren't there some that are more believable?"

## Further Miracles

Not all Bible prophets were associated with dramatic miracles such as raising the dead or walking on dry land through the Red Sea.[18] When they were involved with miracles, often no one else could substantiate them. Who else besides Moses, for instance, saw God writing on the stone tablets which contained his Ten Commandments?

"If Joseph Smith were linked with miracles, especially if witnesses were present, he most certainly could have been a prophet," I concluded. "However, miracles do not necessarily originate with Deity. Magicians work tricks that are seemingly miraculous. Visions have been seen by some who may have been under the influence of hallucinogenics, or who may have been psychotic. Miracles alone, then, even when there are witnesses, are not true indicators that a man has been sent from God."

"Also, Matthew and John inform us that false prophets and devils can deceive us with miracles," Elder Thomas added (Matt. 7:22-23; Rev. 13:14; 19:20). "Pharaoh's wise men and sorcerers duplicated Moses's miracles of changing rods into serpents, water into blood, and causing frogs to come out of the rivers."

Elder Thomas explained that miracles rarely convert. Skeptics do not believe in them no matter what they are or who reports them. God's miracles are generally meant for instruction, for edification, or for the welfare of those who already believe (Mormon 9:24). And, as with predictions, not all Bible prophets were associated with dramatic miracles.

Those miracles with which Joseph Smith was involved, that had no other witnesses than him, are just as authentic as any mentioned within the Bible which have no witnesses (such as Moses seeing the burning bush and hearing the voice of God). Faith in the persons reporting them, or faith in the Bible, are what sustains their authenticity. However, if witnesses were present with Joseph, his claim to being a genuine prophet must be even more seriously examined.

• John the Baptist ordained Joseph and Oliver Cowdery when he restored the Aaronic Priesthood. About that visitation from beyond the veil Joseph matter-of-factly wrote:

> While we were . . . praying and calling upon the Lord, a messenger from heaven descended in a cloud of light, and having laid his hands upon us, he ordained us, saying: 'Upon you my fellow servants, in the name of Mes-

siah, I confer the Priesthood of Aaron, which holds the keys of the ministering of angels, and of the gospel of repentance, and of baptism by immersion for the remission of sins; and this shall never be taken again from the earth.

(Joseph Smith—History 1:68-69)

Contrast Joseph's casual recording of this holy experience with Oliver's. Joseph had been involved with such sacred events many times before; Oliver had yet to experience his first. To hear the Lord and to see an angel of God (John) really turned on his eloquence:

> On a sudden, as from the midst of eternity, the voice of the Redeemer spake peace to us. While the veil was parted . . . the angel of God came down clothed with glory, and delivered . . . the keys of the Gospel of repentance. What joy! what wonder! . . .
>
> Earth, nor men, with the eloquence of time, cannot begin to clothe language in as interesting and sublime a manner as this holy personage . . . The assurance that we were in the presence of an angel, the certainty that we heard the voice of Jesus, and the truth unsullied as it flowed from a pure personage . . . is to me past description and I shall ever look upon this expression of the Savior's goodness with wonder and thanksgiving.[19]

• The ancient apostles, Peter, James and John, ordained Joseph and Oliver to the Melchizedek Priesthood shortly after John the Baptist's visitation.[20] Oliver testified at the October 1848 general conference of the Church: "I was . . . present with Joseph when the Melchizedek Priesthood was conferred by the holy angels of God."[21]

• Wishing to meet the prophet, Elizabeth Ann and Newel K. Whitney prayed for that opportunity in Kirtland, Ohio. Hundreds of miles to the east in New York, Joseph had a vision. Within the Whitney family history is recorded:

> About the first of February, 1831, a sleigh containing four persons . . . drew up in front of the store of Gilbert and Whitney. One of the men . . . walked into the store . . . 'Newel K. Whitney! Thou art the man!' he exclaimed, extending his hand cordially, as if to an old and familiar acquaintance.
>
> 'You have the advantage of me,' replied the merchant, as he mechanically took the proffered hand. 'I could not call you by name as you have me.'
>
> 'I am Joseph the Prophet,' said the stranger smiling. 'You've prayed me here, now what do you want?'[22]

• Within the home of John Johnson in Hiram, Ohio, Joseph and Sidney Rigdon both saw the Father and Son with holy angels while hearing a "voice bearing record that he is the Only Begotten of the Father." It was then that they had a vision of the three degrees of glory (D & C 76:11-24).

• Referring to the Zion's Camp march of volunteer saints enroute to Missouri to aid the besieged Mormons there, Joseph said, "We know that angels were our companions, for we saw them."

Parley P. Pratt wrote about one of those angels:

> I had traveled all night to overtake the camp . . . At noon I had turned my horse loose from the carriage to feed . . . I sank down overpowered in a deep sleep . . . but I had only slept a few moments . . . when a voice, more loud and shrill than I had ever before heard, fell on my ear . . . It said: 'Parley, it is time to be up and on your journey.' In the twinkling of an eye . . . I sprang to my feet so suddenly that I could not recollect where I was or what was before me to perform . . . Brother Joseph . . . [later said] that it was the angel of the Lord . . .[who] awoke me.[23]

• One night five armed men rode into Zion's Camp where Joseph Smith and other Mormons were resting, shouting that the Mormons would "see hell before morning" because hundreds of men were coming "who had sworn the utter destruction" of Mormons. According to Joseph's written history, earlier that day there was not a cloud in the sky. After the five left the camp, "Wind and rain, hail and thunder" drenched those who were coming to attack and soaked their ammunition. Hail "cut down the crops of corn and vegetation . . . even cutting limbs from trees, while the trees, themselves were twisted into withes by the wind." The flashes of lightning were so frequent that "the most minute objects" could be seen. "The earth trembled and quaked, the rain fell in torrents, and . . . it seemed as if the mandate of vengeance had gone forth from the God of battles, to protect His servants from the destruction of their enemies." Those in Zion's Camp hardly suffered.

Wilford Woodruff wrote that when the five men left the camp

> a small cloud like a black spot appeared in the northwest, and it began to unroll itself like a scroll, and in a few minutes the whole heavens were covered with pall as black as ink. [A sudden storm] soon broke upon us with wind, rain, thunder and lightning and hail. Our beds were soon afloat and our tents blown down over our heads. We all fled into a Baptist meetinghouse. As the Prophet Joseph came in shaking the water from his

hat and clothing he said, 'Boys . . . God is in this storm.' We sang praises to God, and lay all night on benches under cover while our enemies were in the pelting storm.[24]

• At considerable sacrifice by the financially destitute saints, the Lord commanded that a temple be built in Kirtland: "Verily I say unto you, it is expedient . . . that the first elders of my church should receive their endowment from on high in my house" (D & C 105:33).

After it was completed, Joseph Smith and many others saw angels within the temple for more than three months, the Celestial Kingdom with the Father and Son was described, many prophesied, and the gift of tongues was manifested. On one occasion, "a noise was heard like the sound of a rushing mighty wind," filling the temple. "The people of the neighborhood came running" when they heard an "unusual sound" inside the temple and they saw "a bright light like a pillar of fire" over the temple. "It was a Pentecost and an endowment . . . long to be remembered."[25]

• On April 3, 1836, Joseph and Oliver Cowdery saw Jesus Christ in the Kirtland temple. Describing what they saw, Joseph wrote that under the Lord's feet

> was a paved work of pure gold in color like amber. His eyes were as a flame of fire; the hair of his head was white like the pure snow; his countenance shone above the brightness of the sun; and his voice was as the sound of the rushing of great waters . . . saying: . . . 'Let the hearts of all my people rejoice, who have, with their might, built this house to my name . . . I have accepted this house, and my name shall be here; and I will manifest myself to my people in mercy in this house . . . if my people will keep my commandments.'[26]
>
> (D & C 110:1-10)

• Within the Kirtland temple, resurrected beings also restored important keys to Joseph Smith and Oliver Cowdery. Moses gave Joseph and Oliver

> the keys of the gathering of Israel from the four parts of the earth, and the leading of the ten tribes from the land of the north. After this, Elias appeared, and committed the dispensation of the gospel of Abraham, saying that in us and our seed all generations after us should be blessed. After this vision closed, another great and glorious vision burst upon us; for Elijah the prophet, who was taken

into heaven without tasting death, stood before us, and said: Behold, the time has fully come, which was spoken by the mouth of Malachi—testifying that he [Elijah] should be sent, before the great and dreadful day of the Lord come—to turn the hearts of the fathers to the children, and the children to the fathers, lest the whole earth be smitten with a curse— Therefore, the keys of this dispensation are committed into your hands; and by this ye may know that the great and dreadful day of the Lord is near, even at the doors.[27]

(D & C 110:11-16)

• In Illinois, many, including Joseph, were stricken with malaria. On the morning of July 22, 1839, Joseph was healed by the Lord and he in turn healed all who lay sick along the banks of the Mississippi River.

According to Wilford Woodruff, Joseph and others then visited the sick in Montrose, Iowa. After Brigham Young was healed, he and Joseph visited others. Elijah Fordham was dying. When the men entered the room, Joseph walked over to Elijah, took him by his hand and spoke to him. The dying man "seemed entirely unconscious" of who was in his room and was unable to speak. Continuing to hold his hand, Joseph "looked into his eyes in silence." He asked Elijah if he had faith to be healed. Elijah answered that he was afraid it was too late. The prophet then asked if he believed in Jesus Christ. Feebly, Elijah answered that he did. "Joseph then stood erect, still holding his hand in silence several moments." Then, in a very loud voice he said, "'Brother Fordham, I command you, in the name of Jesus Christ, to arise from this bed and be made whole.'" Fordham was made whole instantly.

Later that day, "a man from the West" asked Joseph if he would go to his house and heal his infant twins. Joseph could not go, but he said that he would send Wilford Woodruff. Taking from his pocket a silk bandana handkerchief, he gave it to Wilford and told him that if he would wipe the face of the children with it, they would be made whole.[28] "Elder Woodruff did as he was commanded, and the children were healed."[29]

Like Christendom's earliest miracles, those Joseph was involved with were not for show. Never did he advertise that he was a healer or a miracle worker. They were not intended for the theater or the circus tent. Likewise, those who came to him from beyond the veil were not mute, as the "messengers" from other purported visions often are. All had a purpose in their visitations. They came reverently in the presence of those who already believed.

I was astounded that so many of the prophecies and other miracles with which Joseph was involved were also witnessed by others. "It seems to me," I concluded, "that either Joseph Smith and the other witnesses of the seemingly miraculous collaborated in the writing of their journals, he was an astounding magician, or the events recorded actually happened."

"No Bible miracle can be substantiated as well as many of those in which Joseph Smith was involved," Elder Thomas remarked. "Original accounts are available that report many miracles of the restoration, but where are original documents of Bible miracles such as those of Jesus and his resurrection? Where are the original journals of the children of Israel that can verify the parting of the Red Sea and the gathering of manna?"

In spite of what the elders said, since I wasn't there when the miracles took place and I had no access to eyewitness accounts other than Joseph's, it was easy for me to dismiss them as stories created by overzealous Mormon missionaries and historians. I was living proof of what the elders said at the beginning of our discussion: miracles rarely convert, and skeptics do not believe in them no matter what they are or who reports them.

# 14
# The Law of Consecration

When Elders Porter and Thomas returned the following Saturday afternoon I steered them over to the old studio piano in our living room. Having only bikes for transportation, it was difficult getting to appointments on time. Since they were late when they finished the lesson about predictions and miracles, Elder Thomas, who was going to major in piano pedagogy, didn't play as he had promised. I had informed my parents that he was going to bring some of his music the next time. Mother, a fine pianist herself, said she would like to hear him. She and Daddy were sitting on the couch waiting when the elders arrived.

"Hi. I'm Elder Porter," the gentle giant cheerfully announced as he held out his bear paw to my dad.

"And I'm Elder Thomas," said the main attraction, shaking both of my parents' hands.

"I'm Chet Morgan and this is my wife, Herschell," Daddy smiled.

"We appreciate you letting us use your piano this afternoon," Elder Thomas said. "I'm a little rusty since I don't get to play very much on my mission. But I have some music just in case I get an opportunity to practice. I understand you play, Mrs. Morgan."

"A little," she humbly answered. "But we'd rather hear you."

Elder Thomas played beautifully. No one stirred. He had won the hearts of us all. When he was finished, he invited my parents to sit in on their missionary discussion. As I expected, they cordially declined, but said they would listen to him play anytime.

After the three of us went into the dining room, I challenged the elders with an accusation that I'd heard at college. "Do you believe that by paying ten percent of your income you can buy your way into heaven?"

Always the comedian, Elder Porter smiled and said, "Yes. When the bishop signs your tithing receipt it becomes official and is acceptable by the eternal revenue service."

Becoming serious again, Elder Porter assured me that what I had heard about Mormons buying their way into heaven was not true. Joseph Smith received many revelations to look after the poor and needy. Those revelations were the groundwork for building an unselfish and caring people who could eventually live the Law of Consecration that was part of Christ's earliest Church (Acts 2:44; 4:32-37). "I give unto the church . . . a commandment . . . [to] look to the poor and the needy, and administer to their relief that they shall not suffer," the Lord told Joseph (D & C 38:34-35). "The earth is full, and there is enough and to spare . . . If any man shall take of the abundance which I have made, and impart not his portion . . . unto the poor and the needy, he shall, with the wicked, lift up his eyes in hell" (D & C 104:17-18). Accounts from Joseph's day indicate that he himself was quite charitable, despite limited personal resources. He taught that "a religion that does not require the sacrifice of all things never has power sufficient to produce the faith necessary unto life and salvation."[1]

The Master's plan, as revealed to Joseph Smith, is for his saints to be devoted to the Law of Consecration, which means that all they have will be returned to the Lord, and he in turn, through his priesthood leadership, will give back according to the "circumstances" and "wants and needs" of the members.

# The Lesser Law

In the years following my conversion I have learned much about the Law of Consecration and the lesser laws we are now living. The principle has been attempted from time to time, but many Latter-day Saints, like their predecessors in the New Testament and the Book of Mormon, were not yet ready to live it. Therefore, the saints have been commanded to live a lesser law revealed in the Old Testament—the law of tithing—a law that is a "schoolmaster" to prepare for the greater. Members voluntarily give at least ten percent of their increase to the Lord's Church. That tithing is used to build and maintain tens of thousands of buildings, including temples and their grounds, pay utilities, custodians and other employees, purchase educational materials, support Church colleges and other schools, and many other important things.

Once each month Mormons fast and pray for two meals and donate at least the cost of those meals to the needy. Since there are no administrative fees for the collection and distribution of fast offerings (because of unpaid leadership), for each $100 donated $100 is shared with those who lack. Vast LDS welfare projects farms, orchards, ranches and canneries are maintained and operated, mainly by volunteers. Donated goods are retailed to the public through thrift stores known as Deseret Industries. One of the stores' primary purposes is to train the less advantaged so they will be able to market their skills.

"So if I became a Mormon I would have to pay ten percent of my income plus donate more for the fast offering collection?" I frowned. "What would happen if I quit paying?"

"No member is forced to donate to the Church. If Latter-day Saints discontinue paying their tithes and offerings, he or she continues as a member," Elder Porter assured me. "They are not asked to leave. Nobody in the Church coerces anyone else to donate anything."

"The only way to assure entry into the Celestial Kingdom, though," Elder Thomas continued, "is by honestly striving to live all of Christ's commandments. The payment of money will not by itself guarantee a person's being ushered into the Lord's presence. However, tithing is one of the commandments, and if a member of the Church truly desires to live life the Lord's way, he or she will live all of the commandments, including tithing. The Lord challenged us, 'Bring ye all the tithes into the storehouse, that there may be meat in mine house, and prove me now herewith . . . if I will not open you the windows of heaven, and pour you out a blessing, that there shall not be room enough to receive it'" (Mal. 3:10).

"It seems to me that if I become a Mormon I won't have to work anymore. That sounds good. How do I sign up?" I winked.

With all of this charitable industry, the Lord does not encourage dole-seeking. "The ultimate aim of welfare service principles, programs, and activities is to develop Christ-like character in Church members, thus preparing them to live in a society where men and women are of 'one heart and one mind,' where they live 'in righteousness,' and there are 'no poor among them'" (Moses 7:18).[2] "The aim of the Church is to help the people to help themselves."[3] Members are encouraged to store at least one year's supply of food, to stay out of debt, to have some kind of health insurance, to obtain a good education, to learn and improve at least one skill that will support their families, and to financially prepare for retirement.

The Heritage Foundation has noted that the LDS Church focuses "on strengthening the family, teaching a vigorous work ethic, and helping the needy to help themselves. Its themes are ones the secular world would do well to study."[4]

In addition to helping individual members in times of need, wherever community wide catastrophic events such as earthquakes, floods, hurricanes, fire storms, and war have deprived Latter-day Saints of their lives, their livelihood, or their homes, the money given by members of the Church has often been donated for temporary relief. Over the past century millions and millions of dollars worth of food, clothing, blankets, medicine and other important items including money have been rushed to those who are in need through no fault of their own. Not only are members benefited, but much needed help is often extended to non-members of the Church as well.

Soon after World War II, U.S. members of the Church unconditionally sent trainloads of free supplies to starving Europeans. Feeling keenly their responsibility to care for themselves, Mormons in Holland at that time undertook potato projects wherever land could be found. Backyards, road medians, vacant lots, and flower gardens became potato patches.

Like all other Europeans in those demanding days, the Dutch were experiencing a difficult time finding enough food to feed their families. But conditions in Germany were more bleak. Though they had only recently been bitter enemies, the Dutch saints shipped fifteen tons of potatoes, originally intended for their own tables, to destitute German Mormons mainly, but also some to non-Mormons as well. The shipment created a "new spirit of unity and love among the Saints."[5]

A member of the Jewish faith fondly recalls, "brotherhood . . . is that which is practiced by the Latter-day Saints, not simply in words or hospitality [but in] life. My father built the first synagogue [in Salt Lake City] in 1900. The only sizable contribution he got came from the LDS Church. In those years, anything as big as they gave made the difference between success and failure."[6]

The Catholic Community Services of Utah has honored the Church for its sensitive, unselfish, and ecumenical response to the needs of the homeless [and] for the role it has played . . . on behalf of the people and the groups who are not members of the LDS Church, but who have benefited from its charity.

As is typical with true benefactors, much happens that is not in the public eye. On a worldwide scale, we know the Mormon Church has contributed a considerable amount of money to African relief and other causes through the Catholic Relief Services and other agencies. These are very, very significant contributions.[7]

"I didn't think the person was right who told me that Mormons believe they can buy their way into heaven," I said. "But joining your church certainly seems to be an expensive proposition."

On the other hand, the Law of Consecration, as unrealistic an ideal as there ever was, appealed to me. It seemed impractical, but if everyone truly lived the law from their hearts, and were not forced to live it as Marxist communism wants to do, the world would be a wonderful place in which to live. Peace would reign; there would be no more wars. Those who are able would work for the welfare of the community; those who are unable to do a full day's work would do what they could so they would not feel they were a burden on someone else.

Though Bible and Book of Mormon prophets, as well as the Mormon prophet Joseph Smith, taught the Law of Consecration, few were evidently ready for such a concept, I concluded. Still, it seemed to me that the Mormons hadn't given up in preparing to live the law, judging by the hundreds of millions of dollars worth of aid that they donate and the vast volunteer labor going into their welfare projects worldwide.

But I believed that people are generally selfish. Greed, and mistrust seem to be at the core of most everything we do. I felt there would be no way that a whole country, an entire community, a church, or even a neighborhood could live such a law for very long. Shangri-las and utopias have been attempted by other groups from time to time, and they haven't worked either. Yet, where else in the world was there a major religious organization that was actively working toward that ideal? I didn't know of any.

# 15
# Persecution in Print

Whenever I had the opportunity, I tried rattling the brains of my friends at Pasadena College, attempting to find out what they knew about the LDS faith so that I could make a reasonable judgment about the Church. However, it seemed to me that no one that I talked with knew anything about the Mormons except that they were a "cult" and that the men had more than one wife (a practice that had long since been dropped).

However, caring students tried helping me in my dilemma about the LDS religion by directing me to a nearby Christian bookstore. "They have books about all kinds of religions—not just the Mormons," I was told.

And they did. There were books about Christian Science, Catholicism, Jehovah's Witnesses, the Muslims and Hindus; just about every religion in the world, it seemed to me. Purchasing three "authoritative" publications about Mormonism, I eagerly hurried back to my garage apartment to learn some "solid facts" about the LDS Church.[1]

After opening the pages of one book I was immediately disappointed by the literature's obvious lack of objectivity. Not the least bit friendly, sarcastic verbiage liberally saturated page after hate-filled page. All three authors used a continual flow of emotionally charged words and phrases such as "Mormon masquerade," "insidious perversions," "heinous crime," "Christ-denying," "colossal faking," "unholy absurdities," "senseless mental vaporings," "high-handed," "mental instability," and "naked hideousness," to sway readers against seriously examining the Mormon point of view.

## Early Persecution

In addition, the authors of these books appeared to endorse the persecution of early Mormons. One recorded:

As the year 1831 drew to a close [in New York], the new church numbered several hundred members, and shortly thereafter relocated in Kirtland,
Ohio, sending missionaries soon to Jackson County, Missouri, the supposed location of the marvelous city of Zion to be built in the future . . .
All did not go well with the saints, however, in Missouri, and in 1833 the
Mormons were routed from Jackson County having stirred up the populace
against them partly on account of their religion and partly because they
were abolitionists from the North.[2]

Another said:

[Joseph Smith's] following grew. So did his conflicts with the law.
When New York became too uncomfortable for him because of law-suits,
he moved with his 'saints' to Kirtland, Ohio. This was in 1831 . . .
At Kirtland . . . Smith conveniently got a revelation that they should go
to Missouri . . . The stay at Independence, Missouri, did not last long. The
Mormon band proved to be a lawless element there, too. Smith even declared that the 'Saints' were independent of all earthly rules. Finally after
many skirmishes and much conflict, Governor Boggs ordered the Mormons
to leave Missouri. Many were arrested, but Smith and the leaders, together
with 12,000 followers, escaped.[3]

Hardly a tear of sorrow for the treatment of Mormons is detected. It
almost sounds like the saints were vacationing or that they were malic-
iously trying to pick fights with their non-Mormon neighbors. Their
troubles were, according to these authors, brought upon them by
themselves. They were accused of being a "lawless element" in spite of
their devotion to law that was later summarized in their twelfth article of
faith: "We believe in being subject to kings, presidents, rulers and
magistrates, in obeying, honoring, and sustaining the law." The authors
seemed to believe the Saints deserved what they got.

I have since learned that the horrible facts are that Mormons were
almost constantly beaten, tortured, raped, killed, and driven off their land
by disbelievers who thought they were doing God a service or who were
caught up in the frenzy of pernicious gang psychology.[4]

In spite of such persecution, the Lord was able to protect his anointed
prophet through the deeds of the honest in heart who, upon meeting
Joseph, were forced to acknowledge his innocence and integrity. Many
who were initially against the prophet soon felt inclined to defend him. In
New York, bigots destroyed a dam that had been erected for baptismal

services. That evening, Joseph was arrested for preaching the *Book of Mormon*. Finding that he was not a threat, the constable, who until he personally met the prophet was involved in plans to ambush him, warned Joseph that those who had obtained the warrant were lying in wait outside. When jeering armed men surrounded the wagon, as had been previously designed, the officer instead shouted at his horses and they escaped. That night he gave Joseph the only empty bed in the tavern where they stayed, while he slept against the door with a loaded musket to defend his "prisoner."

Soon after his acquittal at midnight the following evening, another deputy from a neighboring county arrested Joseph for similar reasons. For nourishment, the officer "generously" gave him a bread crust and some water. He slept with his arm around his "dangerous" prisoner to keep him from escaping. After Joseph's acquittal, the constable asked his forgiveness and led him safely away from another mob.[5]

John Reid, a non-Mormon who defended Joseph in both trials, said about the second trial:

> On the way to Colesville for another trial, I was again called upon by [Joseph's] friends to defend him against his malignant persecutors, and clear him from the false charges they had preferred against him. I made every reasonable excuse I could, as I was nearly worn down through fatigue and want of sleep; as I had been engaged in lawsuits for two days, and nearly the whole of two nights. But I saw the persecution was great against him; and here let me say . . . singular as it may seem, while Mr. Knight was pleading with me to go, a peculiar impression or thought struck my mind, that I must go and defend him, for he was the Lord's anointed. I said I would go, and started with as much faith as the Apostles had.

After that trial, the court reconvened at 2:00 o'clock in the morning! The judge told Joseph, "Mr. Smith, we have had your case under consideration, examined the testimony and find nothing to condemn you, and therefore you are discharged." The judge then severely reprimanded him "merely to please those fiends in human shape who were engaged in the unhallowed persecution of an innocent man, sheerly on account of his religious opinions." Standing, Reid told the judge:

> This court puts me in mind of a certain trial held by Felix of old, when the enemies of Paul arraigned him before the venerable judge for some alleged crime, and nothing was found in him worthy of death or of bonds. Yet, to

please the Jews, who were his accusers, he was left bound contrary to the law; and this court has served Mr. Smith in the same way, by their unlawful and uncalled for reprimand after his discharge, to please his accusers.

. . . [Afterwards] we got him away that night from the midst of three hundred people without his receiving any injury; but I am well aware that we were assisted by some higher power than man; for to look back on the scene, I cannot tell how we succeeded in getting him away. I take no glory to myself; it was the Lord's work and marvelous in our eyes.[6]

From New York the saints fled to Ohio. While building up their religion there, some went on to Missouri to found and establish their "Zion." When persecution finally drove most from Ohio, the bulk of the Church ended up in Missouri—a frightening thing to more entrenched Missourians.

The generally more-educated Mormons, who were from the Eastern states mainly, brought with them different customs, ideas, habits, and attitudes. More settled Missourians, who often chose to live near the western borders of the United States to escape the law by fleeing to Indian territory if necessary, feared Mormons were buying up all the cheap land. They also worried that Mormon stores might be too much competition for already established businesses. Theologically, Mormon beliefs were foreign to them. Belief in revelation through a living prophet was offensive. LDS enthusiasm for building Zion in the midst of long settled Missourians was misunderstood as clannishness and self-righteousness. Many also believed that Mormons might be abolitionists, they might convert the Indians to their faith, they could form an overwhelming voting block, and they were gaining too much political power. Mormons might take over the state![7]

Drunken mobs, emboldened by overzealous preachers, began mocking Mormons, which led to looting and razing homes and businesses. Unsubstantiated reports of Mormon uprisings reached the ears of the governor. Without investigating for himself, Governor Lilburn Boggs issued his infamous "extermination order" which essentially gave license to anyone to murder Mormons. It reads in part: "The Mormons must be treated as enemies, and must be exterminated, or driven from the State if necessary for the public peace."[8]

When gangs of ruffians learned that the governor was on their side, Mormon homes and businesses were burned and vandalized. Precious livestock and horses were killed or driven off. Goods and wagons were stolen. Defenseless women and children were ravished. Leaders were imprisoned simply because of their beliefs.

At Haun's Mill, a band of butchers slaughtered nineteen helpless boys and men while the frightened women scattered into the brush. "One of the regulators shot down Thomas McBride, an old Revolutionary War soldier, with his own gun, then hacked him savagely with a corn knife. Another . . . found a nine-year-old boy cowering under the bellows in the black-smith shop. He shot him through the head, boasting later that 'Nits will make lice, and if he had lived he would have become a Mormon.'"[9] One man gleefully held an empty ten-gallon keg on his saddle and beat it like a drum. Another took a woman's bonnet for his girlfriend. Survivors returned and threw the bodies of their friends and relatives into an unfinished well, fearing they had no time to dig graves because the marauders might reappear at any time. They then fled to the Mormon settlement at Far West.

In the dead of winter, Mormons were once more forced by mobs to flee from their homes and trudge through the snow across the frozen Mississippi. From malaria-infested swamps, they built the beautiful city of Nauvoo, one of the largest cities in Illinois, rivaling even Chicago in size. A magnificent temple, the wonder of America, was erected. Tourists from all over came to see and left with admiration. Tens of thousands of Latter-day Saints lived in peace and comfort—at last.

An English visitor to Nauvoo described its temple as "the wonder of the world." She was also impressed by Nauvoo's "handsome stores, large mansions and fine cottages" situated on the banks of "the noble Mississippi" where ships brought Mormons from "all parts of the world" to be "welcomed with the tear and joy and the gladdening smile, to share the embrace of all." The tourist described Joseph Smith as "a kind, cheerful, sociable companion" who "has the good will of the community." As she "saw the Prophet and his brother Hyrum conversing . . . one day," she felt that she had "beheld two of the greatest men of the nineteenth century." Reflecting on the derogatory things written and said about Latter-day Saints in the public print, she concluded: "I have witnessed the Mormons in their assemblies on a Sunday, and I know not where a similar scene could be effected . . . While all is storm, and tempest . . . abroad respecting the Mormons, all is peace and harmony at home."[10]

In spite of Nauvoo's peace and harmony, under the "protective custody" of Governor Thomas Ford, Joseph and Hyrum were murdered by a mob of "protectors" in the Carthage jail. The saints, under the inspired guidance of Brigham Young, were then forced to leave their beautiful homes to find safety in a foreign land—the Great Salt Lake Basin.

## Careless Research

Along with their winking at the rapine of innocents, the hate-spreading authors of this anti-Mormon literature often disregarded accuracy in their accusations. Though the slanted tone would be obvious to people unfamiliar with the LDS Church or doctrine, the inaccuracies are often not.[11] Their venomous messages could not help but provoke a loathing toward anything and anyone associated with Mormonism. They did inspire ire. It wasn't until the patient missionaries went over the literature with me that I could see how the authors were twisting the Mormon past and its teachings to fit their warped allegations.

Likewise, newspapers in Joseph Smith's day continually printed slanderous stories about him. Most who turned against him did so because of the media's warped information. Few editors or readers had the courage to investigate for themselves who he was and what he taught. Because of the general nature of the scorn heaped upon him by people who didn't even know him, much of the character assassination in anti-Mormon literature can be thrown out as hearsay and scandalmongering.

Several obvious cues marked the disregard for accuracy in the books I purchased:[12] The Church of Jesus Christ of Latter-day Saints was officially founded with a membership of "thirty souls" instead of *six men;*[13] Oliver *Cowdery's* name is changed to "Mr. Cowderly" by one author and misspelled "Cowdry" by another;[14] David "Witmer" instead of *Whitmer;*[15] the Book of Mormon was published "in 1930" (instead of *1830*) with the name, *"The Golden Bible"* instead of *Book of Mormon;*[16] the Book of Mormon is divided into "sixteen" books instead of *fifteen;*[17] John the Baptist ordained "Cowderly" and Smith to the "Aaronitic" instead of *Aaronic* priesthood;[18] "Mormon [was] a direct descendant of Levi" instead of *Lehi;*[19] reference is made to a scripture found in "3d Levi, chapter 11" when there is *no such book* nor even one that resembles it;[20] at "Hawn's

Hill" instead of at *Haun's Mill* was the "famous" instead of *infamous* massacre of helpless old men and children.[21]

Other inaccuracies were more lengthy. According to Casper Nervig, Joseph "came from a shiftless family which moved from place to place leaving a poor reputation behind. Superstition and epilepsy were family traits. His father was a peddler, fortune teller, and water witch. The son Joseph continued his father's practice but went him one better by practicing divination for lost and stolen articles. Joseph received practically no education and at the age of fourteen could barely read and write. He was a disorderly and lazy boy sharing the bad reputation of his father and brothers . . . At about the age of fifteen he began to have 'visions' and epileptic fits."[22] Walter Martin says that "Joseph was entirely destitute of moral character "[23] William Biederwolf writes, "It was commonly understood in the community where Joe Smith lived that a lie had to be a mighty big one to be a bigger one than Joe Smith could tell."[24]

I later learned that all of these accusations were fabrications or distortions of the truth. Joseph was not an epileptic, although his body was subject to other physical maladies like anyone else. An epidemic of typhoid fever contributed to a drastic leg operation when Joseph was seven. Doctors bored into the diseased bone and broke off pieces while he endured the full brunt of the pain without an anesthetic. For three years he walked with crutches. When, as an adult, Joseph was dragged from his bed and tarred, some of the tar and a vial of some unknown substance was forced into his mouth and a tooth was chipped. From then on he had a faint whistle in his speech. He did not suffer from epilepsy, but even if he had, that would have nothing to do with whether or not he was a prophet. The author seemed to believe that epilepsy is the result of sin—as though the afflicted person brought the malady upon him or herself.

There is no evidence that Joseph's father did water witching or fortune telling, although he did market foodstuffs and hired himself out. Peddling is merely another name for selling—the backbone of America's free enterprise system. The Smith family was poor. Cord wood, vegetables, baskets and brooms, maple sugar, gingerbread, root beer, pies and boiled eggs were sold from their home, at camp meetings and other gatherings. "From twelve to fifteen hundred sugar trees" on their land produced about "one thousand pounds" of maple sugar each year, and it was no small chore collecting it. Joseph's mother, Lucy, painted "designs on oilcloth [and] sold

. . . table covers." Joseph Sr. and his older sons "hired out on local farms" and did odd jobs such as "gardening, harvesting and well digging to supplement their income." All the while they were building a home and clearing sixty acres of heavy timber for a farm.[25] This hardly sounds like he or his family were "disorderly and lazy," and "destitute of moral character."

Even if his family had "a poor reputation" and was thought of as "shiftless" (and there are numerous accounts that attest to the high regard his family received from non-Mormon neighbors), it would not disprove that Joseph was a prophet. Moses's adoptive family—the Pharoah's—certainly had "a poor reputation" and he must have been considered "shiftless" among enslaved Jews. Jesus had a "poor reputation" among the Sanhedrin who most certainly thought him "shiftless."

## Joseph Smith's Character

Not all non-Mormons who knew the family of young Joseph Smith spoke against them. Orlando Saunders said:

> I knew all of the Smith family well. They have all worked for me many a day. They were very good people. Young Joe (as we called him) has worked for me, and he was a good worker . . . They were the best family in the neighborhood in case of sickness; one was at my house nearly all the time when my father died. I always thought them honest. They were owing me some money when they left here. One of them came back in about a year and paid me.[26]

Thomas Taylor, a lawyer and lecturer, knew the Smiths "very well. They were very nice men, too. The only trouble was they were ahead of the people; and the people . . . turned to abuse them because they had the manhood to stand for their own convictions."[27]

A woman named Mrs. Palmer says that her parents

> were friends of the Smith family, which was one of the best in that locality —honest, religious and industrious, but poor. The father of the family, was above the average in intelligence. I have heard my parents say that he bore the appearance of having descended from royalty. Mrs. Smith was called 'Mother Smith' by many. Children loved to go to her home.

Mrs. Palmer recalls the time when one of the church leaders warned her father to keep from associating with Joseph. Her father

> defended his own position by saying that Joseph was the best help he had ever found. He told the churchman that he always fixed the time of hoeing his large field to that when he could secure the services of Joseph Smith, because of the influence that boy had over the wild boys of the neighborhood, and explained that when these boys, or young men, worked by themselves much time would be spent in arguing and quarreling, which often ended in a ring fight. But when Joseph Smith worked with them, the work went steadily forward, and he got the full worth of the wages he paid.[28]

Non-Mormons who knew Joseph as an adult also spoke highly of him. James Gordon Bennett, editor of the New York *Herald*, wrote after visiting Nauvoo: "Joseph Smith . . . is a man of the highest order of talent and great independence of character, firm in his integrity, and devoted to his religion."[29]

During Joseph's visit to Washington, D.C., Congressman Mathew Davis wrote to his wife, Mary, that he had heard "Joe Smith" give a lecture.

> During the whole of his address, and it occupied more than two hours, there was no opinion or belief that he expressed, that was calculated, in the slightest degree, to impair the morals of society . . . He displayed strongly a spirit of charity and forbearance. I have changed my opinion of the Mormons. They are an injured and much-abused people.[30]

The Masonic Grand Master in Illinois wrote after visiting Nauvoo for three days:

> I had supposed, from what I had previously heard, that I should witness an impoverished, ignorant and bigoted population, completely priest-ridden and tyrannized over by Joseph Smith.
> . . . On the contrary, to my surprise, I saw a people apparently happy, prosperous and intelligent. Every man appeared to be employed in some business or occupation. I saw no idleness, no intemperance, no noise, no riot: all appeared to be contented . . . [and were] hospitable, polite, well-informed and liberal.
> . . . With Joseph Smith, the hospitality of whose house I kindly received, I was well pleased. Of course, on the subject of religion we widely differed, but he appeared to be quite as willing to permit me to enjoy my right of opinion as I think we all ought to let the Mormons enjoy theirs. But instead of the ignorant and tyrannical upstart, judge my surprise at finding him a sensible, intelligent companion and gentlemanly man.[31]

Native Americans often visited Nauvoo and were warmly welcomed by the saints. Helen Mar Whitney remembers a time when a deputation of Pottawatamie chiefs came to see Joseph Smith in June, 1843. "The Prophet had an ox killed for them, and some horses were also prepared for them." Remembering the kindness of Joseph and the Mormons, the Pottawatamies made the saints welcome upon their land after they were driven from Nauvoo.[32]

Jane James, a free black woman, led her mother, two sisters, a brother and his wife and two children, one thousand miles on foot from Connecticut to Nauvoo after they had joined the Church. After meeting him for the first time Jane reported that the prophet Joseph "was the finest man I ever saw."[33]

## Other Witnesses to the Book of Mormon

The books I read contained numerous other claims which do not hold up under scrutiny. Nervig says of the Book of Mormon, "This 'new revelation' is based solely on the testimony of one . . . illiterate man,"[34] but how could an "illiterate man" create an ancient religious history that hosts of scholars believe is true? How was an "illiterate man" able to produce a book that, in the words of a former clergyman, would aid theologians to learn "more in a few weeks about the Bible" than was learned from all their "years of study [of] man-made theologies and ancient languages?"[35] Further, this new revelation was not based solely on the testimony of one man. Numerous witnesses saw the gold plates and saw and heard Jesus Christ as well as angels bestowing important priesthood keys.

Nervig also describes Oliver "Cowderly" [sic] as "a degenerate school teacher."[36] But who, that personally knew Cowdery, has ever left such a description? William Lang, a non-Mormon colleague of Oliver's when the two practiced law, wrote, "Mr. Cowdery was an able lawyer and a great advocate. His manners were easy and gentlemanly; he was polite, dignified, yet courteous . . . His addresses to the court and jury were characterized by a high order of oratory with brilliant and forensic force. He was modest and reserved, never spoke ill of any one, never complained."[37]

## Ancient Book of Mormon History

William Biederwolf reports that "The Book of Esther [sic] tells us that the Jaredites occupied Central America until 600 B.C., when they were wholly exterminated, but the entire scholarship of the world tells us that the Mayas are living today in Central America exactly where they did in ancient times . . . in spite of the fact that they were declared extinct by Joe Smith . . . The Book of Mormon tells us that for 600 years before Christ, Central America was entirely desolate and that the Nephites then occupied it until A.D. 384, when they and their Christian civilization were utterly annihilated by the wild and barbarous Lamanites . . . According to all reputed scholarship the Mayans who occupy this land today were in possession of it even before the days of Abraham."[38]

Joseph has never said that the Mayans became extinct. Neither does the Book of Mormon say anything about Central America; nor does The Book of Ether (not "Esther") say "the Jaredites occupied Central America until 600 B.C;" nor does it say that "for 600 years before Christ, Central America was entirely desolate and . . . the Nephites then occupied it until A.D. 384;" and neither can the Nephites at the end of the story be considered a "Christian civilization." They rejected Christ, and their wickedness exceeded that of the Lamanites. Moreover, archaeological evidence points to the Olmecs as appearing long before the Mayans came on the scene.

In fact, the Olmecs[39] seem to fit the Jaredite description as put forth in the Book of Mormon. They "stretched over the period from perhaps 2500 BC to just after 600 BC." Their remains are located "primarily in a semi-circular area in and just north of the Isthmus of Tehuantepec . . . The San Lorenzo Tenochtitlan site . . . displays the most spectacular remains credited to this culture."[40]

What is referred to by anthropologists as the Preclassic and Early Classic Mayans appeared later than the Olmecs. It "had developed its essential form by 100 B.C., it continued through an unsteady career to a slow decline, then gasped to an end before A.D. 600." The earlier Mayans seem to describe Lehi and his posterity who, according to Sorenson, "reached peak vigor between A.D. 250 and 300 [which was then] followed quickly by a precipitous decline."[41]

The LDS Church does not claim to know exactly where the Book of Mormon lands were located. However, chronologically the Olmec, Preclassic Mayan, and Early Classic Mayan time frames snugly fit the Book of Mormon's history. Topographically, the Mesoamerican (southern Mexico/northern Central America) terrain and natural geography ("narrow neck of land," rivers, highlands, lowlands, seas, "many waters," etc.)

conform to the book's descriptions. (The "narrow neck of land" might well be the Isthmus of Tehuantepec). Geologically, there were upheavels from earthquakes and volcanoes around the time of Jesus's death, as Third Nephi implies. In all of the ancient Americas a written language was developed only among Mesoamericans during the time frame of the Book of Mormon —an important criterion for identification of Book of Mormon cultures. Tradition and written codices among pre-Columbian natives tell about earlier transoceanic migrations that began their history. The nearly two centuries of peace among Book of Mormon peoples after Jesus's appearance is born out archaeologically and from native tradition. "Precipitous decline" is graphically illustrated when the book abruptly ends in 421 AD.

## Language of the Book of Mormon

The three anti-Mormon writers claimed that there is "no such language as 'Reformed Egyptian Hieroglyphics,'" "Modern Egyptian," nor "neo-Egyptian."[42] The first Nephi in the Book of Mormon recorded that he was making his "record in the language of my father, which consists of the learning of the Jews and the language of the Egyptians," not in "reformed," "modern" or "neo" Egyptian (1 Nephi 1:2). A millennium later Moroni wrote:

> We have written this record according to our knowledge, in the characters which are called among us the reformed Egyptian, being handed down and *altered by us,* according to our manner of speech . . . But the Lord knoweth the things which we have written, and . . . because that *none other people knoweth our language,* therefore he hath prepared means for the interpretation thereof.
>
> (Mormon 9:32-34)

Most people today could not read a ten-centuries-old text in any language. Before modern dictionaries were developed, written languages changed even more dramatically than they do now, but they continue to change nevertheless. Moroni clearly understood that the Egyptian written language that Lehi and Nephi used had changed over the centuries into what he and his people called "reformed Egyptian."

Originally, Lehi and his family spoke Hebrew. Perhaps because they were educated merchants, they learned to write the kind of Egyptian known as demotic which "could be written in less space than Hebrew...

Demotic was actually a shorthand, extremely cramped and abbreviated; and . . . peculiarly adapted to the sounds and thought processes of one language . . . only. It could be used very economically for writing Egyptian, but not for any other language."[43] Perhaps Egyptian, and not his beautiful Hebrew, was used by Nephi to save precious space on metal plates.

By the time Moroni came along a thousand years later, both the Hebrew and the Egyptian had been altered so that no one except those living in his society could read them. Moroni informs us that the Lord "hath prepared means for the interpretation" of the plates because no one in the future could understand them, either. When the anti-Mormon authors write that "there is no such language as Reformed Egyptian Hieroglyphics," they are partially right. Today archaeologists know of no such language. Perhaps someday, with better deciphering methods, "reformed Egyptian" will be rediscovered. But it won't be in Egypt.

## Other Anti-Mormon Claims

Anti-Mormon writers often accuse Mormons of disparaging the Bible. According to Biederwolf, "The Mormons say the Bible is so polluted that scarcely a single verse has escaped so as to convey the same sense now as it did in the original."[44] An authoritative statement from the LDS Church reads,

> The Church of Jesus Christ of Latter-day Saints accepts the Holy Bible as *the foremost* of her standard works . . . Nevertheless, the Church announces a reservation in the case of erroneous translation . . . and . . . we are not alone, for Biblical scholars generally admit the presence of errors . . . An impartial investigator has cause to wonder more at the paucity of error than that mistakes are to be found at all.[45]

Some have been led to believe that "The Church of Jesus Christ of Latter Day Saints [sic] requires . . . each young member [to] support himself during a two-year missionary tour,"[46] or that "[missionary work] is binding upon every male member . . . for at least two years."[47] No Latter-day Saint is *required* to do anything in the Church. Young men (not "each young member") from 19 to 26 are encouraged to serve a mission, but they are not reprimanded in any way if they choose not to. In addition, unmarried women over the age of 21 may also serve. Mature couples often serve as missionaries and mission presidents. In 1995 an average of over 25,000 unpaid missionaries annually entered the mission field. Since the Church's inception, more than half a million have gladly served.[48]

Martin notes that "The Book of Mormon speaks out most pointedly against polygamy . . . and states that polygamy in the sight of the Lord 'was abominable.'"[49] He then wonders why it was practiced in the 19th century LDS Church. True, the Book of Mormon does speak out against the men in the Book of Mormon having more than one wife: "There shall not any man *among you* have save it be one wife." However, Jacob further records: "For *if I will,* saith the Lord of Hosts, *raise up seed unto me, I will command my people;* otherwise they shall hearken unto these things" (Jacob 2:27-30). The Lord may, if he wishes, command plural marriage as he has in ages past.

Ashley Bartlett has preserved a dramatic episode regarding polygyny—the correct term for having more than one wife—that occurred during a water rights case in Craig, Colorado, many years ago. A fierce blizzard was raging while the court took a two-hour lunch intermission and recess to await the arrival of an important witness from forty miles away. Mrs. Lamb, the hostess and owner of the hotel where lunch was being served, was pouring coffee. Bartlett turned his cup over so she wouldn't waste her coffee on him.

> 'Oh, Mr. Bartlett, you must have some hot coffee on this bitter day.'
>
> I [Bartlett] had occupied the same chair [at the table] for a week. Next to me was an old gentleman who asked her, 'Mrs. Lamb, didn't you know he is a Mormon?'
>
> Everybody heard, even the judge. 'So, we have a Mormon here. How do you justify lustful polygamy of the Old World in this modern time?' After some silence, he went on: 'I'm not surprised at your reticence to speak for anything so un-Christian and so abhorent to decency!'
>
> At this point Mrs. Lamb spoke out, 'Mr. Bartlett, you are in my house. I give you full permission to defend yourself.' Then, she turned to her bookcase and getting her Bible, handed it to me, adding, 'I demand that you defend yourself.'
>
> **Bartlett**: 'It must be well known to His Honor that plural marriages were discontinued by the Mormon church in 1890. That ought to be a sufficient answer.'
>
> **Judge**: 'But the stink still remains. Young man, show us from the New Testament any shred of justification for such an unholy marital relationship.'

I handed the Bible to the judge and asked him to read, beginning with the first verse of the 21st chapter of the Book of Revelation.

(There was pin-drop silence among the hundred or more guests as he read): 'And I saw a new heaven and a new earth: for the first heaven and the first earth were passed away; and there was no more sea.' He paused, then asked, 'Tell us, what has this to do with the question?'

**Bartlett**: 'If your honor please, read verse two.'

'And I John saw the holy city, new Jerusalem, coming down from God out of heaven, prepared as a bride adorned for her husband.' (The judge leaned over the table toward me). 'Much as I enjoy reading the Holy Book, I ask you, What point is there in all this?'

**Bartlett**: 'If your Honor please, Let me ask. Do you, along with all other Christian believers hope to enter, and have place in this Holy City when it comes?'

**Judge**: 'Yes, I do! But there won't be anyone there who is tinged with the slime of polygamy!'

**Bartlett**: 'Will you read verse three, then verses 10, 11 and 12?'

'And I heard a great voice out of heaven saying, Behold, the tabernacle of God is with men, and he will dwell with them, and they shall be his people, and God himself shall be with them . . . And he . . . shewed me that great city, the holy Jerusalem, descending out of heaven from God, having the glory of God: and . . . had a wall great and high, and had twelve gates . . . and names written thereon, which are the names of the twelve tribes of the children of Israel.'

**Bartlett**: 'Please read the last two lines of verse 22, then verses 23 to 26 in the thirty-fifth chapter of Genesis so we may know the names of those twelve men whose names will be on the gates of God's holiest city.'

'Now the sons of Jacob [Israel] were twelve: The sons of Leah; Reuben . . . Simeon . . . Levi . . . Judah . . . Issachar . . . Zebulun: The sons of Rachel; Joseph and Benjamin: And the sons of Bilhah . . . Dan and Naphtali: And the sons of Zilpah . . . Gad and Asher.'

**Bartlett**: In closing I said, 'When God chose the names to grace the gates of his holiest city, he set aside all the one-wife families of the earth, and chose twelve men who had one father and four mothers, for this honor. Furthermore, when God chose the lineage for his Only Begotten Son he passed over all the one-wife families of the earth, and chose Mary of the lineage of David, a polygamist, for the highest honor ever given to women. Now, Sir, I do not care what others may think of plural marriage, but that is what God thinks of it, and that is all that really matters.'

Putting down the Bible the judge held out his hand and apologized.[50]

## Responses to Anti-Mormon Literature

A story from former owners of a Christian bookstore demonstrates how reasonable people ought to respond to anti-Mormon literature:

As in other Christian bookstores, the couple's store included a great deal of anti-Mormon literature. While reading some of it, they "could not understand why Christian people could write such vicious things about a church [they] had only heard good things about." Whenever the store owners mentioned placing pro-Mormon material in the store, their Christian friends told them that "Mormons were a cult and didn't believe in Jesus."

Sending for the book, *Mormon Doctrine,* the writer "read it from cover to cover. It was so close to things I had believed all my life," she says. "My friends tried to discourage such thinking. Convincing my husband this was the true Church was the hard part. Many times we stayed up until 2 or 3 a.m.—he with the Bible and I with *Mormon Doctrine* and the standard works [LDS scriptures] I had later picked up.

"For more than a year" they talked. During the earliest discussions, their 9-year-old sat on the couch next to his father. As the months went by, he moved closer to his mother. His father "began to see the truthfulness of the gospel through the innocence of his son."

It was then that they stopped ordering anti-Mormon material.

On their way to Disneyland, the family stopped in Salt Lake City. They never got to California, they were so impressed. Purchasing several LDS tapes and books they listened to every tape on their way back home. By the time they got home, they were all "convinced this was the true Church."

After the family was taught by "the finest young men we have ever known," they were ready for baptism. As persecution from family and friends increased, they sold their store to buyers who agreed to not handle anti-Mormon literature.

Though they lost friends and family, they feel that that "has only made us stronger and we are only sorry that it took us this long to find the one true Church. Owning a Christian bookstore was how we . . . came to know the true Church. Instead of the anti-Mormon material driving us away. . . the literature drove us to it."[51]

Anti-Mormon literature also helped me. Its authors seemingly didn't care to convey the truth about the LDS faith and its first prophet, Joseph Smith. Their aim seemed to be to slander rather than to objectively analyze. A similar conclusion was made by a former military chaplain who joined the Church after reading anti-Mormon literature: "Either those writers were grossly ignorant of what Latter-day Saints really believe or else they were intentionally malicious."[52]

Upon comparing what I read to what I knew of the LDS Church, I concluded that those who use this trash cannot represent truth and therefore could be false prophets. True religion would teach truth, not pick fights. I decided it would be a waste of time for me to continue reading it, especially *when the authors offered absolutely nothing better than what the LDS Church already offered.*

As I read the anti-books, I felt—in order to be fair   equal time must be spent in pro-Mormon literature. So, purchasing copies of James Talmage's *Articles of Faith* and *The Great Apostasy,* along with LeGrand Richards's *A Marvelous Work and a Wonder,* I began learning more about Joseph Smith and what Mormons truly believe from LDS scholars. The Sunday School class and the missionaries were helpful, but I could now turn to these texts whenever I had a question.

Nevertheless, as important as Latter-day Saint literature was, I still could not bring myself to reading the one work that really mattered.

# 16
# The Search Intensifies

## An "Expert" on Mormonism

For about a year I devoted myself to studying Latter-day Saint theology along with trying to keep up with my college studies. The more I studied the theology, the more the previously unbelievable LDS doctrines became believable. The Godhead, premortality, the need for prophets and further revelation, the purpose of life, a spirit world, proselytizing among those who have left this life, rewards based on faith and works, families being together forever, all seemed to be more biblical than their counterparts in "orthodox" and traditional Christianity. The concepts of a mysterious Trinity, the magnificent human personality having no previous existence before the womb, no further need for prophets and revelation, rewards based on belief alone, family relationships ending at death, a heaven reserved only for those fortunate enough to have been raised in a Christian home or who were converted before death, furious fires awaiting those who have never heard of Christ: none of these things seemed biblical or reasonable. Still, I wasn't a theologian. What if the seemingly irrational is true? Hell and its infernal fumes might be my next home if I embraced Mormonism.

Knowing of my dilemma, a professor at Pasadena College took a personal interest. Approaching me one day he asked, "Would you like to speak with an expert on Mormonism, Bill? I'll give you a note of introduction if you'd like." Leaping at the opportunity, I practically flew to the office of this master of Mormon thought.

## Dr. Ludcliffe

Dr. Ludcliffe,[1] Dean of Fuller Theological Seminary, was a tall, warm, dignified man. Shelves of scholarly volumes lined the walls of his office. Papers and more books were neatly stacked on his desk. Surely if anyone could steer me straight, he was the one. Putting me at ease, Dr. Ludcliffe invited me to sit near him at the side of his huge desk.

Eagerly I listened while the good dean began explaining LDS doctrine and history. As the hour slipped by, though, I became more and more disappointed. Here and there he slipped in something I'd never heard of or had forgotten, but the "expertise" he was supposed to have had was merely a regurgitation of the old, worn-out anti-Mormon thoughts I had already heard.

As he finished, I grew more discouraged. The discussion was reminiscent of the three earlier clerics. As I was leaving, though, he perked me up by putting his arm around me and making an interesting challenge. If I would bring a pair of Mormon elders to his office he would disprove the LDS faith. "You know," he revealed in a whisper as if I didn't already know, "they call them 'elders,' but they're really only 19- or 20-year-old boys."

Latter-day Saint missionaries are assigned to specific areas, and the ones teaching me were in Fontana. I didn't know any in Pasadena, but they were not hard to find. I made contact with the missionaries assigned to the Pasadena area and explained my situation. A week or two later the three of us visited Dr. Ludcliffe's office.

## Meeting the Challenge

Even though Dr. Ludcliffe warmly welcomed us, the scene must have been threatening to the young elders: a doctor of divinity challenging two youths who had barely graduated from high school. If they were nervous, they didn't show it, though. Elder Elliott did most of the talking. Elder Stephenson was new to the mission field, but he was attentive and enthusiastic during the visit.

The drama unfolded with a planned and prepared friendly attack by a learned man and a spontaneous, unplanned defense by a comparatively uneducated young adult. The dean knew in advance what he was going to say; Elder Elliott had to think about and be inspired to answer without preparation. Each time a scriptural or historical assault on Mormonism was made, the elder would humbly and dispassionately parry with what seemed to be a sensible defense. He calmly offered what answers he could, often claiming that what the dean accused the Church or Joseph Smith of believing or doing simply was not true. A few times he had to plead ignorance, but there was no obvious embarrassment on his part because he didn't know. He merely answered what he could and let those things he didn't know drop. Neither the elder nor the dean argued. At no time did the missionary counter with an attack on orthodox Christianity.

Never did Dr. Ludcliffe disprove the LDS faith, but neither did Elder Elliott persuade me to believe his way. I left that hour's encounter, however, with a deeper admiration for the young, unlettered "stripling warriors" of the Church. No longer were they "mere boys." It was truly remarkable how easily the young man could come up with credible answers to most of the amiably antagonistic accusations about his faith. He ably fulfilled William George Jordan's thought: "The man who has a certain religious belief and fears to discuss it, lest it may be proved wrong, is not loyal to his belief; he has but a coward's faithfulness to his prejudices. If he were a lover of truth, he would be willing at any moment to surrender his belief for a higher, better, and truer faith."[2] I was profoundly impressed. I had witnessed LDS doctrine logically being defended in an unruffled manner by a still wet-behind-the-ears youth as his church was being assailed by a trained theologian.

I came away with the enlightened realization that during the past year of intense study I had received a groundwork in biblical interpretation that obviously could withstand any severe test such as the good dean gave to that elder on my behalf. No longer did I worry about my lack—or the missionaries' lack—of theological training. That discussion gave me the important assurance that even I could explain Mormon belief without being embarrassed.

## The Keystone

Many wonderful saints in Fontana helped by patiently answering my questions about Joseph Smith and Mormonism, some of which I'm sure must have seemed rather foolish. Jack and Joyce Larkin were two.[3] Their oldest daughter, Wendy, was away at college, a son, John, was serving a mission, and three—Don, Ron, and Misty—were living at home. They seemed to have an ideal family life. Their example and genuine happiness were part of what convinced me that there has to be something good to Mormonism. One Saturday evening, after Jack and I spent the afternoon splitting wood for a ward project, Joyce served us a delicious roast beef dinner. Elder Porter and his new companion, Elder Randolph from Enterprise, Utah, were also there.

Elder Porter had received a "Dear John" letter that week and was not his happy-go-lucky self. After a heartfelt discussion in the hall between the two of us we all sat down in the living room for a couple of hours and discussed the restored gospel. Two extremely precious gemstones in my search for truth were introduced to me that evening.[4]

"It is certainly obvious to me," I didn't have to remind anyone, "that if the Book of Mormon is true, Joseph Smith must have been a prophet. And, if Joseph Smith was a prophet, then the gospel of Jesus Christ must have been restored through him as he said it was. But, why are Latter-day Saints so sure the Book of Mormon is true? Four ministers, a seminary dean, a number of professors and students I have known, all say it was plagiarized. Why do you insist it came from early Israelites?

"And what about the anachronisms within the book? Horses were introduced to the Americas by the Spaniards; indigenous natives in the Western Hemisphere had no knowledge of the wheel, as is evidenced by the use of the travois by Plains Indians; the smelting of iron was unknown to them; and whoever heard of pre-Columbians knowing about elephants?"

"You've certainly hit upon some sticklers, Bill," Jack admitted. "There do seem to be some modern things that are wrongly attributed to ancient times. But simply because details have not yet been discovered about something does not mean that that article is out of place historically. However, there is a great deal of evidence that the things you have mentioned were indeed known before Columbus discovered America."

Opening the first gemstone I discovered that night—an emerald-green paperback called *Book of Mormon Message and Evidences*—Joyce showed me some fascinating statements by respected authorities that pre-Columbian skeletons of horses, mastodons and mammoths associated with man in the Western Hemisphere have indeed been found. "Elephants are mentioned only once in the Book of Mormon and that was among the earliest people, the Jaredites," Joyce pointed out. "And the latest mention of horses being used by Book of Mormon people was prior to the crucifixion of Christ" (Ether 9:19; 3 Nephi 3:22). The authorities also wrote that the use of iron, along with copper, brass and gold, was known by early natives. Turning to the front of the book Joyce then showed me photographs of ancient American wheeled toys and a petroglyph of an elephant, as well as the engraved gold and silver records in a stone box of the Persian king, Darius.[5] "Archaeologists and paleontologists have barely scratched the surface of what is yet to be discovered."

Jack took from his bookshelf *The Americas Before Columbus* and showed me photographs of temples, pyramids and other buildings, precisely cut and fitted stone walls, and other remains and artifacts of ancient South, Central and North Americans. Besides the wheeled toys that Joyce showed me, photos of four stone wheels as tall as a man and remains of cement roads were displayed.[6]

"This is fascinating," I conceded. "I wonder why such discoveries are not widely known. These photographs of wheeled toys are remarkable. I wonder why the knowledge of wheels seems to have been lost by the time the conquistadors arrived."

"Someone has said that occasionally a man stumbles upon the truth, but he picks himself up and hurries on as if nothing has happened," Joyce recalled. Turning to another section of the green paperback, she read aloud: "In 1946, in New York City, the Grolier Club displayed 100 books and writings published before the 20th century that most influenced the American people. Among them were the *Gettysburg Address; The Autobiography of Benjamin Franklin;* Noah Webster's *An American Dictionary;* and the *Book of Mormon.*"[7] Most at that exhibit stumbled upon the truth and hurried on, not realizing what God perhaps placed before them to be examined.

Jack went on to say that some refuse to read the Book of Mormon because they have been told that it is satanic. However, if the contents of the Book of Mormon were originally part of the Bible, there would be no criticism of it. If the books of Matthew, Mark, Luke, John or any other books of the Bible came forth in our time in the way Joseph Smith described, they would no doubt be rejected by the same Christians who reject the Book of Mormon. If the Book of Mormon were unearthed by archaeologists, there would be little criticism of it. It would be thought of the same way that the Dead Sea Scrolls or the ancient library at Nag Hammadi in Egypt are. Its moral teachings are in perfect harmony with all the Lord had previously revealed. Only its setting, personalities, geography, method of coming forth, and Jesus's visit to the Western Hemisphere are unprecedented.

Christ's true disciples are always eager to discover anything new he might have said or done. Joyce read that F. S. Spaulding—a non-Mormon —declared: "If the Book of Mormon is true, it is, next to the Bible, the most important book in the world . . . If this book is what it claims to be it throws light upon matters of the first importance . . . It is inexcusable that the book has never had the serious examination which its importance demands."[8]

## Bible Prophecies Concerning the Book of Mormon

Turning to his Bible, Elder Randolph showed me a prophecy about the Book of Mormon coming forth: "And thou [Israel] shalt be brought down, and shalt speak out of the ground, and thy speech shall be low out of the dust" (Isaiah 29:4). From "out of the ground," from beneath "the dust," the Book of Mormon has come forth to "speak," on behalf of ancient Israelites who were its authors.

The Lord also promised that he "will . . . do a marvelous work among this people, even a marvelous work and a wonder: for the wisdom of their wise men shall perish, and the understanding of their prudent men shall be hid" (Isaiah 29:14). What is his marvelous work and wonder if it is not the restoration of the gospel of Jesus Christ with its Book of Mormon? Only the prophets can tell because "the wisdom of . . . wise men shall perish, and the understanding of . . . prudent men shall be hid."

Don eagerly showed me what Ezekiel testified:

> The word of the Lord came . . . unto me, saying . . . thou son of man, take one stick [Hebrew: 'wood'] and write upon it,[9] for Judah, and for the children of Israel . . . Then take another stick, and write upon it, for Joseph, the stick of Ephraim, and for all the house of Israel . . . And join them one to another into one stick; and they shall become one in thine hand. And when the children of thy people shall speak unto thee, saying, Wilt thou not show us what thou meanest by these? Say unto them, Thus saith the Lord God; Behold, I will take the stick of Joseph, which is in the hand of Ephraim, and make them one stick, and they shall be one in mine hand.
>
> (Ezekiel 37:15-22)

The stick of Judah is the Bible since it was largely written by prophets who came from the tribe of Judah. The stick of Joseph is the Book of Mormon since Lehi and his progeny were descendants of Joseph. The two "sticks" have become "one stick" (book or "wood") in the Lord's "hand" to help bring more to Christ.

"Surely," I said, "other religionists must interpret these scriptures differently."

"Others do interpret these passages differently, both with the LDS faith and with each other, but they differ by what authority?" Elder Porter asked, still being the missionary in spite of his sadness. "Who is their prophet? Theologians dare not claim such an office; the heavens are closed and God no longer speaks, according to them. Since prophets penned scripture, prophets need to interpret them in order for us to know what they truly mean. Joseph Smith claimed to be a prophet. If he was a prophet, then his interpretations can be considered authoritative. If he wasn't, who is?"

## Moroni's Promise

Misty called my attention to a bold promise that Moroni made near the end of the Book of Mormon:

> When ye shall receive these things, I would exhort you that ye would ask God, the Eternal Father, in the name of Christ, if these things are not true; and if ye shall ask with a sincere heart, with real intent, having faith in Christ, he will manifest the truth of it unto you, by the power of the Holy Ghost. And by the power of the Holy Ghost ye may know the truth of all things.

(Moroni 10:4-5)

Knowing that I liked to read, Joyce handed me the green paperback and encouraged me to study it so that I would gain an appreciation for the Book of Mormon. Turning to one of its pages, while I held it, she showed me that though he didn't realize it because he was not LDS, former vice President of the United States Henry Wallace spoke of the power about which Moroni wrote:

> Of all the American books of the nineteenth century, it seems probable that the Book of Mormon was the most powerful. It reached perhaps only one percent of the United States, but it affected that one percent so powerfully and lastingly that all the people of the United States have been affected, especially by its contribution in opening one of our great frontiers.[10]

I later read of a Protestant missionary who "was amazed that any group of people would put that kind of test on their particular religion or book." He read the Book of Mormon and, after sincere fasting and prayer, was converted "by the power of the Holy Ghost."[11]

The power of the Holy Ghost has worked in millions of others who have taken the time to prayerfully read the Book of Mormon and ask if it *is true*. There have also been instances when that power has worked with sincere people who have asked the Lord to show them that the Book of Mormon *is not true,* as in the experience of a college theology teacher in Freiburg, Germany, who invited Mormon elders to her classes. When they told her students about the book, it "sounded too fantastic" to her. However, she felt an overpowering urge to read it. She reports, "In my fear to read the Book of Mormon, I knelt down and asked God to forgive me for wanting to read it. How fast that prayer was answered! The words started to light up. The testimony of Jesus Christ in the Book of Mormon started to burn within me. The power of the Holy Spirit surrounded me."[12]

Joyce told of another convert—Peggy—whose parents had attended a church-run college and whose father was an ordained minister. They "worshipped together as a family and often discussed their beliefs." Peggy "had received a thorough grounding in the Bible and was very happy . . My father was not violently anti-Mormon and yet it was firmly impressed upon me that the only thing worse than being a Catholic was being a Mormon."

Several years after she was married, she became frustrated by the "glaring gaps" between what the ministers taught and her understanding of what the Bible taught. Perplexed, Peggy began searching in earnest for a church she could accept. She checked out books about the beliefs of various Christian religions from the library, but "each church was missing some element of the gospel." Reluctantly, she finally checked out two books about Mormon doctrine. After reading them she "couldn't find any faults." Even more hesitatingly she checked the Book of Mormon out. In her home

> I began with a prayer on my knees: 'Oh Lord, I know this book is a product of the devil made to lead people astray. I ask thee to protect me from its evil and let my eyes see the dangers that I might not be misled.' I was safe now. And I believed that it would only take a few pages to expose the book as a fraud. Instead it only took a few pages to scare me out of my wits! The Lord hadn't protected me! What I read was in praise of Christ, a statement of His power, glory, and mission. I took the book back that afternoon.
>
> The next two weeks were murder. Every time I relaxed, the words of the book would come back to haunt me. I checked it out again. Again I prayed: 'Lord I'm scared of this book but I have to know the truth about it. Please give me guidance.' A few more pages and I couldn't sit still. Back to the library again and another two weeks of agony.

Saturday she checked it out "one last time." She and her husband decided to call an LDS meetinghouse for answers. Shortly after missionaries were sent, both were certain the Church was true, and were baptized.[13]

Elder Porter testified that that same power of the Holy Ghost would even work in me if I would sincerely ask God for help. "If the book of Mormon is true, Joseph Smith most certainly was a prophet of God. And, if he was a prophet, the gospel of Jesus Christ was restored through him. That's why he called it the keystone of our religion."

Still, I resisted. "There are those who claim Joseph Smith made up the book, himself. He could have written that promise. Some readers of the book might try praying and talk themselves into believing the book came from God."

"Do you know what I would like to tell people that believe Joseph Smith wrote the Book of Mormon?" Jack asked. "I'd like to challenge them to try it themselves. I'd like to ask them to write an original book themselves without any research—a subject that no one else has ever thought about and in an area of the world about which there is virtually no scholarship—complete with original characters, stories, setting, and theme. Then get a friend to put up the thousands of dollars of their own money that would be needed to have it published. Finally they must talk others into taking it out into the world without any remuneration. Then they must get tens of thousands of scholars to believe it and authenticate it and get millions to believe that it is not a fictional account."

## Authoring a Historical Novel

Many believe that in order to write a book all they need to do is sit down with a pen or a typewriter and it is practically done. "It's easy," they say.

Ron pointed out that when he had to write reports in school, he realized how much more difficult it would be to write an even larger work like the complex Book of Mormon. Nathaniel Hawthorne once said, "Easy writing is damned hard writing."[14] Maya Angelou has described writing as "not natural. It is very hard work . . . To write well means that one rewrites 20 to 50 times . . . Quite often if I've got six pages, I have to cull out four."[15]

Again turning to her paperback, Joyce read:

Around 1840, an article about the difficulty of writing the Book of Mormon appeared in the *New Yorker:* 'One of the greatest literary curiosities of the day is the much abused Book of Mormon. That a work of the kind should be planned, executed and given to the scrutiny of the world by an illiterate young man of twenty—that it should gain numerous and devoted partisans . . . seems scarcely credible . . . yet such is the fact.

'It is difficult to imagine a more difficult literary task than to write what may be termed a continuation of the Scriptures, that should not only avoid all collision with the authentic and sacred word, but even to fill in many chasms that seem to exist.'[16]

Helen Jones, an LDS historical novelist, recognized, "The more I write the more I realize that the most competent writer would fail at writing a book like the Book of Mormon. Most people do not understand the writing process and therefore do not fully appreciate what Joseph Smith did."[17] At least four things—research, characterization, writing, and theme—are fundamental to creating a good historical novel.

## Research

"Research . . . is the basis for all worthwhile historical writing, both fiction and non-fiction," Jones advises.[18] Joseph Smith had not enjoyed enough schooling to have developed the skills needed to perform thorough investigation on any subject, not to mention the involved Book of Mormon. More importantly, no one in his time could have done much research for such a manuscript: no documents existed anywhere in the world that authentically explained the Book of Mormon's setting and culture. The world would have to wait until nine years after the publication of the book for an American attorney, John Lloyd Stephens, and an English artist, Frederick Catherwood, to reveal the existence of the long forgotten pyramids and temples of Central America where some scholars believe the Book of Mormon people most probably lived.[19]

## Literary Forms

Within the book, I later found out, are numerous literary forms, few of which could have originated on their own. Psalms and allegories were known in his day, but Joseph Smith could not have authored such complexities. Other literary devices such as the "chiasmus" were unknown even to most specialists in ancient languages at the time. It was not until after the publication of the Book of Mormon that chiasms were brought to the attention of most Western scholars. John Welch writes:

> Although all knowledge of this form lay dormant for centuries, it was rediscovered and reexplored in the nineteenth century when formal criticism began to emerge. But by the time the concept of chiasmus received currency or recognition, the Book of Mormon had long been in print. Since the Book of Mormon contains [more than 300] chiasms, it thus becomes logical to consider the book a product of the ancient world and to judge its literary qualities accordingly.[20]

Chiasmus is an inverted type of parallelism. Simply put, although it usually becomes more involved, elements of the last phrase or sentence correspond with elements of the first phrase or sentence; elements of the next to last phrase or sentence correspond with elements of the second phrase or sentence; etc., building up to a "turning point" at the center of the structure. Alma 5:20-25 is an example:

**a** . . . can ye think of being saved when you have yielded yourselves to become *subjects to the devil?*
  **b** . . . Ye will know at that day that *ye cannot be saved*
    **c** for there can no man be saved except his *garments are washed white;* yea, his *garments must be purified* until *they are cleansed* from all stain,
      **d** through the blood of him of whom it has been spoken by *our fathers,* who should come to redeem his people from their sins.
        **e** . . . how will any of you feel, if ye shall stand before the bar of God, having your garments stained with blood and *all manner of filthiness?*
          **f** . . . what *will these things testify* against you?
          **f** . . . *will they* not *testify* that ye are murderers,
        **e** . . . and also that ye are guilty of *all manner of wickedness?*
      **d** . . . do ye suppose that such an one can have a place to sit down in the kingdom of God, with *Abraham,* with *Isaac,* and with *Jacob,* and also all the holy *prophets,*
    **c** whose *garments are cleansed and are spotless, pure and white?*
  **b** . . . Nay; except ye make our Creator a liar from the beginning, or suppose that he is a liar from the beginning, *ye cannot* suppose that such can *have place in the kingdom of heaven;*
**a** but they shall be cast out for they are the *children* of the kingdom *of the devil.*

The entire 36th chapter of Alma is a chiasm which Welch describes as an amazing passage of scripture, both in its rich content and in its complex structure. Alma has skillfully framed the story of his conversion with chiastic panels for the sole purpose of drawing our attention to the centrality of Jesus Christ in that conversion. Compared with any chiastic passage in Hebrew literature, Alma chapter 36 equals or betters them all in terms of balance, rhythm, impact, and fluency in this artistic form.[21]

Handing me the second gemstone—Nibley's *Lehi in the Desert and the World of the Jaredites*—Jack challenged me to read it along with Harris's book. Joseph Smith pulled off some other stunningly impossible phenomena if the Book of Mormon is not true. Unbelievable treasures are buried within its golden chest.

From those two jewels that I was introduced to that night, plus *The Americas Before Columbus* and a number of others that I read in later years, I learned that scattered extensively throughout the Book of Mormon are many things about which Joseph Smith could never have dreamed.

Original **spiritual elements** from Hebrew antiquity such as prophecy, revelation, dreams and their interpretations, angels, and visions make up much of the book.

Magnificent **sermons, debates, discourses, and oratory** are widely quoted.

As in the Bible, scores of refreshingly wise **proverbs and other bits of aphoristic wisdom** are there, such as:

O the vainness, and the frailties, and the foolishness of men! When they are learned they think they are wise, and they hearken not unto the counsel of God (2 Nephi 9:28);

Come unto the Holy One of Israel, and feast upon that which perisheth not, neither can be corrupted, and let your soul delight in fatness (2 Nephi 9:51);

Do not spend money for that which is of no worth, nor your labor for that which cannot satisfy (2 Nephi 9:15);

When ye are in the service of your fellow beings ye are only in the service of your God (Mosiah 2:17);

How knoweth a man the master whom he has not served and who is a stranger unto him, and is far from the thoughts and intents of his heart? (Mosiah 5:13);

How blind and impenetrable are the understandings of the children of men; for they will not seek wisdom, neither do they desire that she should rule over them (Mosiah 8:20);

Blessed are they who humble themselves without being compelled to
be humble (Alma 32:16);
Wickedness never was happiness (Alma 41:10);
Let your sins trouble you with that trouble which shall bring you down
unto repentance (Alma 42:29);
Greater is the value of an endless happiness than that misery which
never dies (Mormon 8:38);
A bitter fountain cannot bring forth good water; neither can a good
fountain bring forth bitter water (Moroni 7:11);
Charity is the pure love of Christ, and it endureth forever; and whoso
is found possessed of it at the last day, it shall be well with him (Moroni
7:47).

**Fascinating stories** about battle tactics, courage, devotion, escape,
faith, honesty, initiative, inspiration, integrity, intrigue, kindness, leadership, loyalty, miracles, missionary work, murder, mystery, obedience,
preaching, preparation, prophesying, revelation, reverence, righteousness,
sacrifice, trust, etc. make up the bulk of the book.

**Cultural components and customs** are mentioned, such as agriculture,
apparel, domesticated animals, architecture, astronomy, banners, battlefield
clothing and makeup, building material, cloth, a spiritual compass, covenants, ethics, fasting, food, fortifications, genealogies, geography and
geographical directions, governments, human relations, law and law
enforcement, artificial lighting, mathematics, a sophisticated medium of
exchange,[22] medicine, oaths, place names, primogeniture, prisoners of
war, prisons, shipbuilding, taxes, tools, trade, transportation, warfare,
weapons, writing, and writing material.

More than two hundred **strange words and names,** the roots of which
are mainly Hebrew and Egyptian, are there:[23] Abinadi, Abish, Alma,
Amulek, Bethabara, Coriantumr, curelom, deseret, Ethem, ezrom,
Giddianhi, Hagoth, Helaman, Irreantum, Jarom, Kim, Kishkumen, Lamoni,
Liahona, Lib, Limnah, Melek, Morianton, Mormon, Moroni, Moronihah,
Mosiah, Mulek, Nahom, neas, Nehor, Nephi, Ogath, Orihah, Paanchi,
Pahoran, Rabbanah, Riplakish, Ripliancum, Sariah, senine, Shemlon,
sheum, shiblon, Shilom, Teancum, Zarahemla, Zeezrom, Zemnarihah,
Zeniff, Zenock, to name a few.[24]

Interestingly, all of the Jaredite names except two end in consonants
and most of the Nephite names end with a vowel;[25] the Jaredite noun "deseret," meaning honeybee, is "associated . . . very closely with the symbol

of the bee" which is *dsrt* in the classical Egyptian culture (vowel sounds were not written in Egyptian);[26] the wide use of *Mor-* "is in striking agreement with the fact that in lists of Egyptian names the element *Mr* is, next to *Nfr* by far the commonest";[27] the most common proper noun in the Book of Mormon is Amon (or Ammon) which is also the most common "and most revered name in the Egyptian Empire." The name is so popular that it appears "in compounds as well as alone, [and] is the commonest element in compound names." It is seen in the Book of Mormon with various forms such as Amon, Amun, Amen, Aminidab, Aminadi, Aminihu, Amnor, Helaman, Kishkumen and Lamoni.[28]

Familiar **biblical names** are used in entirely **different contexts than in the Bible:** Aaron, Amos, Benjamin, David, Ephraim, Gilgal, Gideon, Helam, Heth, Isaiah, Ishmael, Jacob, Jared, Jeremiah, Jerusalem, Jonas, Jordan, Joseph, Joshua, Judea, Kish, Laban, Lehi, Lemuel, Levi, Midian, Nimrah, Nimrod, Noah, Omer, Ramah, Samuel, Seth, etc.

Other Bible names tie that book and the Book of Mormon together because they refer to **the same persons and places recorded in the Old World** scriptures.

Prophecies and prayers from Neum, Zenock and Zenos, three **forgotten Old Testament prophets,** are cited.[29]

**Lost Bible scriptures** of Joseph, the son of Jacob, are quoted (2 Nephi 3:6-21).

Prophetic sections of **Isaiah with important commentaries** are strategically placed. In the Bible, "Isaiah is the most quoted of all the prophets, being more frequently quoted by Jesus, Paul, Peter, and John (in his Revelation) than any other Old Testament prophet. Likewise the Book of Mormon . . . [quotes] from Isaiah more than from any other prophet."[30]

Original **Hebrew literary forms** saturate its pages, including allegory, epistles, genealogy, lamentations, mimation, nunation, parallelisms (synonymous, simple, alternate, synthetic, synonymia, repetition, prosapodosis, polysyndeton, paradiastole, numbers, exergasia, epistrophe, epibole, duplication, cycloides, climax, catabasis, antimetable, anaphora, anabasis, amoebaeon, antithetical, chiasmus),[31] and psalms.

According to Parry, the most prevailing poetic form in Hebrew scripture is parallelism. Basically, poetic parallelisms are "words, phrases, or sentences which correspond, compare or contrast one with another, or are . . . in repetition one with another." One of many excellent examples is an *extended alternate parallelism* found in Mosiah 1:18-2:1. In this type of parallelism, three or more lines contain basic elements which are repeated or contrasted in an **a-b-c**-etc./**a-b-c**-etc. pattern. Elements of the "**a**" lines correspond with one another as do the "**b**" lines with "**b**" lines, etc:

**a** . . . *Mosiah*
  **b** . . . *did as his father had commanded him,*
    **c** and *proclaimed unto all the people* who were *in the land* of Zarahemla
     **d** that . . . *they* might *gather themselves together,*
      **e** to *go up to the temple*
       **f** *to hear the words which his father* [king Benjamin] *should speak unto them.*
**a** . . . after *Mosiah*
  **b** *had done as his father had commanded him,*
    **c** and had made a *proclamation throughout all the land,*
     **d** . . . *the people gathered themselves together* throughout all the land,
      **e** that they might *go up to the temple*
       **f** *to hear the words which king Benjamin should speak unto them.*

Other **shorter Semitic literary devices** are found on virtually every page such as cognate accusatives, compound prepositions, a prophetic perfect tense[32] and qasids.[33]

**Other literary devices** are also scattered throughout the book: colophon, description, enallage, epic, exposition, hyperbole, idioms, logic, lyric, metaphor, narration, oratory, simile, and sorite.[34]

**Archaeologists** are continually unearthing artifacts and sites that seem to indicate that the places and people referred to in the book were probably living in Mesoamerica.[35]

**Codices of early native Americans**[36] such as Title of the Lords of Totonicapan, Popol Vuh, Annals of the Cakchequels, the Nuttall Codex, and the works of Ixtlilxochitl refer to significant elements mentioned within the Book of Mormon: Adam and Eve, a worldwide flood, the tower of Babel, transoceanic migrations, and the mysterious appearance of a fair god.[37]

**Legends** of a bearded god of virtue seem to refer to someone like Christ visiting the Americas near the time of Jesus's resurrection.[38]

**Wordprint analysis,** using unbiased computers, have shown by comparison of large blocks of words that the Book of Mormon was written by a variety of authors, not just one or two as detractors believe. None of its writing matches Joseph Smith's or Sidney Rigdon's styles.[39]

Other **fascinating facts** which Joseph Smith would not have known if he were the author of the Book of Mormon: Within the first two books are six times more "eth" suffixes than any subsequent book; within the book of Mosiah are 559 words not found in the preceding 144 pages, and 203 of them are not used anywhere else in the following 324 pages; in Alma's book alone are 675 words found nowhere else in the Book of Mormon; Alma is located approximately midway through the book, yet more words are introduced there than in any other book before it (most words in novels are introduced toward the beginning); Moroni, the last author, introduces the second highest number of words. The Book of Mormon has 5,665 different words, the Bible approximately 6,000, but the Book of Mormon is less than half the size of the Bible;[40] the word "and" occurs about 6 percent of the time in the Bible and the Book of Mormon, but only about 3.5 percent in Joseph Smith's own prose.

The book's common phrase "and it came to pass" is typical of an abridgment phrase used in ancient languages, and where material is summarized in both the Bible and the Book of Mormon. Every time this phrase occurs in the Book of Mormon it is within reviewed material. Within Moroni's own writings the phrase does not occur at all since they are not abridgments, but in his synopsis of Jaredite history, the phrase occurs 114 times. Ezra, one of the Bible's scribes, did the same thing in his abridgment but never in his own writing.[41] It is interesting to note that at least three Mayan glyphs at Palenque have been translated "then it came to pass," "it had come to pass," and "it shall come to pass."[42]

## Characterization

Along with the researching that must be done in order to write a historical novel, there is characterization. John Henry Evans explains that "character drawing . . . is admittedly the most difficult thing to do in imaginative work. As a rule, great writers live because of their skill in creating characters rather than because of any talent they may have for plot, setting, purpose, or style."[43] According to Jones, building characters into a story is such "a complex problem . . . that most writers build fewer than a dozen three-dimensional characters for a book." An author must live with his or her characters day and night so they can realistically meet their expectations and react to their problems. Jones points out that "there are more three-dimensional characters [100+] in the Book of Mormon than most writers can create in a long writing career."[44]

Besides the *named* characters in the Book of Mormon there are quite a number of important *unnamed* men and women such as: King Lamoni's parents, the Lamanite king who was killed by the servants of Amalickiah, the widowed queen who married Amalickiah, the brother of Jared, the brother of Kim, the brother of Shiblom, three mysterious disciples who shall never taste death, and others. Anyone making up such a book would certainly have named every character that stands out.

Within the book are "at least twenty-eight names and titles" for Jesus the Christ such as Good Shepherd, Holy One of Israel, Immanuel, Jehovah, Lamb of God, Lord of Hosts, Lord, Messenger of the Covenant, Messiah, Only Begotten Son, Redeemer, Savior, Son of God, Son of Man, etc.[45] The name "Jesus Christ" is used four hundred seventy-six times, averaging nearly once per page. Only the four gospels (Matthew, Mark, Luke, John), which are synopses of Jesus's life, average more. Though the Book of Mormon has "1,349 fewer verses than the New Testament, it makes 108 more references to the Lord." Within the thirteen and one-half pages of the final book alone—the Book of Moroni—Jesus Christ is referred to 215 times.[46]

## Writing

Usually, the actual sitting down and writing of a book begins only after a lengthy period of researching, thinking and dreaming. An important part of the writing process is the vital *rewriting*. Over and over, a writer must revise, cross out, rearrange, add to, and squeeze in words and phrases. All writers insist that this going back and forth inside the book while the writing is in progress is absolutely essential.[47]

Joseph Smith, however, never asked his scribes to repeat back the wording to him. Using the Urim and Thummim, he was translating, not creating a novel.[48] He "was *reading* the Book of Mormon, not writing it," Jones believes.[49]

According to Joseph's more educated wife, Emma, who was his scribe before Oliver Cowdery came along, "No man could have dictated the writing of the manuscripts unless he was inspired; for, when acting as his scribe, [Joseph] would dictate to me hour after hour, and when returning after meals, or after interruptions, he would at once begin where he had left off, without either seeing the manuscript or having any portion of it read to him. This was a usual thing for him to do. It would have been improbable that a learned man could do this, and, for one so ignorant and unlearned as he was, it was simply impossible."[50]

It has been estimated that 60 to 90 working days were all that Joseph used during the translation process.[51] After the 116 pages of the Book of Lehi were lost by Joseph's first scribe, Martin Harris, the translation had to continue under another scribe. Emma acted in that capacity for a while, but the translation began in earnest two days after Oliver Cowdery's arrival on April 7, 1829. Less than two months later, before June 11th, they had at least finished the Plates of Mormon. This is known because Joseph used the words from the title page as his legal description when he applied for a copyright on that day. By June 30th the book was completed and ready for publication. From Emma's service just prior to April 7th to June 30th was no more than 85-90 days—an astounding feat for writing any book of such magnitude.

The actual number of working days must have been even fewer. Three or four days for moving to Fayette, New York from Harmony, Pennsylvania, had to be taken. Supplies were purchased in Colesville, New York which was 30 miles away. Time was also needed to compose thirteen sections of the Doctrine and Covenants. People were taught and baptized by Joseph. With all of the distractions, it has been estimated that the total time for translating would then be reduced to a phenomenal 60-75 days to write today's 531 pages—averaging an incredible seven to nine pages each day!

## Theme

As important as research, characterization, and writing are, the most important part of a book is its theme. Like the Bible, righteousness, as defined by Jesus Christ, is the heart and theme of the Book of Mormon. Realizing this, Perry Benjamin Pierce notes that "Mormons have been slandered and traduced, unjustly and without warrant, for an immoral 'Bible.' There is nothing immoral in the book."[52] Mark Twain also concluded, "There is nothing vicious in [the Book of Mormon's] teachings.

Its code of morals is unobjectionable."[53] Again and again standards of righteousness are underscored in story after interesting story.

Like its cousin, the Holy Bible, the Book of Mormon's theme is the *source of inspiration,* not only in building individual lives, but in giving impetus to the creation of countless enriching segments of Latter-day Saint culture. Novels, histories, journals, articles, magazines, stories, poetry, commentaries, apologies, archaeological texts, biographies about people within the book, dissertations, greeting cards, hymns, plays, movies, choral arrangements, symphonies and other kinds of instrumental music, art, pageants, names of streets, cities, people, and geographical sites have their roots in this one tantalizing text.

Translated into scores of languages, the Book of Mormon may readily be studied throughout the world. It is one of the great filtering agents, helping the Lord sift his wheat from the tares and his sheep from the goats before his second coming (Matthew 13:24-30, 36-43; 25:31-46).

The Book of Mormon is God's gift to mankind; what we do with it individually is our gift to God. Its intricate interweaving of stories, its originality, its wisdom and fundamental message of salvation through the atonement of Jesus Christ demand that the serious student meticulously examine it again and again. Someone has pointed out that, like all true classics, the Book of Mormon will wear out the thoughtful reader long before he or she could ever wear it out.

"What you have shown me is most impressive," I said. "I can't think of any retort to such an array of fascinating facts about the Book of Mormon except that Joseph Smith must have been an extremely brilliant young man to have created such a novel. Or, he had the help of some well-educated person who anti-Mormons have not yet found out about. Or, just maybe, his story about the angel Moroni delivering the plates to him is true. Perhaps there was an original Book of Mormon that was engraved on gold plates. It's almost easier for me to believe the angel story than the other possibilities. They seem to be even more impossible.

"I have another hang-up though," I continued. "Witnesses swore they saw the plates. But were those witnesses reliable? I have read that all of them left the LDS Church and denied their testimonies."

# 17
# Witnesses

"That's not true!" everyone chorused. "None of the witnesses ever denied their testimonies."

"Most of the witnesses were always faithful to the Lord and his Church," Jack testified. "Some left and came back and a few stayed away and never came back. But not one of the twelve (including Joseph Smith) who saw the plates ever denied his testimony about the Book of Mormon."

"If they saw the angel and the gold plates why would they ever leave in the first place? Who would dare turn their backs on such miracles?" I asked.

All of us are weak in one way or another. Though he was there when Jesus was involved in miracles, including hearing the voice of God and seeing two angels (Moses and Elijah) on the Mount of Transfiguration, Peter denied knowing his Lord in the face of danger. Judas Iscariot betrayed Christ after he also saw the miracles the Lord had performed. Jonah was heading away from the area which the Lord had personally called him to when he was dramatically turned around by a great fish. In spite of that traumatic miracle, he then dared to become displeased with God and was angry with him because God would not destroy Nineveh. Aaron, the brother and companion of Moses who saw the miraculous plagues brought upon Egypt, who was there when the Red Sea parted, who ate the manna, encouraged the Israelites (who also saw many miracles) to make gods of gold when he felt Moses was too slow in coming down from the mountain.

Sometimes we get our feelings hurt, our leaders don't do things the way we think they should, or they do things we believe they shouldn't. There are many excuses for turning our backs on what we know deep inside is right. The witnesses of the Book of Mormon were just as human as people in the Bible and the rest of us. A few became disgruntled with Joseph Smith—not with the Book of Mormon—because in their eyes he was a fallen prophet.

If Joseph was the author of the Book of Mormon, how did he persuade three men to affix their signatures to a statement that they saw an angel, had heard God, and had seen a golden text in the first place? How did he get eight others to say that they had handled the engraved plates? No money was involved, for Joseph had none. There was little hope of distributing the book because of a threatened boycott against it. Even when it was sold no profit could be made; the cost of printing was too high.

## Three Special Witnesses

Joseph's relief at finally being allowed to show the plates to others can readily be sensed when he exclaimed to his parents, "Father, mother, you do not know how happy I am: the Lord has now caused the plates to be shown to three more . . . They have seen an angel, who has testified to them, and they will have to bear witness to the truth of what I have said, for now they know for themselves, that I do not go about to deceive . . . I feel as if I was relieved of a burden which was almost too heavy for me to bear . . . It rejoices my soul that I am no longer to be entirely alone."[1]

For the remainder of their mortal lives the three witnesses who saw an angel with the plates never denied what they had seen and heard, though all of them were out of the Church at one time or another. They dared not deny their testimonies. Their eternal exaltation depended on it. If they had lied about seeing the angel with the engraved gold, their period outside of the Church would have been the opportune time to admit their deception. Their friendship with Joseph was on the wane. Surely they could have exposed him as the deceiver others thought him to be.

### Martin Harris

Martin Harris was the first of the three to become interested in Joseph's work. A well-to-do farmer of respectability, he was probably the only one of Joseph's acquaintances who could afford to financially back the printing of the book. Fearful that he could be aiding a fraud, Martin obtained a copy of some characters from the plates and took them to college professors in and around New York City. Martin returned to Joseph in Harmony, Pennsylvania, thoroughly convinced from his conversations with professor Charles Anthon of Columbia University and others that the plates were from antiquity.

For two months Martin personally wrote the manuscript as the translation fell from the prophet's lips. His stenographic effort brought forth 116
pages of the Book of Lehi. Anxious to prove to his skeptical wife, Lucy,
that he was involved in God's work, he pleaded with Joseph to be allowed
to take the pages home to show her. After repeated denials by the Lord,
Martin was finally allowed to take the work to Palmyra on condition that
he would show it to no one else except Lucy's sister, Martin's brother, and
his parents. While he was away, Martin betrayed that trust and showed the
manuscript to others, which resulted in its loss.

Why would such a respected and embarrassed man return to Joseph and
donate thousands of dollars for the publication of the book unless he was
convinced that Joseph's work was divine?

Years later, when the body of the Church left Kirtland, Ohio for
Missouri, Martin stayed behind. Living in the midst of those who ridiculed
the Church, he continually bore fervent testimony that the Book of
Mormon was true. Asked in 1869 why he still had a testimony after
leaving the Church, he replied, "I never did leave the Church, the Church
left me."[2] An octogenarian when he came to Utah in 1870, Martin Harris
died in full fellowship on July 10, 1875, at the age of ninety-two.

Many people visited Martin while he lived in Kirtland, wanting to know
if he had changed his mind about his sworn statement. One such visitor
was William Homer. When Homer asked if he still believed the Book of
Mormon to be true and that Joseph Smith was a prophet, Martin replied,

> Do I believe it! Do you see the sun shining? Just as surely as the sun is
> shining on us and gives us light, and the moon and stars give us light by
> night, just as surely as the breath of life sustains us, so surely do I know
> that Joseph Smith was a true prophet of God, chosen of God to open the
> last dispensation of the fulness of times; so surely do I know that the Book
> of Mormon was divinely translated. I saw the plates; I saw the Angel; I
> heard the voice of God. I know that the Book of Mormon is true and that
> Joseph Smith was a true prophet of God. I might as well doubt my own
> existence as to doubt the divine authenticity of the Book of Mormon or the
> divine calling of Joseph Smith.[3]

## Oliver Cowdery

After the loss of the 116 pages, the translation nearly ceased. While
Joseph and Emma were scratching out a living in Harmony, Oliver Cowdery arrived in Palmyra to work as a schoolteacher. Living in the Smith

home, he heard the fascinating stories of Joseph's work and wondered about it, so he went to Harmony to find out for himself what it was all about. While there, Oliver volunteered his services and became Joseph's new scribe. Most of the Book of Mormon manuscript is in his handwriting.

Why would Oliver leave his teaching responsibilities and his needed revenue to take part in a work that would pay him nothing and that was receiving so much negative publicity, unless he believed there might be something truthful about it?

In 1838, Oliver was excommunicated from the Church for accusing Joseph Smith of "treating the Church with contempt," and because Oliver refused to be governed by the Church in his temporal affairs.[4]

After practicing law and working as editor of a Democratic paper in Ohio, as well as being nominated to the Wisconsin state assembly during the next decade,[5] Oliver and his wife, Elizabeth, with their daughter, Maria Louise, traveled to the October 1848 general conference of the Church at Kanesville, Iowa. Fully repentant, he humbly asked to be readmitted into the Church. At that conference he testified:

> For a number of years I have been separated from you. I now desire to come back. I wish to come humbly and to be one in your midst. I seek no station. I only wish to be identified with you.[6] I was present with Joseph when an holy angel from God came down from heaven and conferred, or restored, the Aaronic Priesthood . . . I was also present with Joseph when the Melchizedek Priesthood was conferred by the holy angels of God.[7]

On November 12, 1848, Oliver Cowdery was again baptized. Why would he leave a successful life in public affairs to return to an unpopular church if he did not believe Joseph Smith was the prophet of the restoration? Joseph Smith could not have persuaded him to return because he was long dead.

## David Whitmer

Prior to meeting the prophet, Oliver met David Whitmer in Palmyra and told him what he had learned from the Smith family. He promised David that he would write and tell him what his impressions were when he became acquainted with Joseph in Harmony. Converted, Oliver wrote David. Though they had never met, Joseph later sent a note to David asking him to come to Harmony and take them to the Whitmer home in Fayette so the translation could be completed in peace.

When David received Joseph's request, he was getting his land ready for planting. It would be impossible to leave. Certain things then occurred that were regarded by David and his devout German Reformed father, Peter Whitmer, Sr., as miraculous and as signs that David was to do as Joseph had requested. The night that he received the message, five to seven acres of land were mysteriously plowed. Later the following day, after harrowing a field of wheat, David realized that he had done more in a few hours than he normally would do in two days. David's father urged him to hurry and fetch the prophet when he finished spreading some plaster of Paris. The next day David went to his sister's house where the plaster was stored and discovered that it was missing. She informed him that three mysterious strangers had come by and had taken the plaster to the field. "In amazement" she and her children watched them "scatter the lime with remarkable skill and rapidity."[8]

Why would the devout Peter, Sr., go against Christianity's orthodox advice and encourage his equally pious son, David, to travel by horse and wagon 200 dusty miles round trip to bring to his table someone he had never met and who was the laughed-at sensation of the region? Peter, Sr., had been elected "overseer of highways" and school trustee. One of his sons, Christian Whitmer, had been appointed ensign, one of three commissioned officers in the Seneca Grenadiers of the 102d New York Regiment of militia. He was also elected one of six constables of Fayette township. Peter, Jr. was an excellent tailor who later made a suit for General Alexander Doniphan.[9] Why would this Bible-reading family risk their reputations in allowing Smith's "gold Bible" under their roof unless they sincerely felt the hand of heaven might be involved?

Unlike in unharmonious Harmony, the Whitmers and their Fayette neighbors treated Joseph and Oliver kindly. Joseph wrote: "We found the people . . . friendly, and disposed to enquire into the truth of these strange matters."[10]

Years later, when the saints left Missouri, David stayed. He lived in Richmond, Missouri for the rest of his life.[11] Having served as mayor and on the city council, he was well respected by the local citizenry. On March 25, 1881, a statement appeared in the Richmond *Conservator* which read: "We, the undersigned citizens of Richmond, Ray Co., Mo., where David Whitmer, Sr., has resided since the year 1838, certify that we have been long and intimately acquainted with him and know him to be a man of the highest integrity and of undoubted truth and veracity." The statement was signed by twenty-one honorable men including "judges, lawyers, a bank president, the postmaster, a doctor, and many other prominent citizens." In that same edition, David wrote:

> Those who know me best know well that I have always adhered to [the Book of Mormon] testimony. And that no man may be misled or doubt my present views in regard to the same, I do again affirm the truth of all my statements as then made and published . . . In the spirit of Christ, who hath said, 'Follow thou me, for I am the Life, the Light, and the Way,' I submit this statement to the world; God in whom I trust being my judge as to the sincerity of my motives and the faith and hope that is in me of eternal life.[12]

How did David entice the town's most prominent citizens to testify that he was "a man of the highest integrity and of undoubted truth and veracity" if they felt otherwise?

Six years later, David published a pamphlet: *An Address to All Believers in Christ, by a Witness to the Divine Authenticity of the Book of Mormon.* It was an effort to refute charges that he had denied his witness:

> That the world may know the truth, I wish now, standing . . . in the very sunset of life, and in the fear of God, once for all to make this public statement: That I have never at any time denied that testimony or any part thereof . . . I also testify to the world, that neither Oliver Cowdery or Martin Harris ever at any time denied their testimony. They both died reaffirming the truth of the divine authenticity of the Book of Mormon.[13]

Why bother if the whole story was a hoax? It had been nearly half a century since David left the Church. Why not keep his mouth shut? Or, why not go to the grave with a clear conscience and admit that the witnesses had tried to hoodwink the public? He was the last living witness; none of the others could contradict him. Obviously he truly believed that he had seen an angel holding an engraved golden text and had heard the voice of God, for he had every chance to deny his testimony.

## Eight Other Witnesses

Soon after the three special witnesses saw the angel and viewed the plates, Joseph showed the plates to eight others. No celestial glory enveloped them. No voice from the heavens spoke as with the original three. No angel stood in their midst. Joseph merely handed the engraved records to the eight who then handled and "hefted" them.

Five of the eight remained faithful to the Lord and his Church (Joseph's father, his brothers Hyrum and Samuel, and two of the Whitmer brothers, Christian and Peter). John and Jacob Whitmer, together with their brother-in-law, Hiram Page, became alienated from the Church. John was excommunicated when he refused to appear before a high council court to examine certain of his financial activities. Jacob and Hiram sided with John and David. Though no formal Church hearings were held for them, the two went their separate ways.

The Whitmer family had sacrificed much for the restored religion. Leaving their Fayette homes, they followed the prophet to Kirtland, then on to bitter persecution in Missouri. Time, money and effort were gladly given. It was not easy being a Mormon in those days. When one looks at all they did for the kingdom, it is somewhat understandable why a few of the Whitmers became disgruntled when, to their way of thinking, some of their Mormon friends turned against them. But they knew that priesthood authority must be followed if the Lord's kingdom was to prosper. The fact that the four who never came back were discontented makes it even more remarkable that they stayed strong and unwavering in their testimonies.

In his "manuscript history," John Whitmer wrote of his hope for salvation "'in the Kingdom of God, notwithstanding my present situation, which I hope will soon be bettered and I find favor in the eyes of God." He closed with a prayer for forgiveness "of my faults."[14]

John Whitmer, son of Jacob, said, "My father . . . was always faithful and true to his testimony to the Book of Mormon, and confirmed it on his death bed."[15]

In reply to questioning about his written testimony, Hiram Page pointed out, "It would be doing injustice to myself, and to the work of God of the last days, to say that I could know a thing to be true in 1830, and know the same thing to be false in 1847."[16] Hiram's son, Philander, said in 1888, "I knew my father to be true and faithful to his testimony of the divinity of the Book of Mormon until the very last. Whenever he had an opportunity to bear his testimony . . . he would always do so, and seemed to rejoice exceedingly in having been privileged to see the plates . . . I can also testify that Jacob, John, and David Whitmer and Oliver Cowdery died in full faith in the divinity of the Book of Mormon. I was with all these witnesses on their deathbeds and heard each of them bear his last testimony."[17]

"Only four of the twelve witnesses of the engraved records—not all of them—had left the Church never to return," Joyce summarized. "And, no one who intimately knew those four has ever said that they denied their testimonies. On the other hand, many have pointed out that they were the happiest when they could testify that what they had sworn to was true."

## A Family Affair

"It seems Joseph made witnessing the plates a friend and family affair," I argued. "Claiming to be witnesses were his father and two brothers, his friends Martin Harris and Oliver Cowdery with their friends the Whitmers. Even Hiram Page was a brother-in-law of the Whitmers. To someone like me who is very skeptical in the first place, such closeness sounds like a neighborhood collaboration to mislead the world."

"Some may accuse Joseph of making it a friend and family affair," Elder Porter said. "But, if that is supposed to mean that the witnesses weren't reliable, then Jesus's work wasn't reliable, either. At least a few of the twelve apostles were also friends and relatives. The sons of Jona, Simon (named Peter by Jesus) and Andrew, were brothers as well as James and John, the sons of Zebedee. All four were partners in the same fishing business. Matthew and another James were the sons of Alphaeus and therefore brothers also. Philip and Nathaniel were good friends before being called to the apostleship. Philip at one time lived in the same fishing village of Bethsaida as Peter, Andrew, James and John. All except one—Judas Iscariot—were from Jesus's home province of Galilee. James, who may have been Jesus's brother, was later called to be an apostle also. Others could have been related. In addition, the mothers of John the Baptist and Jesus were cousins."

Once again I had to hang my head as my arguments against Mormonism were countered by even stronger ones. It seemed to me that if anyone doubted the veracity of the witnesses, the burden of proof had to be placed on the doubter's shoulders. Eight of the twelve went to their deathbeds in full Church fellowship with vibrant willingness to reaffirm their testimonies about seeing the Book of Mormon plates. Even the four who never returned to the Church remained true to their testimonies.

Of course, by now I was convinced that none of the witnesses was brilliant enough to have created the Book of Mormon as a historical novel.

The questions that were uppermost in my mind were how did Joseph Smith ever come up with such a complex book when he had only the rudiments of a formal education and so little time in which to write it? And then, how did he get his father, two brothers, and eight others to stick with what has to be one of history's most insolent and involved schemes if Joseph made it all up?

# 18
# My Next Stumbling Block

As a youth, I lived in a bigoted environment. Adults and other youth, by their example, taught me to rarely refer to a person belonging to another ethnic or racial group by the correct name. I, in turn, must have taught others. Instead of calling an Italian an Italian, he was a "wop." Jews were "kikes," Japanese were "Nips" or "Japs," Chinese were "coolies" or "chinks," Indians were "redskins," Mexican Americans were "spics" or "wetbacks," Germans were "krauts," British were "limeys," and blacks were "coons" or "niggers." Whenever I called someone by one of those slang words my conscience screamed, but I continued to do it anyway.

When I was a Boy Scout, our assistant scoutmaster was a Jew, as was at least one of my violin teachers. No two finer individuals ever lived. At Dorsey High in Los Angeles, where I attended school for two years, a large block of the student body was Jewish and another huge group was African-American. It was there that I began to see how wrong I was in my prejudices as I developed friendships with wonderful Jewish and African-American individuals. It hurt to hear my black friends tell the other students in class what it was like to be treated like second class citizens. Though I was by no means perfect, in those high school years I began half-heartedly defending people of other backgrounds when someone tore them down. As the years wore on, though, I became more vocal in upholding them.

During the months of study about the Church I had met Latter-day Saints of various races and ethnic groups. But never had I met a black person within the Church.

My best friend and supervisor at Vroman's wholesale book warehouse was Jesse Henderson—a black man.[1] Every so often I tried talking to Jesse about the Church. He was friendly and let me ramble, but he didn't get enthusiastic about religion the way I did. I knew it was not true, but non-Mormons were constantly telling me that blacks were not allowed to become members of the LDS Church. Jesse may have heard that gossip and didn't want to hurt my feelings by asking me about it.

196

"Why are there so many rumors about the Church being bigoted against blacks?" I asked the elders one day.

"Over the years, many members claiming African heritage have become Latter-day Saints," Elder Randolph answered.[2] "But because so many non-Mormons of their race have heard that Mormons are prejudiced against them, they often won't investigate the teachings of the Church, and therefore won't give themselves a chance to become converted."

## Church Attitude Toward Blacks

The LDS Church was born during times of slavery.[3] In spite of that fact, the Book of Mormon boldly states that it is "against the law . . . that there should be any slaves," and, the Lord invites all to come unto him and partake of his goodness, "black and white, bond and free, male and female" (Alma 27:9; 2 Nephi 26:33).

In the 1840's, Joseph Smith proposed that slave owners "Petition . . . your legislators to abolish slavery by the year 1850, or now . . . Pray congress to pay every man a reasonable price for his slaves out of the surplus revenue arising from the sale of public lands, and from the deduction of pay from the members of Congress. Break off the shackles from the poor black man, and hire him to labor like other human beings; for 'an hour of virtuous liberty . . . is worth a whole eternity of bondage' . . . Make honor the standard with all men."[4]

Ralph Waldo Emerson received acclaim for his suggestion that the government purchase slaves and set them free. The mayor of Boston, Josiah Quincy, nephew of John Quincy Adams, commented:

> If [Emerson] was in advance of his time when he advocated this disposition of the public property in 1855, what shall I say of . . . [Joseph Smith] who had committed himself . . . to the same course in 1844? . . . [If] men's opinions were stirred by such a proposition when war clouds were discernible . . . was it not a statesmanlike word eleven years earlier, when the heavens looked tranquil?[5]

Joseph taught that blacks born into slavery "came into the world slaves, mentally and physically. Change their situation with the whites, and they would be like them. They have souls, and are subjects of salvation. Go into . . . any city, and find an educated Negro . . . and you will see a man who has risen by the powers of his own mind to his exalted state of respectability."[6]

# Early Blacks in the Church

## Elijah Abel

Blacks became Latter-day Saints even in the earliest days of the restoration. In fact, three—Elijah Abel, Jane James, and Green Flake—were welcomed to live in the home of Joseph and Emma Smith in Nauvoo. Elijah, a Nauvoo mortician, was "a fine . . . speaker [and] a man of great knowledge." He was ordained a Seventy on April 4, 1841. After arriving in Salt Lake, he and his wife managed the Farnham Hotel. In 1883 he served a mission in Canada and the U.S.[7]

## Sam and Amanda Chambers

Samuel ("Sam") and Amanda Chambers were baptized in Virginia while still slaves. When he was young, Sam had the tragic misfortune of seeing his mother sold.

In Salt Lake, the couple purchased twenty acres where they grew fruit and alfalfa. Years later Sam returned to Mississippi and brought back relatives. After that he sold the farm and gave his fortune of $60,000 to various charities.

Amanda was famous for her delicious dinners and chicken pies. Everyone in the community came to their home for a "bounteous supper" during Sam's and Amanda's golden wedding celebration. After Amanda's death, Sam's white neighbors and friends cared for him until he died in 1925.[8]

## Green Flake

Green Flake was a North Carolina slave who chose to remain with his master and mistress, James and Faithy Flake, after they joined the Church. The other slaves were freed. Green accompanied the Flake family to Nauvoo where he married Martha Crosby who came with the Crosby family from Mississippi. Green (Brigham Young's wagon driver), and Martha entered the Salt Lake Valley in July, 1847. The pioneer couple had two children, Lucinda Vilate and Abraham.[9]

## Abner Howell

Abner Howell was the son of Paul and Mary Howell who came to Utah from Kansas in 1888 when Abner was almost twelve. For twenty years, Paul was employed as a police officer in Salt Lake City. Neither he nor Mary ever joined the Church.

Because his parents were not Latter-day Saints, Abner did not join the Church until after he was married. The first black man to graduate from high school in Salt Lake City, Abner had many friends, but not many of his race because there weren't many. He wrote:

> Before I was in my teens I wondered many times why I was a different color to the other boys. Little by little I was told [by other boys] that I was cursed and could not go to heaven when I died, but was doomed to go to hell with the devil and burn forever . . . One day, when the boys were telling me these things, I was so touched that I began to cry. While in this frame of mind, Bro. John Henry Smith came along and wanted to know what was wrong and why I was crying. So I told him. He comforted me with a few kind words and took me to his house a block away. He got the Book of Mormon and turned to the 26th chapter of 2nd Nephi, and last verse. He then said read this, which I did.

That verse says, "[The Lord] inviteth . . . all to come unto him and partake of his goodness; and he denieth none that come unto him, black and white, bond and free, male and female; and he remembereth the heathen; and all are alike unto God."

"When I was through reading," Howell continues, "a great load was lifted from my heart and mind, and my eyes were opened, and I read more and more. I thought how great that was! The words 'all are alike unto God.' I could not find anything in the Bible that pleased me so much as what I had just read in the Book of Mormon."[10]

Abner "spent most of the forties with organized labor being a member of the city federation of labor." He also served on the executive board of the Salt Lake Boy Scouts, the community chest, the welfare board, and on the State Senate floor.

When the Howells arrived in Cincinnati during a vacation trip, they were shocked to discover that the evils of "society had crept into religion. Most of the members lived across the river on the Kentucky side and some . . . did not want the [Len and Mary Hope] Negro family to come to church." The family was permitted to attend only once each month. During one of those Sundays, the Howells went to church with the Hopes. Brother Howell was invited by the bishop to speak.

> That afternoon I asked the Lord to lead me . . . Somehow that last verse in the 26th chapter of 2nd Nephi said 'Read me.' I talked a short while on brotherhood. Then I took the Book of Mormon and . . . read . . . Those

people [afterward] came to shake my hand and greeted me as a good Latter-day Saint. One man said, 'I did not know there were such things in the Book of Mormon.' [The Hope] family was . . . made welcome from then on.

When Martha died in May 1954, Abner continued his vigorous life by becoming a guide at the dedication of the Los Angeles Temple and in speaking at many firesides, seminaries, and the University of Southern California Institute.[11]

In 1913, Booker T. Washington visited Salt Lake City. After his visit he wrote that he "had never been among a more healthy, clean, progressive set of people" than Mormons. He said that like the Negro, Mormons have been misrepresented. "The Negro is suffering today just as the Mormons have suffered and are suffering." He then said, "I think it will interest my readers to know that there are colored 'Mormons' in Utah. I met several of these. Many of them came here in the old days. In fact, Brigham Young brought colored people with him to this country, and they or their descendants have remained . . . I met one colored man who came out here in the early days. He is now eighty-two years of age. He is a staunch 'Mormon' . . . from Mississippi."[12]

That was impressive. The fact that so many white Latter-day Saints, including Joseph and Emma Smith, would invite blacks to stay in their homes and put their arms around them and make them feel welcome, helped me feel good about Mormons. "Why then," I asked the missionaries, "is there so much gossip that blacks are not welcome in the LDS Church?"

## Priesthood

Elder Porter taught me that ancient Israel was comprised of twelve tribes. Under the Law of Moses, only Levite men were ordained to the priesthood. No man belonging to another tribe could be ordained. Neither could a woman of any tribe be given the priesthood. Other men from the remaining eleven tribes may have been prophets, but were they ordained? The Bible does not clearly document the answer to that question. However, it is clear that prophets in the New Testament who did not belong to the tribe of Levi received the priesthood.[13]

The prophet Moses and his brother, Aaron, were Levites and therefore held the Levitical priesthood. The names, Levitical and Aaronic, are often used interchangeably. However, I learned later, within the tribe of Levi, only men descended from Aaron could hold the office of priest. Priests were the only ones who could "offer sacrifices for the people, burn incense on the altar, and teach the law, whereas the other Levites were employed in more menial tasks, such as the housekeeping of the tabernacle, keeping oil in the lamps, transporting the Ark of the Covenant."[14]

After the wholesale captivity of ten of the tribes into Assyria as well as centuries of apostasy, only a shell of a Levitical priesthood remained in Palestine during Jesus's time. A glimpse of it is found in the New Testament when, in the temple, "a priest named Zacharias" was informed by an angel that he and his wife, Elizabeth, were to have a son, John.

"Jesus, a Jew, later ordained twelve apostles," I pointed out. "Where did he obtain that right? He obviously wasn't a Levite."

Paul addressed that question: "If perfection had been attainable through the Levitical priesthood, (for under it the people received the law [of Moses]), what further need would there have been for another priest [Christ] to arise after the order of Melchizedek? . . . For when there is a change in the priesthood, there is necessarily a change in the law as well . . . [Christ] belonged to another tribe, from which no one has ever served at the altar . . . Our Lord was descended from Judah, and in connection with that tribe Moses said nothing about priests" (Hebrews 7:11-14, RSV).

Jehovah had placed the law of Moses (with its Levitical priesthood) among Israelites as a schoolmaster to bring them unto Christ with his higher Melchizedek priesthood. That lesser Levitical priesthood was then set aside by Christ because of its weakness. "For it was fitting that we should have such a high priest [as Christ], holy, blameless, unstained, separated from sinners, exalted above the heavens" (Hebrews 7:18, 26-27, RSV).

Jesus was Jehovah. He was the source of all priesthood authority. Therefore he had the authority to ordain others to a higher priesthood. With the Melchizedek priesthood authority he ordained the apostles.

"What about gentiles?" I wanted to know, still sticking up for the underdog. "You've implied that they could not hold the priesthood in Old Testament times. Could they during the time that Jesus lived in Palestine?"

On one occasion, a gentile woman asked Jesus to heal her daughter. If the scriptural account is correct, Jesus ignored her. ("But he answered her not a word.") His apostles haughtily "begged him to send her away, for she crieth after us." Jesus answered them: "I was sent *only* to the lost sheep of the house of Israel." In the future, missionaries would teach the gentiles as a group, converting many thousands of them.

Desperately, the woman pleaded: "Lord, help me!" Jesus said, "It is not meet to take the children's bread, and to cast it to dogs."[15] Instead of calling Jesus a bigot, she swallowed her pride and humbly agreed, knowing that he had the power to heal her daughter. He was the Master Physician and could heal by merely saying the word. What he had told her was the truth, she diplomatically agreed. But even "dogs eat of the crumbs which fall from their masters table," she plead. Recognizing that he was sent only to Israelites, couldn't she have a portion of his magnificent healing ability just this once for her ailing daughter? "Then Jesus answered and said unto her, O woman, great is thy faith: be it unto thee even as thou wilt. And her daughter was made whole from that very hour" (Matthew 15:22-28).

Jesus fully understood that the time would eventually come when gentiles would receive the gospel and its attendant priesthood. But for the moment gentiles, as a group, must patiently wait: "Go not into the way of the Gentiles, and into any city of the Samaritans enter ye not," he instructed his apostles, "But go rather to the lost sheep of the house of Israel (Matt. 10:5-6)." As far as the scriptures show, no gentile during Christ's personal ministry was ordained.

In these latter days Joseph Smith and Oliver Cowdery have left eyewitness accounts of ancient prophets who came back and ordained them to both the Aaronic and Melchizedek Priesthoods. Not only was the priesthood restored, but through Joseph Smith one of the most beautiful and gentle verses of scripture known reveals the Lord's will concerning the use of his priesthood:

> No power or influence can or ought to be maintained by virtue of the priesthood, only by persuasion, by long-suffering, by gentleness and meekness, and by love unfeigned;
>
> By kindness, and pure knowledge, which shall greatly enlarge the soul without hypocrisy, and without guile—
>
> Reproving betimes with sharpness, when moved upon by the Holy Ghost; and then showing forth afterwards an increase of love toward him whom thou has reproved, lest he esteem thee to be his enemy;

That he may know that thy faithfulness is stronger than the cords of death.

Let thy bowels also be full of charity towards all men, and to the household of faith, and let virtue garnish thy thoughts unceasingly; then shall thy confidence wax strong in the presence of God; and the doctrine of the priesthood shall distil upon thy soul as the dews from heaven.

The Holy Ghost shall be thy constant companion, and thy scepter an unchanging scepter of righteousness and truth; and thy dominion shall be an everlasting dominion, and without compulsory means it shall flow unto thee forever and ever.

(D & C 121:41-46)

Just as the gospel was temporarily withheld from gentile nations in the meridian of time, the priesthood was also temporarily withheld from blacks after the restoration. But even then, Brigham Young promised that the "time will come when they will have the privilege of all we have the privilege of."[16]

"Elijah Abel held the priesthood," I argued.

The missionaries had no authoritative answer to my challenge, but they did have personal opinions. They told me that when the Kingdom of God was restored, it was built "precept upon precept; line upon line . . . here a little, and there a little," just as it was during Jesus's earlier ministry (Isaiah 28:10). Everything was not brought back in one magnificent swoop. It takes time to organize and staff a worldwide organization. Perhaps because it was not yet time (as in the case of the New Testament's gentiles) or because whites in the LDS world were not yet ready for it, blacks could not, as a body, receive the priesthood. Just as the Canaanite woman's daughter was special, Brother Abel may have been a special individual, who, for some reason, was able to be ordained. For now, the reasons for priesthood "restrictions have not been revealed" regarding either the gentiles in Jesus's time or blacks in ours.[17]

"Though it's an ear scratcher, a hundred other 'why's' must be asked," Elder Porter pointed out. "Why were the sons of Aaron the only Levites ordained as priests? Why did the Lord deny the priesthood to eleven of the twelve tribes during Old Testament times, but later gave it to all twelve? Why did he wait to preach to and ordain gentiles? Why couldn't women receive the priesthood?"

"Let me throw that one your way," I interrupted. "Why can't women have the priesthood in your church?"

"Again, the Lord has chosen not to reveal the answer to that question," Elder Randolph said. "What he has clearly shown throughout the Bible, as well as in modern revelation, is that men must bare the burden of priesthood—the authority to govern the kingdom of God under the direction of the Lord. This is not to say that women have no voice in the Lord's Church. They freely express their opinions in various Church councils, in their homes where they are co-partners with their husbands, communities, and other places. In fact, more than fifty years before the U.S. Constitutions's 19th Amendment, which extended the right to vote to women, the Utah Territorial legislature, controlled by Mormons, gave that right to women. But the ultimate governing power in our Father's patriarchal system, rests with men. Women have been preordained to motherhood in order for others to have the opportunity to enter this life. If we wanted to be picky, we might also ask why God did not preordain men to motherhood since the scriptures say he is no respecter of persons (Acts 10:34).

"Motherhood and priesthood are two of the most important responsibilities our Father has given to his children. In fact, it seems to me that bringing children into the world and nurturing them is an even greater responsibility than being ordained to the priesthood."

It was quite a dilemma. Here I was, becoming more involved in the LDS faith and its Book of Mormon, and this priesthood problem held me back. How could I tell Jesse that he could not be ordained to the priesthood in the LDS Church?[18] Still, if the Church is not true, the problem shouldn't make any difference to a person honestly seeking truth. Who would want to be ordained to a counterfeit priesthood?

Because of what seemed to be obvious discrimination by the LDS Church, though, my enthusiasm for the Church faded quickly. The perceived inequity toward blacks grew in my mind until I could not bear to listen to the missionaries anymore. I asked them to not waste any more of their time with me if they couldn't come up with better answers than what they had already given me. Other pews would have to be investigated if there was such a thing as truth out there; or I would have to resolve this thing about the priesthood on my own. It just didn't seem right that a group of people would be discriminated against if this were the Lord's true religion.

Though I had no more discussions with the elders for a while, I continued to have a friendly relationship with them by attending their church as well as the Nazarene Church. I enjoyed the people in both organizations—especially the single girls. Then, too, I was learning more about the Bible and the doctrines of the two faiths, thus maintaining my religious orientation.

Still haunting me were the things I had read about the Book of Mormon. I could not force them from my mind no matter how hard I tried. How did the world get that book unless Joseph Smith was a prophet of God?

# 19
# The Road Back

## The Altar

Every Wednesday, the students at Pasadena College attended a worship service where, at times, guest speakers were invited by the administration to woo us to Christ. The services were highly emotional and couldn't help but stir the attentive listener into thinking seriously about the Lord. At least that's the way they affected me.

As evangelists like to do, altar calls were made at the height of their zeal. Dozens came forward to give themselves to Christ. Friends knelt with them while they wept and prayed.

On occasion I was moved to go, but it was too embarrassing. I'd have to crawl over the legs of people in order to reach the aisle. Then I'd have to feel stares as I walked to the altar, which was really a low railing. On top of that, I'd have to see those stares on the way back.

One day the "spirit" was intense. For many months I'd been studying and earnestly praying, wanting answers. "Has the gospel been restored through Joseph Smith? Or is truth somewhere else? Must we wait until that awful day of death before we discover what's beyond that mystery of mysteries?" I needed answers.

Others were going up. Students were crawling over me to get to the aisle; it didn't seem to bother them. No one was alone as they knelt in anxious prayer. There was always someone there to comfort them. Blindly, without even remembering the long walk, I found myself at the altar. I had no problem wondering what to say; I'd been praying about it for so long. Hands of others were laid on my shoulders as I quietly knelt. Audible sobbing could be heard from those surrounding me. That was okay; I appreciated their concern. Now and then, one of the men would say, "Amen" or "Yes, Lord," as their hands warmly rested on my bent back.

No tears trickled from my eyes, but I felt good about the care that those men manifested. I don't know who they were, but I'll forever be grateful to them for coming forward to comfort me during that moment at the rail. It was a special time that I'll forever cherish.

At the time no answers came—at least no answers that I could discern. It was an interesting experience, but that's all that it was. I'd never do it again. "Why, Lord? Why, if you're out there, can't I get answers? The LDS faith seems to be so true except for the priesthood problem, but I don't want to devote my life to an untruth. Are there answers?"

The next few events proved the importance of that prayer.

## The Letter

Over the months of investigation of the Mormon faith I continued to frequently discuss the gospel with LDS friends. One was May Jackson,[1] a young LDS school teacher who, with her mother, tried to help me. They understood that I could not feel right about joining the Church without having the priesthood problem resolved in my mind. Like Jack and Joyce and the elders, they tried to encourage me to read the Book of Mormon so I would receive a testimony of it. I did try a few times, but I would get bogged down because of the King James English or some other reason that I didn't understand.

One Sunday afternoon May invited me to dinner. In my pocket was a letter from Elder Porter.[2] He had been released from his mission for about three months and was enrolled at Brigham Young University. I told May how moving the letter was. She asked me to read it aloud to her while she helped her mother prepare the food. It read:

Dear Bill,

You're continually on my mind, so I thought I'd drop you a line. I've told my friends about you and how much you've impacted my life. I'll never forget the night you put your arm around me and tried to comfort me because of the Dear John from Becky. You're a special friend.

After my mission I continued helping my dad in the fish hatchery that he runs. Then I enrolled in college.

I haven't heard from any of the missionaries in your area so I don't know whether or not you have been baptized, yet. I hope so. You asked us not to return because your enthusiasm for the restored gospel of Jesus Christ was fading over the priesthood problem. I still don't have any solid answers, but I do know that what we taught you is from God.

You're a good man, Bill. I'll always remember your honest approach to finding the truth. If you haven't joined the Church yet, don't let unanswered questions lead you away. We always have them. You know from the bottom of your heart that the Book of Mormon is true. I could sense it when I was there. At least you know it intellectually. You know more facts about the gospel than anyone else I've ever helped teach.

But when I left you hadn't yet prayerfully read the Book of Mormon for some reason. You circled it like one of the wolves in a pack circles its prey, by reading things about the book. But you didn't go in for the kill. With your knowledge about the restoration, you have actually sinned if you haven't yet read the book prayerfully because you have knowingly neglected the things of God. If you're not a member yet, you're probably still going hungry as you continue to stalk your dinner.

Please, Bill. I plead with you to take the time to prayerfully read the Book of Mormon. I promise that you will be touched by the Holy Spirit and he will bear witness to you that it is true. That's what really counts—the Spirit. Knowing facts is important, but the Spirit gives life to those facts. Repent and be baptized in the name of Jesus Christ for the remission of your sins and you will receive the gift of the Holy Ghost. The real joy of the gospel of Jesus Christ will then forever enter your life as long as you live righteously. You will then know, as I know, that Jesus is the Christ, the Son of the living God.

Your friend,
Simon Porter

"You know he's right, Bill," May said. "Read the Book of Mormon. Find out for yourself that it's true. Why fight it?"

"I'll keep on trying," I responded. "But every time I try, something stops me someplace in one of the early chapters. I can't seem to get back to it after that."

The phone rang. May answered it. "Hello. Hi, Linda. Is that right? At the stake center tonight? At seven? Great. I'll tell Bill. He'll want to know. Ok. Bye, Linda.

"Bill! Guess what? A Negro member of the Church is going to speak at a stake fireside tonight? Why don't we go?"[2]

May's enthusiastic invitation was an answer to prayer. After months of intense study, my emotions were strongly involved in the Church, and it tore me up to know that the priesthood was denied to blacks. I eagerly looked forward to listening to the speaker.

## Abner?

It was an older man who stood at the pulpit that Sunday evening. I don't recall who he was. I have often wondered if Abner Howell was the man behind the microphone because Brother Howell was a popular speaker at California firesides then.

Most of what he said that night I have long since forgotten, but I will never forget the essence of what he mentioned about the priesthood and its meaning to him. He had often been sympathetically asked by members of the Church how he felt because he could not be ordained. "That really doesn't concern me," he said. "Someday, either in this lifetime or the next, I will be able to hold the priesthood."

Very special to me was his next thought: "Having the priesthood is not a badge worn to show off rank; using it in the service of others is its significance. 'What can I do with my life?' should be the critical question. 'How can I be of service?'" He then asked, "Have you ever realized that Joseph Smith was able to translate the Book of Mormon without having the priesthood?"

Of course! That was pure revelation! Joseph Smith did not have the priesthood when he talked with God in the grove of trees. He wasn't even a member of the Church; there was no LDS Church then. It wasn't until he was nearly finished translating the Book of Mormon that he and Oliver Cowdery were ordained by John the Baptist and a little later by Peter, James and John.

It occurred to me that Jesus said, "Let your light so shine before men, that they may see your good works, and glorify your Father which is in heaven." He never said we must have the priesthood for our light to shine.

That brother—whoever he was—showed me the right kind of attitude. I'll be forever indebted to him for his thoughts and insights that night.

## Testimonies of Others

Other Church members of African heritage have had similar attitudes. A former Jehovah's Witness tells of learning about the Church from a colleague and his feelings about not being able to be ordained: "I shall never forget that evening. It was as if a messenger from God had come to visit. The message he brought was exactly what I had been looking for." When he discovered that blacks at that time could not hold the priesthood, he was hurt. However, he reminded himself that he had a "strong feeling that the message was the truth, and more was involved than pride and vanity." Kneeling alone in his backyard, he prayed. "The answer came back loud and clear. It was the truth!"[3]

While visiting his brother in Toronto, Canada, a crusader who was widely known throughout the Caribbean wished to attend a church other than his own. Letting his fingers do the walking, he noticed "The Church of Jesus Christ of Latter-day Saints" listed in the phone book.

While he attended the Church's meetings he felt "the love of the people" and found "tremendous emphasis on family life." This led him to want to know more about Joseph Smith and the restoration. For as many as fifteen hours a day he compared the Book of Mormon with his Bible.

Interestingly, the difficult problem of the priesthood did not bother him. He says, "I have always done evangelical missionary work in the broad sense and was never hooked on the ceremonial part of my ministry, performing baptisms and so on.

"The priesthood holder has his calling and I have my faith. If I develop my faith, I'll be as effective as the priest in terms of doing things for my fellow man."[4]

## The Announcement

On June 8, 1978, as Peter must have done when he announced to the Hebrews that the gentile nations could be taught the gospel, a modern Peter—Spencer W. Kimball—announced that divine revelation had been received

> to extend to every worthy member of the Church all of the privileges and blessings which the gospel affords. Aware of the promises made by the prophets . . . who have preceded us that at some time, in God's eternal plan, all of our brethren who are worthy may receive the priesthood, and witnessing the faithfulness of those from whom the priesthood has been withheld, we have pleaded long and earnestly in behalf of these, our faithful brethren, spending many hours in the Upper Room of the Temple, supplicating the Lord for divine guidance.
>
> He has heard our prayers, and by revelation has confirmed that the long-promised day has come when every faithful, worthy man in the Church may receive the holy priesthood, with power to exercise its divine authority, and enjoy with his loved ones every blessing that flows therefrom.[5]

As President Kimball stated, the promise had long been made that blacks would someday be able to be ordained. Few Mormons believed it would happen during their lifetimes, though. It seemed to be like the promise of the Second Coming: it will occur, but not today. Then, suddenly, we were stunned by the impossible. It did happen today.

I was shocked and didn't believe it the first time I heard it. I thought the person who told me must be mistaken. But others called or came to me at church and told me the same thing. Tears freely flowed when I finally realized it was more than a rumor. For days, in fact, whenever I thought about it, my throat closed down as I choked up. It still does.

Others felt the same way. In those days I didn't know any black members of the Church. But the whites I knew were thrilled and joyfully dazed the way I was. In church or at other Mormon get-togethers, that was the main topic of conversation.

After the revelation about the priesthood was received, the gospel has rolled forth as never before. Blacks all over the world have heard the good news and are being baptized. Natives in certain African countries, for instance, were being prepared to receive the priesthood in interesting ways. Before branches of the Church were officially within most of Africa, many Nigerians and Ghanans organized unempowered "LDS" groups in their villages. They had heard of the Church from magazine articles, from friends who had traveled to America who had joined the Church, and in other ways. The villagers desired to be a part of it.

Before receiving direction from Salt Lake, many mistaken, yet moving and heartwarming symbols, customs and acts were introduced or retained from other churches. When Mormon missionaries finally arrived in their villages, they gladly gave up their mistaken practices and waited in long lines to be baptized into the true Church.[6]

Mary Frances Sturlaugson, an African American and at one time a Mormon-hater, became converted and attended Brigham Young University. She captured the feelings she and other Mormons felt on the day of the announcement. "Not only did I feel the heavens rejoicing, but I saw and heard the Saints around me doing the same. That special feeling radiated in the air." Immediately after hearing the announcement, "cold chills went completely through" her when she saw a young man who was talking on the phone stand up, throw his fists into the air and shout, "All right!" All she could say to herself was, "I don't believe it's happened." Another man near her kept repeating happily, "I'll be darned, I'll be darned."

Out on the street, "horns were honking like crazy" as Mary cried "like a happy kid at Christmas." At a stop light, a driver leaned out of his car and asked if she had heard. Half mumbling through tears of joy, she "nodded a disbelieving yes. He whooped and started blowing his horn as he drove off."

At her apartment Mary's roommates ran outside to meet her. Jumping up and down they hugged and screamed. Inside, they knelt and "each said a prayer, sobs punctuating every one."

Mary later reflected, "I . . . never expected to see this prophecy fulfilled in my day or even in a yet future generation. No one was more surprised nor skeptical than myself . . . This was a revelation from God in fulfillment of that promised day."

Mary reminds us that the Lord has said, "For my thoughts are not your thoughts, neither are your ways my ways . . . For as the heavens are higher than the earth, so are my ways higher than your ways, and my thoughts than your thoughts" (Isaiah 55:8-9).[7]

# Embarrassed

As the older black gentleman at that fireside helped eliminate one of the largest obstacles in my mind, another person I met at another fireside shamed me into overcoming the biggest obstacle of all. Like a streaking meteor flashing through the night's sky, a diminutive missionary swept into my life and then vanished. Unsmiling eyes framed with horn-rimmed glasses fixed on his uplifted face will remain forever etched in my memory.

After that fireside, I began spouting off to one of the adult leaders of the youth about the Book of Mormon being plagiarized. That was the only conclusion I could accept unless it was true. And I wasn't quite ready to believe that. I was filled with a sense of self-importance as young men and women gathered around.

The elder finally had heard enough. As eyeballs lifted to my eyeballs, he asked, "Have you ever read the Book of Mormon?" That's all he said. That's all he needed to say. Embarrassed, I left. In that humiliating moment I knew what I had to do, whether I liked it or not. I'll forever be grateful to that young elder whoever he was and wherever he may be. To me he'll always stand tall.

## Getting Down to Business

At first it was a struggle to get through the mysterious barrier that had kept me from continuing during earlier efforts. The missionaries, May,

Jack, Joyce, and others had made the same challenge that the unnamed elder had made. Every time they urged me to read the Book of Mormon I vowed I would do it. But I didn't carry out my promises; I didn't read the entire book. This time I begged and pleaded with God for help as I struggled to keep from putting it aside as I had before. I didn't ever want to be embarrassed again in front of my friends like I had been on the night of the fireside. As the days went by and I continued to persist in reading and prayer, I actually found myself not wanting to put the book down. Good feelings came over me and I knew the Book of Mormon was true. But after I'd lay it down to do homework, to sleep, to work, or for some other reason, I'd talk myself out of those feelings. "You're being brainwashed, Bill. You only hope it's true."

And oh how I did. How I hoped with all my heart that the book was true.

## Special Thoughts

Thoughts flooded my mind. The Book of Mormon is certainly unique. When in all of the annals of story writing has a writer seriously asserted that his book was copied from gold leaf? What author has ever soberly claimed that his book was entombed for centuries inside a stone box? Who else has dared to claim that his or her writing is an authentic record of the Messiah's visit to far off places? Has anyone else ever had the audacity to maintain that his publication is "the most correct of any book on earth?" How could an uneducated youth attempt such an undertaking, then get a congregation of clergy and other erudites to swear their allegiance to his book? Obtaining the unqualified endorsement from such a distinguished array would truly be a miracle if the text actually originated with Joseph Smith.

Could Quetzalcoatl, also known by various other names such as Kukulkan and Itzamna, have been Jesus? "The doctrines of the benign and saintly Quetzalcoatl or Kukulcan must be classed among the great faiths of mankind, and their author, alone of all the great teachers of morals except Christ himself, inculcating a positive morality, must be granted a precedence of most of the great teachers of Chinese and Hindu antiquity."[8] "Thus passes Itzamna, this reputed son of a god, perhaps our Christian God under another name, and the Itzas believed that his soul went to dwell with his Heavenly Father."[9]

Who was Mexico's Messiah about whom the Spanish padre, Juan de Torquemada, wrote in the 16th century? "He was perfect in moral virtues and they [the natives] say that He is alive and that He is to return."[10]

Was the mysterious being of light that the early natives told the conquistadors about actually the altered story of Jesus descending from the heavens? They said that

> a great light came from the northeastern sky. It glowed for four days in the sky, then lowered itself to the rock; the rock can still be seen at Tenochtitlan de Valle in Oaxaca. From the light there came a great, very powerful being, who stood on the very top of the rock and glowed like the sun in the sky. There he stood for all to see, shining day and night. Then he spoke, his voice was like thunder, booming across the valley . . . He . . . told us how to pray and fixed for us days of fast and days of feasting. He then balanced the 'Book of Days' (sacred calendar) and left vowing that he would always watch down upon us his beloved people.[11]

Why was Jesus's name changed to Quetzalcoatl, Itzamna, or Kukulcan if he, indeed, was the same person as they? Over time, the Hebrew name and title "Yehoshua" and "Messiah" evolved into the Greek "Jesus" and "Christ." Could it be that the same kind of thing had occurred among the ancestors of the modern Mayans?

Quetzalcoatl means "feathered serpent." It is a compound word derived from Guatemala's national bird, the emerald and crimson "quetzal," and "coatl," meaning "serpent."[12] Throughout Mesoamerica are carvings of a feathered serpent decorating ancient pyramids and other sites.

The cross and crucifix are symbols of Jesus the Christ. If he visited another people nearly 2,000 years ago, is it possible that their progeny also devised symbols to represent him? Could the feathered serpent be a symbol in the same way that the cross is symbolic?

When the Lord instructed Moses, "Make thee a fiery [brass] serpent, and set it upon a pole," he symbolized the saving power of the future, crucified Messiah. "'It shall come to pass, that every one that is bitten [by snakes], when he looketh upon [the brazen serpent], shall live' (Numbers 21:8-9).

In the Bible, Jesus referred to that incident: "And as Moses lifted up the serpent . . . even so must the Son of man be lifted up: That whosoever believeth in him should not perish" (John 3:14-15).

Book of Mormon Israelites asked: "Did [Moses] not bear record that the Son of God should come? And as he lifted up the brazen serpent in the wilderness, even so shall he be lifted up who should come. And as many as should look upon that serpent should live, even so as many as should look upon the Son of God with faith, having a contrite spirit, might live" (Helaman 8:14-15).

The legend of Quetzalcoatl, about a bearded white man who came down from the sky, might logically be reconstructed to arrive at an actual event. Like the beautiful quetzal, Jesus Christ came down from above. Whoever looked to him as their Savior would not die but would inherit eternal life. In the same way the cross represents Christ, the resplendent bird was juxtaposed with Moses's brazen serpent into one symbol—the feathered serpent—to remind the faithful of Jesus Christ's historical descent from the heavens. Whoever looked to the feathered serpent would live.

As I had already determined, two and only two conclusions were obvious: *either Joseph Smith was a monumental genius to have composed such an elaborate scheme, or his tale is true.* For him to have created such a mind-boggling set of elements ingeniously snuggled together within the framework of history and the Bible, then to keep track of them so they flow into a complex yet coherent story, would be more of a miracle than his strange account of how it all happened.

# 20
# Peace

One sacred Sunday, as I slouched in an overstuffed chair meditating about the Book of Mormon and quietly imploring God, an indescribable influence calmly intruded. Silently circulating through my entire self, serene tranquility subtly embraced me. Afraid to twitch an eyelid for fear of disturbing that peaceful presence, I surrendered.

Enveloped in that hallowed glow, I knew! Tears washed away all doubt. With that holy gleam came the angelic assurance that the Book of Mormon is true and was translated by an anointed prophet. Man's maker and master is the Messiah. Sweet tranquil certainty bathed me with the understanding that all that the missionaries had taught me, all of the concepts I had learned from LDS literature, everything my Mormon friends had led me to were divine. The Church of Jesus Christ has been restored. His prophets speak again. The Kingdom of God is upon the earth once more to prepare mankind for the coming reign of its Sovereign. Basking in the enlightenment of God I became acquainted with the Spirit. I knew the Prince of Peace. If this was what The Church of Jesus Christ of Latter-day Saints had to offer, *I wanted more.* After fifteen months I had opened my heart to the answer to that prayer on Mt. Rubidoux.

Seven years passed before I was privileged to be sealed to my eternal bride, Barbara. From that union have come seven magnificent children— Bill, Beverly, Bernice, Brenda, Bonnie, Belinda and Bobbi. Like most moms and dads, we are everlastingly grateful for our children and adore them more than our limited tongues can express. They have begun their own eternal families and are bringing ever increasing joy to us through their companions and our grandchildren. Barbara and I also share the deepest affection for our parents and grandparents. Though they did not raise me in the Church, my parents' and grandparents' exemplary lives cannot be overlooked. They lived as righteously as they knew how, as did Barbara's Mormon forebears. Together we hope to pass on the same wonderful heritage of goodness to our posterity. It is marvelous to realize that the possibility is available for us to be together in the one family reunion that truly matters.

I invite anyone reading these thoughts to come to the same sacred knowledge that millions like me have come to by sincerely petitioning God as you study the latter-day miracle known as the Restoration. I would have known earlier if I hadn't been so stubborn and resisted the whisperings of the Spirit. How close I came to not hearing! I was looking for something that would convince me; what I found was Someone who converted me.

The doctrines of the Restoration are as eternal as the heavens and come from the God who dwells within them. His precepts stand alone as preeminent above all the philosophies and sophistries of men. They are true and need no apology nor defense. They make sense because they spring from the source of sense. They are the root of happiness now and forever.

Not all of my ever-accumulating questions have even come close to being answered. I am confident, though, that my Father in heaven knows the answers, he will reveal them in his own time. I am satisfied, too, that I have found authoritative answers that I could have found in no other place. The flood of unique answers I have received with the aid of the Spirit has dramatically helped me to realize my true identity and my relationship to God and his children. They have shown me the purpose of life.

Although I didn't realize it while I was involved, Jesus's formula for discerning his prophets by examining their fruits was critical in helping me to know that Joseph Smith was truly a prophet. Though other fruits can no doubt be considered, those that are outlined in this work—especially the Book of Mormon—are a substantial accumulation of nourishing and refreshing fruit that cannot be easily dismissed. By prayerfully examining Joseph's fruits, I learned that not only he, but his ancient Bible and Book of Mormon colleagues were also prophets. Most notably, I came to know the most eminent prophet of them all—Jesus the Christ.

Along with Parley P. Pratt, I believe that had Joseph Smith "been spared a martyr's fate till mature manhood and age, he was certainly endued with powers and ability to have revolutionized the world . . . As it is, his works will live to endless ages, and unnumbered millions yet unborn will mention his name with honor, as a noble instrument in the hands of God, who, during his short and youthful career, laid the foundation of that kingdom spoken of by Daniel, the prophet, which should . . . stand forever."[1]

Though I am not anxious to experience it, no longer do I fear death. It is merely a breath away from the world of spirits. It is only a heartbeat from where my parents and grandparents dwell. Death is only one brief instant within an everlasting drama. Every mortal is a probationary performer in two critical scenes of life. Because of the atoning sacrifice of Jesus Christ, each is a playwright for his or her own destiny. When the curtain closes on this act, another act begins. We are auditioning for him who is our divine director and critic. Whatever plaudits and acclaim we generate after our next scene will truly be deserved for we will have fully demonstrated that how we performed is the way we wish to perform forever. Many will voice concern that they have received no curtain calls nor standing ovations. Others will bow to the adoring adulation of a celestial audience welcoming their triumphant return. As proven stars they will appear with their director and his already established cast in an eternal dramaturgy when he announces, "Well done, thou good and faithful servant: thou hast been faithful over a few things, I will make thee ruler over many things: enter into the joy of thy Lord" (Matthew 25:21, 23).

# Notes

## Preface

1. *Church News.* 3 June 1989.
2. I have tried my best to recall details as they occurred during my conversion experience. Since nearly four decades have passed, much has been forgotten, I'm afraid. Information has been added that was not available in those days, and a few incidents and events for the sake of simplicity. The overall story of my conversion, however, is completely true. A few names have been changed to protect those who wish to remain anonymous and to protect friends who would be hurt if I forgot their contributions!

## 1. Searching for Truth

1. Mother and Daddy eventually became Latter-day Saints.
2. *Liahona: The Elder's Journal,* 20 April 1926, p. 424; as quoted in *A Marvelous Work And A Wonder,* p. 28.

## 2. The Beginning of Answers

1. I didn't like coffee and tea, so when the Mormons later explained the "Word of Wisdom"—to eat wholesome and nutritious foods and to not drink alcohol, tea, coffee, nor use tobacco and illicit drugs—I had no problem. (See D & C 89).
2. "My Confrontation with Mormonism." *Era,* September, 1970, pp. 24-25.
3. Ordinarily the King James Version of the Bible (KJV) is used by Latter-day Saints and will be largely used throughout this work. However, the Revised Standard Version (RSV) is used in a few places because in those particular places it seems to be clearer.
4. *Joseph Smith—History,* pp. 47-50.
5. In looking back, I realized that I *had* asked for these visitors. When I prayed on Mt. Rubidoux I went there looking for answers.

## 3. Christ's New Testament Church

1. *Joseph Smith, An American Prophet,* p. vi.

## 4. Why Prophets?

1. *His Many Mansions,* Comparative Chart of Adventist, Baptist, Eastern Orthodox, Episcopalian, Lutheran, Methodist, Presbyterian, Roman Catholic, Unitarian and Latter-day Saints churches.
2. *The New Republic,* 9 April 1956; as quoted in *The Dead Sea Scrolls audio tape.*
3. Revillout, *Patrologia Orientalia, II,* pp. 123-7; as quoted in *Since Cumorah,* p. 49.
4. The following books are mentioned in the Bible but are not to be found in present Bibles: the Wars of the Lord (Num. 21:14); Jasher (Josh. 10:13; 2 Sam. 1:18); the Acts of Solomon (1 Kgs. 11:41); Samuel the Seer (1 Chr. 29:29); Gad the Seer (1 Chr. 29:29); Nathan the Prophet (1 Chr. 29:29; 2 Chr. 9:29); Prophecy of Ahijah (2 Chr. 9:29); Visions of Iddo the Seer (2 Chr. 9:29; 12:15; 13:22); Book of Shemaiah (2 Chr. 12:15); Book of Jehu (2 Chr. 20:34); Sayings of the Seers (2 Chr. 33:19).
5. *Know the Bible,* p. 239.
6. *Introducing the Bible,* p. 79.
7. *His Many Mansions,* Comparative Chart.
8. *A Guide to the Religions of America.*
9. See also Matt. 22:29; Mark 12:24; Luke 2:46-47; 4:21; 16:29; 24:32; 24:45; John 2:22; 5:39; 10:35; 20:9.
10. *Letters Exhibiting the Most Prominent Doctrines of The Church of Jesus Christ of Latter-day Saints,* pp. 1-33. Spencer was a renowned Baptist minister in New England during Joseph Smith's time who was later converted to the restored gospel.

## 5. Fruits of a Prophet

1. Shortly after beginning my investigations into the LDS Church, my mother's doctor, Dr. Cherry, sensed something was bothering her. When she told him that she was worried because I was learning about "those Mormons," Dr. Cherry chuckled. "Herschell [Mother's name!], if I were you I would learn about the Mormons, too. Some of my finest patients are Mormons."
2. *From Clergy to Convert,* pp. 92-97.

## 6. When Reasoning Replaced Revelation

1. See, for instance, James E. Talmage, *The Great Apostasy;* James L. Barker, *Apostasy from the Divine Church;* T. Edgar Lyon, *Apostasy to Restoration; By Study and Also by Faith, Vol. 1,* pp. 81-117.
2. *Apostasy to Restoration,* pp. 89-91.
3. During the early part of the fourth century, Eusebius quoted Hegessipus: Eusebius, *"Ecclesiastical History," Book IV,* chapter 22; as quoted in *The Great Apostasy,* p. 72.
4. *Ibid.,* p. 73.
5. *Apostasy to Restoration,* p. 97.
6. *No More Strangers, Vol. 4,* pp. 69-91.
7. *Apostasy to Restoration,* p. 150.

## 7. The Restoration of Revelation

1. Bryant, *Picturesque America, or the Land We Live In,* p. 503; as quoted in *A Marvelous Work and a Wonder,* p. 29.
2. The doctrine of predestination did not originate with Calvin as is commonly believed. It is also found in the earlier writings of Augustine and Luther.
3. Bible references: "angel having the everlasting gospel" (Rev. 14:6); "dispensation of the fullness of times," "gather all things in one" (Eph. 1:10); "Elijah" and "great and dreadful day" (Mal. 4:5); "latter day . . . kingdom" (Dan. 2:28, 44); "restitution" (Acts 3:21), "restore all things" (Matt. 17:11; Mark 9:12); "suddenly come to his temple," (Mal. 3:1); "time of the harvest," "the tares," "gather the wheat" (Matt. 13:24-30; 36-43).

## 8. A Visit to a "Mormon" Church

1. The instrument of death is not the essence of Christ's atonement. If he had been stoned to death it would be ludicrous to believe that rocks would be mounted on Christianity's steeples.
2. Instead of splitting Sunday meetings into two sessions as they did when I began looking into the Church, all Sunday meetings today are consolidated into one three-hour block of time.

3. One convert pointed out that he "felt strange" when he was a clergyman in northern Virginia, "being paid to visit the sick and share the gospel" when he "was telling others to do" it for nothing. *Clergy to Convert,* p. 3.

4. Surprising to some is the fact that Latter-day Saints are numbered among the world's highly gifted and educated. People from astronauts to Olympians to Pulitzer Prize and Academy Award winners to educators, statesmen, scientists, inventors, physicians to Miss and Mrs. Americas call themselves Mormons.

5. The topic of that first Sunday School class was the Book of Mormon. Because it occurred nearly forty years ago, I cannot recall every detail that was discussed. Details that were probably not covered are discussed here as if they were covered.

6. Awaking "from a deep dream of peace," Abou Ben Adham discovered an angel writing in "a book of gold" the names of those who love the Lord. When he asked if his name was included, the angel replied that it was not. Ben Adham then asked him to write his name as one who loves his fellow men. The next night the angel reappeared and showed Ben Adham "the names who love of God had blessed; And lo! Ben Adham's name led all the rest!" James Hunt. *Abou Ben Adham.*

7. *Biblical Archaeology Review,* Nov/Dec. 1993, p. 44: "Unlike the other Dead Sea Scrolls, [the Copper Scroll] is inscribed on copper . . . an indication that it was very important and meant to outlast the ravages of time."

8. See *Ancient Writing on Metal Plates* for photographs of metal plates.

9. See *These Early Americans,* pages 129-136, for photographs of early stone boxes.

10. *Joseph Smith's First Vision,* p. 149.

11. *Ensign.* January, 1988, pp. 46-47.

12. Frontispiece of the Book of Mormon.

13. *Ibid.*

14. "Conversion Hard for Jewish Rabbi." *Church News,* 8 November 1975, p. 13.

15. *Church News,* 4 May 1991.

16. Stark, *Contemporary Mormonism: A Social Science Perspective,* May 1994; as quoted in *The [Provo, Utah] Daily Herald,* 2 April 1994, p. 1. Rodney Stark, a non-Mormon professor at the University of Washington, believes "we are observing an extraordinary event. After a hiatus of fourteen hundred years, in our time a new world faith seems to be stirring."

17. Winged angels didn't make sense to me, so the concept of the wingless Moroni was not a problem. Wings on angels were an invention of early artists and theologians because the only flying creatures they knew about had wings. Angels, it seemed to me, must travel through space where there is no atmosphere. Therefore, some other means of transportation than wings must have been used by them. Why not a light beam?

## 9. Expert Opinions

1. Dr. Grant's name has been changed. I don't recall whether or not the dean's name was actually Broadbent, although I believe that it was.

2. Interestingly, approximately a quarter of a century later, a Mormon —David Gardner—became the president of the entire University of California system.

3. I don't remember which denominations the four clergymen represented.

4. This is only one of a number of different versions of the story created by anti-Mormons.

5. For a photographic reproduction of Spaulding's story, *Manuscript Found,* see *They Lie in Wait to Deceive, Vol. 2,* pp. 393-428.

6. *Ibid.,* p. 431.

7. *Ibid.,* p. 431.

8. *Ibid.,* p. 432.

9. *Ibid.,* p. 433.

10. *Ibid.,* p. 433.

11. *Ibid.,* p. 434.

12. *Ibid.,* p. 434.

13. Rice, *The "Manuscript Found,"* pp. 7-8; as quoted in *Ibid.,* p. 394.

14. *A New Witness for Christ in America, Vol. II,* pp. 208-209.

15. *Faith and My Friends,* pp. 255-256.

16. *The Distant Prize,* p. 205; as quoted in *The Book of Mormon Message and Evidences,* p. 12.
17. John A. Tvedtnes, Preliminary Report of *The Isaiah Variants in the Book of Mormon,* p. 136, Foundation for Ancient Research & Mormon Studies (FARMS), Provo, Utah, 1984.
18. *Book of Mormon,* 1981 edition, footnote, p. 82.
19. *The Isaiah Variants in the Book of Mormon,* p. 102.
20. See *Research* section of *The Keystone* chapter in this work for an explanation of chiasmus.
21. *The Isaiah Variants in the Book of Mormon,* pp. 72-73.
22. *The Legacy of the Brass Plates of Laban,* p. 65. The ten chiasma compared in the BM and the KJV were: 2 Nephi 8:3/Isaiah 51:3; 2 Nephi 8:4-7/Isaiah 51:4-7; 2 Nephi 15:11-22/Isaiah 5:11-22; 2 Nephi 24:9-20/Isaiah 14:9-20; Mosiah 14:1-12/Isaiah 53:1-12; 1 Nephi 20:1-12/Isaiah 40:1-12; 1 Nephi 20:1-12/Isaiah 48:1-12; 1 Nephi 20:13-22/Isaiah 48:13-22; 1 Nephi 21:1-5/Isaiah 49:1-5; 2 Nephi 7:1/Isaiah 50:1. The first five chiasma "are essentially identical" but the last five have major chiastic differences, especially 2 Nephi 7:1/Isaiah 50:1.
23. "Thy kingdom come" and "Give us this day our daily bread" are not written in the Book of Mormon's version.

## 10. Clerical Converts

1. *Hayden's History of the Disciples,* pp. 250-251; as quoted in *History of The Church, Vol. I,* pp. 215-216.
2. *Church News,* 28 September 1986, pp. 8-12.
3. "Jane Johnston: Methodist Minister to Mormon Pioneer." *Ensign,* April 1981, pp. 65, 68.
4. *Autobiography of Parley P. Pratt,* pp. 13-20; Brooks, *LDS Reference Encyclopedia,* pp. 386-388.
5. *Joseph Smith: The First Mormon,* p. 120.
6. *A New Witness for Christ in America, Vol I,* pp. 317-326.
7. *Letters Exhibiting the Most Prominent Doctrines of the Church of Jesus Christ of Latter-day Saints.*

8. I have within my personal files the stories of nearly ninety, which is probably only a small portion of those who have joined the Church. I keep hearing about others who are not in my collection.
9. *From Clergy to Convert,* pp. 61-66.
10. *Ibid.,* pp. 74-81.
11. *Ibid.,* p. 73.
12. *Ibid.,* pp. 1-8.
13. *No More Strangers, Vol. I,* p. 138.
14. *Ibid.,* p. 82.
15. See *Clergy to Convert,* p. 74; *No More Strangers, Vol. 2,* p. 110; *Latter-Day Sentinel,* 21 May 1988.
16. *Ibid.,* Vols. 1, 2, pp. 104-120; 26-32 respectively.
17. *No More Strangers, Vol. 3,* p. 151.
18. *Ibid.,* pp. 41-53.
19. *No More Strangers, Vol. 4,* pp. 69-91.
20. *Ibid.,* p. 1.
21. "Nun Disturbed by Family's Baptisms, Then Joins Ranks." *Church News,* 17 September 1977, p. 12.
22. "Former Monk Describes Route to LDS Conversion." *Ibid.,* 11 August 1979, pp. 12-13.
23. Personal letter from the former minister within my files.

## 11. Who Are We?

1. One of the most interesting interpretations I have heard about "the Word" was from a converted Jewish dentist, Dr. Irving Cohen. Anciently, it was forbidden for a Jew to write or say the sacred name of Jehovah. John, raised a devout Jew, could not in good conscience write the Lord's name in his Gospel. Instead, he substituted "the Word" for the word that could not be written—Jehovah. (Irving Cohen, PG Third Ward fireside, Pleasant Grove, Utah, Aug. 29, 1993).
2. *Jesus the Christ,* p. 35.
3. Luke says that "Adam . . . was the son of God" also (Luke 3:38). Adam's father is the same as Jesus's, but he had no mortal mother.
4. Lodge, *Science and Immortality,* p. 184; as quoted in *The Life Before,* p. 11.

5. Proust, *Homo Viator, in Gabriel Marcel,* p. 8; as quoted in *Ibid.,* p. 10.
6. Thirteenth Article of Faith of The Church of Jesus Christ of Latter-day Saints.
7. Taylor, *Mediation and Atonement,* pp. 160-161; as quoted in *Mormon Doctrine,* p. 248.
8. An immortal person can never die; an "unmortal" one can live forever but also can die under certain conditions (from Dr. Daniel Ludlow in a private conversation).
9. Second Article of Faith of The Church of Jesus Christ of Latter-day Saints.
10. *From Clergy to Convert,* pp. 98-103.
11. *Ibid.,* pp. 23-30.
12. *History of the Church, Vol. V,* pp. 134-135.

## 12. Eternal Family Relationships

1. *No More Strangers, Vol. 3,* pp. 41-53.
2. *From Clergy to Convert,* pp. 61-66.
3. *No More Strangers, Vol. l,* pp. 131-138.
4. Matt. 7:24-27; Matt. 9:14-15 (Mark 2:18-20, Luke 5:33-35); Luke 6:37-42; Matt. 13:3-23 (Mark 4:3-25, Luke 8:5-18); Matt. 18:12-14; Matt. 18:23-35; Luke 10:25-37; Luke 12:13-21; John 10:1-18; Luke 14:7-11; Luke 15:11-32; Luke 16:19-31; Matt. 20:1-16; Matt. 21:33-46 (Mark 12:1-12, Luke 20:9-18); Matt. 25:1-13; Matt. 25:14-30; Matt. 25:31-46.
5. *No More Strangers, Vol. 2,* pp. 110-115.
6. *The Words of Joseph Smith,* p. 169.
7. *LDS Bible Dictionary,* King James Version of the Holy Bible. Angels of God are spirits and resurrected persons. Many "angels of God"—righteous couples in the spirit world, as well as the unborn spirits—have not yet been joined eternally.
8. *Among the Mormons,* p. 159.
9. *Peloubet's Bible Dictionary,* p. 671.
10. *Ibid.,* p. 675.
11. *Biblical Archaeology Review,* November/December 1993, p. 39.
12. *LDS Bible Dictionary,* p. 781.
13. See Genesis 17:22, 15-18; 26:1-4, 24; 28, 35:9-13; 48:3-4; Gal. 3:29.

## 13. Predictions and Other Miracles

1. U. C. Riverside at that time had no college of education because it was a new university.
2. Pasadena College no longer exists in the Pasadena, California area. It moved its facilities to Point Loma, California.
3. *Introducing the Bible*, p. 79.
4. *Mormon Doctrine*, p. 602.
5. *History of the Church, Vol. 4*, p. 540.
6. See Amos 3:7; Deut. 30:3-5; Psalms 107:1-7; Isaiah 5:26; Ezekiel 34:12; Ephesians 1:10.
7. *History of the Church, Vol. 4*, p. xxxi.
8. *Ibid.*, p. xxxii.
9. *The World Book Encyclopedia, Volume 3*, p. 482.
10. *History of the Church, Vol. 4*, p. 40.
11. *Ibid., Vol. 5*, p. 393.
12. *The Journal of Joseph*, p. 176.
13. *History of the Church, Vol. 4*, p. 89.
14. *Ibid.*, pp. 356-357.
15. *Ibid., Vol. 5*, pp. 393-394.
16. *Ibid.*, pp. 395-398.
17. Many books have been written concerning Joseph's predictions. For examples see Cleon Skousen, *Prophecy and Modern Times;* Duane S. Crowther, *Prophecy, Key to the Future;* Roy W. Doxey, *Prophecies and Prophetic Promises from the Doctrine and Covenants.*
18. Zechariah, Malachi, and John the Baptist are three.
19. *Joseph Smith—History*, pp. 68-69.
20. *Times and Season, Vol. 2*, p. 201; as quoted in Footnote to *Joseph Smith—History.*
21. *Essentials in Church History*, p. 69.
22. *Joseph Smith and the Restoration - A History of the LDS Church to 1846*, p. 105.
23. *History of the Church, Vol. 1*, p. 146.
24. *Autobiography of Parley P. Pratt*, pp. 122-123.
25. Woodruff, *Ms. History of the Church, Book A*, p. 332; as quoted in *History of the Church, Vol. 2*, pp. 103-105.
26. *Ibid.*, pp. 380, 387, 428, 432-433.

27. *Ibid.*, p. 435.
28. *Ibid.*, pp. 435-436.
29. This experience was similar to Paul's when "from his body were brought unto the sick handkerchiefs or aprons, and the diseases departed from them" (Acts 19:10-12).
30. Woodruff, *Leaves from my Journal,* Ch. xix; as quoted in *History of the Church, Vol. 4,* pp. 3-5.

## 14. The Law of Consecration

1. *Lectures on Faith,* p. 58
2. *Welfare Service Resource Handbook,* p. 1.
3. *Ibid.,* p. 3
4. "Foundation Honors Welfare System." *Ensign,* May 1992, p. 112.
5. *Netherlands' Mission Historical Report,* Feb./March 1948; as quoted in "War and Peace and Dutch Potatoes." *Ensign,* July 1978, pp. 19-23.
6. *Church News,* 16 September 1984.
7. "Catholics Honor Church." *Ensign,* February 1988, pp. 78-74.

## 15. Persecution in Print

1. The three books were *Mormonism Under the Searchlight, Mormonism,* and *Chaos of Cults (Chaos of Cults* is not quoted here since it is no longer in my possession). A fourth publication was given to me: *Christian Truth and Religious Delusions,* parts of which are quoted in this chapter. I have also examined a number of other anti-Mormon pamphlets, books and tapes. Perhaps the best known is the movie, *The God Makers,* by Decker and Hunt (For a concise review of this movie see Gilbert W. Scharffs, *The Truth About "The God Makers,"* Publishers Press, 1986).
2. *Mormonism,* pp. 8-9.
3. *Christian Truth and Religious Delusions,* pp. 114, 116, 117.
4. Jesus warned his apostles, "The time cometh, that whosoever killeth you will think that he doeth God service. And these things will they do unto you, because they have not known the Father, nor me" (John 16:2).
5. *History of the Church, Vol.,* pp. 95-96.

6. *Times and Seasons, Vol. V,* 17 May 1844, pp. 439-552; as quoted in *Emma's Glory and Sacrifice,* pp. 25-26.

7. *History of the Church, Vol. 4,* p. 538.

8. *Among the Mormons,* pp. 102-103.

   In 1976—138 years later—the governor of Missouri, Christopher S. Bond, rescinded the extermination order. In a letter to the LDS First Presidency he wrote: "Expressing on behalf of all Missourians our deep regret for the injustice and undue suffering which was caused by this 1838 order, I hereby rescind Executive Order No. 44 dated October 27, 1838, issued by Governor Lilburn W. Boggs."

9. *Ibid.,* pp. 103-104.

10. *Life of Joseph Smith the Prophet,* pp. 354-355.

11. Only three of the four anti-Mormon books that I read before I was a convert are quoted in this chapter. Many of today's anti-Mormon books are more sophisticated and are not so blatantly obvious in their attacks. Even though their modern literature is often more scholarly-looking, with the twists and half-truths more carefully executed, in general the thrust has not changed. Their underlying message is similar—hate for the Mormon message mixed with liberal inaccuracies and half-truths.

12. Quotes from anti-Mormon sources are in quotation marks; correct spellings and facts are italicized.

13. *Mormonism,* p. 8.

14. *Mormonism Under the Searchlight,* p. 7; *Christian Truth and Religious Delusions,* p. 112.

15. *Mormonism,* p. 8.

16. *Christian Truth and Religious Delusions,* p. 112.

17. *Ibid.,* p. 113.

18. *Ibid.,* p. 114.

19. *Mormonism,* p. 15.

20. *Ibid.,* p. 15.

21. *Mormonism Under the Searchlight,* p. 48.

22. *Christian Truth and Religious Delusions,* p. 110.

23. Howe, *Mormonism Unveiled,* p. 261; as quoted in *Mormonism,* p. 7.

24. *Mormonism Under the Searchlight,* p. 6.

25. *Joseph Smith the First Mormon*, pp. 41-43.
26. *The Saints' Herald, XXVIII*, 1 June 1881, p. 165; as quoted in *They Knew the Prophet*, pp. 2-3.
27. *Ibid.*, p. 167; as quoted in *Ibid.*, pp. 3-4.
28. "Stories from the Notebook of Martha Cox, Grandmother of Fern Cox Anderson"; as quoted in *They Knew the Prophet*, pp. 1-2.
29. *New York Herald*, 19 February 1842; as quoted in *Joseph Smith's First Vision*, p. 149.
30. *History of the Church, Vol. 4*, pp. 78-81.
31. *Life of Joseph Smith the Prophet*, pp. 351-352.
32. Whitney, "Scenes and Incidents in Nauvoo," *Woman's Exponent, X*, 1 December 1881, pp. 97-98; as quoted in *They Knew the Prophet*, pp. 175-176.
33. *Young Woman's Journal, XVi*, December 1905, pp. 551-553; as quoted in *Ibid.*, pp. 159-160.
34. *Christian Truth and Religious Delusions*, pp. 111-112.
35. *No More Strangers, Vol. l*, pp. 104-120.
36. *Christian Truth and Religious Delusions*, p. 112.
37. Lang, *History of Seneca County*, p. 365; as quoted in *Investigating the Book of Mormon Witnesses*, p. 41.
38. *Mormonism Under the Searchlight*, pp. 17-18.
39. The name the people themselves used is unknown. "Olmec," meaning "people of the land that produces rubber," is merely a convenient modern term used for them.
40. *An Ancient American Setting for the Book of Mormon*, pp. 108-114.
41. Levey, *Early Teotihuacan, An Achieving Society*, p. 52; as quoted in *Ibid.*, pp. 121-131.
42. *Mormonism*, p. 16; *Mormonism Under the Searchlight*, p. 12; *Christian Truth and Religious Delusions*, p. 113.
43. Th. Noeldeke, *Die Semitischen Sprachen*, p. 34; as quoted in *Lehi in the Desert and the World of the Jaredites*, pp. 14-15
44. *Mormonism Under the Searchlight*, p. 12.
45. *Articles of Faith*, pp. 236-237.
46. *Mormonism*, p. 13.
47. *Mormonism Under the Searchlight*, p. 46.

48. *Church News,* 4 May 1991.
49. *Mormonism,* p. 11.
50. Letter to the author from Ashley Bartlett, dated 8 Dec. 1959.
51. McKellar, Joyce, *Church News,* (Date unknown).
52. *No More Strangers, Vol. 2,* pp. 1-20.

## 16. The Search Intensifies

1. Not his true name.
2. *The Power of Truth,* p. 16; as quoted in *A Marvelous Work and a Wonder,* p. 438.
3. The names are fictitious although similar settings were part of my conversion. So many LDS people helped me by referring to the books and many of the facts mentioned here that I have created this chapter as a tribute to all of them. I hesitate to name actual names for fear I will leave someone out.
4. *Book of Mormon Message and Evidences* and *Lehi in the Desert and the World of the Jaredites.*
5. *Book of Mormon Message and Evidences,* pp. 4, 6, 79-94.
6. *The Americas Before Columbus,* pp. 38-39, 94, 136-138, 156-160.
7. *Book of Mormon Message and Evidences,* p. 7.
8. *Joseph Smith, Jr. as a Translator,* pp. 3-4; as quoted in *Ibid.,* p. 152.
9. Beeswax on wooden writing tablets as well as scrolls wrapped around wooden sticks were in common use in Ezekiel's day. (See Keith H. Meservy, *Ensign,* September 1977, pp. 22-27 for a discussion about the use of beeswax in wooden tablets).
10. *New York Times,* 5 November 1937, p. 3; as quoted in *Book of Mormon Message and Evidences,* p. 13.
11. *No More Strangers, Vol. 2,* pp. 47-48, 52-53.
12. *The New Era,* April 1975, pp. 11-12.
13. Personal note to the author from "Peggy" (Peggy and George are fictitious names).
14. *USA Today,* 5 March 1986.
15. *Ibid,* 5 March 1986.
16. *Times and Seasons 2,* 1840, pp. 305-806; as quoted in *Book of Mormon Message and Evidences,* p. 123.
17. "A Writer Looks at the Book of Mormon." *Improvement Era,* November 1960, p. 798.

18. *Ibid.*, p. 799.

19. *Mysteries of the Ancient Americas,* pp. 144, 148-152, 214-215, 232-234, 238-240.

20. "Chiasmus in the Book of Mormon." *Book of Mormon Authorship,* p. 51.

21. "Chiasmus in the Book of Mormon." *The New Era,* February 1972, p. 9.

22. It is not known whether the various gold and silver values named in Alma 11:5-19 were measures, weight, or coinage.

23. Brookbank, *Improvement Era,* vols. 13, 17, 18; as quoted in *Book of Mormon Message and Evidences,* p. 118.

24. By comparing these Book of Mormon words with those in any good Bible dictionary, it may easily be seen that, because of their striking similarities to Biblical words, they would go unnoticed if mingled in the midst of Bible words.

25. *Book of Mormon Message and Evidences,* p. 115.

26. Nibley. *Lehi in the Desert and the World of the Jaredites,* pp. 184-188; as quoted in *Ibid.,* p. 115.

27. *Ibid.,* p. 31.

28. A. Moret, *Hist. de l'Orient* 11, p. 787; as quoted in *Ibid.,* p. 23.

29. Neum: 1 Nephi 19:10; Zenock: 1 Nephi 19:10; Alma 33:15-16; 34:7; Helaman 8:19-20; 3 Nephi 10:16; Zenos: 1 Nephi 19:10, 12, 16; Jacob 5:1-77; Alma 33:3-13; 34:7; Helaman 15:11; 3 Nephi 10:15-16.

30. *LDS Bible Dictionary;* 1 Ne. 15:20, 2 Ne. 6:4-9:3; 11:2-25:20; Mosiah 15:6; Hel. 8:13-20; 3 Ne. 16:17-20; 20:11-12; 22:1-17; 23:1; Mormon 8:23.

31. See *Poetic Parallelisms in the Book of Mormon, Supplement,* pp. 1-16, 25-27.

32. Examples are seen of allegory in the entire fifth chapter of Jacob; epistles in Alma 54:5-14, 16-24; 56-61; 60:1-36; 61:2-21; 3 Nephi 3:2-10; Moroni 8:2-30; 9:1-26; a genealogy list in Ether 1:6-33; a lamentation in Mormon 6:17-22; mimation in the ending of words with *m* by the earliest Book of Mormon and Near East peoples as in curelom, cumom and *shelem;* nunation in often ending proper names with *n* as did the classic Arabs and Nephites; a psalm in 2 Nephi

4:16-35. (See *Book of Mormon Message and Evidences,* pp. 118-119, 125-129; *Lehi in the Desert and the World of the Jaredites,* p. 243; entire *The Book of Mormon Text Reformatted According to Parallelistic Patterns; Book of Mormon Authorship,* pp. 33-52, 53-74; *Our Book of Mormon,* pp. 111-112; 125-133).

33. "Hebraisms in the Book of Mormon." *The Zarahemla Record,* Angela Crowel; *Lehi in the Desert and the World of the Jaredites,* pp. 102-103. A cognate accusative is a noun and a verb used in the same phrase that are taken from the same root: "I have dreamed a dream"; "yoketh them with a yoke";" taxed with a tax." Compound prepositions is the use of two prepositions as "did not flee *from before* the Lamanites." Prophetic perfect tense is the representation of action in the past while a prophet looks ahead to the future: "These are they whose sins *he has borne;* these are they for whom *he has died,* to redeem them from their transgressions." (Spoken in 148 B.C. in Mosiah 8:44 before Christ's atonement). Qasids are shown in 1 Nephi 2:9-10: "O that thou mightest be like unto this river, continually running into the fountain of all righteousness" and "O that thou mightest be like unto this valley, firm and steadfast, and immovable."

34. See *Book of Mormon Message and Evidences,* p. 125; *Lehi in the Desert and the World of the Jaredites,* pp. 17-18.

35. See *Exploring the Lands of the Book of Mormon; Ancient Writing on Metal Plates; The Keystone of Mormonism; These Early Americans; The World of the Book of Mormon; Stela 5, Izapa Chiapas, Mexico; Izapa Sculpture; In Search of Cumorah; An Ancient American Setting for the Book of Mormon.*

36. A Mesoamerican codex usually consisted of folded pages of tree bark or animal skins and was written with dye.

37. See *Exploring the Lands of the Book of Mormon,* pp. 25, 74, 132-134, 137-147, 268, 274; *Ancient America and the Book of Mormon.*

38. See *The Messiah in Ancient America; Book of Mormon Message and Evidences,* pp. 139-150; *Christ in Ancient America, Vol. II.*

39. "Who Wrote the Book of Mormon? An Analysis of Wordprints." *Book of Mormon Authorship,* pp. 157-188.

40. *Book of Mormon Message and Evidences*, pp. 121-122.

41. *Book of Mormon Message and Evidences*, pp. 116-122.

42. *Exploring the Lands of the Book of Mormon*, p. 32.

43. *Joseph Smith An American Prophet*, p. 401.

44. "A Writer Looks at the Book of Mormon." *Improvement Era*, November 1960, p. 800.

45. *Book of Mormon Message and Evidences*, p. 158; *Dictionary, of the Book of Mormon*, 1891, p. 178.

46. *Ensign*, April 1992, p. 63.

47. *Improvement Era*, November 1960, p. 801.

48. Urim and Thummim are Hebrew words meaning lights and perfections (Peloubet and Adams, *Bible Dictionary*, p. 715). They were "objects carried inside the breastplate of the chief priests of ancient Israel and used as oracular media to divine the will of God" (Morris, *American Heritage Dictionary*, p. 1409). The historian "Josephus and the rabbis" believed the Urim and Thummim answered inquiries when the stones gave out "preternatural illumination." Others believe answers were given "by the word of the Lord to the high priest . . . when clothed with the ephod and the breastplate" (Peloubet and Adams, *Bible Dictionary*, p. 716). Joseph Smith described the Urim and Thummim as "two stones in silver bows . . . fastened to a breastplate . . . God had prepared them for the purpose of translating the book" (JSH 1:35).

49. *Improvement Era*, November 1960, p. 801.

50. *Saints Herald*, 1 October 1879, pp. 289-90; as quoted in *Joseph Smith and the Beginnings of Mormonism*, p. 91.

51. "Study, Faith and the Book of Mormon." *BYU Today*, September 1988, p. 20; *Insights, An Ancient Window*, Foundation for Ancient Research & Mormon Studies (FARMS), February 1986.

52. *American Anthropologist, 1*, 1899, p. 694; as quoted in *Book of Mormon Message and Evidences*, p. 192.

53. *Roughing It*, 1913, pp. 1, 119; as quoted in *Book of Mormon Message and Evidences*, pp. 10-12.

## 17. Witnesses

1. *History of Joseph Smith,* p. 152.
2. *A New Witness for Christ, Vol. I,* p. 252.
3. *Ibid.,* pp. 251-252.
4. *LDS Reference Encyclopedia,* p. 82.
5. *Joseph Smith and the Restoration,* p. 105.
6. *LDS Reference Encyclopedia,* p. 83.
7. *Reuben Miller Journal,* 21 October 1848; as quoted in *A New Witness for Christ, Vol. I,* p. 72.
8. *Joseph Smith and the Restoration,* pp. 97-99.
9. *Investigating the Book of Mormon Witnesses,* pp. 125-126.
10. *History of the Church, Vol. I,* p. 51.
11. David was excommunicated for not observing the Word of Wisdom, exhibiting "unchristian conduct by neglecting to attend Church meetings" while he held higher offices in the Church, for defaming "the character of Joseph Smith . . . while in office as president of the Missouri Saints," deliberately neglecting his duties, and "after his release from that office, he had persisted in signing himself president of the Church" (*Restoration,* pp. 370-371).
12. *A New Witness for Christ, Vol. I,* p. 248.
13. *Joseph Smith and the Restoration,* p. 108.
14. *Investigating the Book of Mormon Witnesses,* p. 128.
15. *Ibid.,* p. 129.
16. *Ibid.,* p. 129.
17. *Joseph Smith and the Restoration,* p. 112.

## 18. My Next Stumbling Block

1. Besides "blacks," "African-American" seems to be the current name preferred by people of African heritage living in the United States. My sincere and deepest apologies if a word used in this work should offend.
2. Since LDS membership records do not identify an individual's race, it is unknown exactly how many black members have been converted or were born into the Church (except in areas where the predominant population is black).

3. It wasn't until the Emancipation Proclamation was issued in 1863 and the 13th Amendment of the U.S. Constitution was passed in 1865 that slaves were legally set free nationwide.
4. *History of The Church, Vol VI*, p. 205.
5. Quincy, *Figures of the Past;* as quoted in *The Glory of Mormonism,* p. 138.
6. *Teachings of the Prophet Joseph Smith*, p. 269.
7. *The Story of the Negro Pioneer*, pp. 15-16.
8. *Ibid.*, pp. 51-53.
9. *Ibid.*, pp. 4-7.
10. *Ibid.*, p. 57.
11. *Ibid.*, pp. 55-60.
12. "Booker T. Washington's Views of the Mormons." *Improvement Era,* November 1970, pp. 62-63.
13. See John 15:16; Acts 14:23; Ephesians 4:11; Hebrews 5:4-6, 7:11-12; Titus 1:5.
14. *LDS Bible Dictionary*, pp. 599-600.
15. "Dogs" was a metaphorical term for gentiles just as "sheep" was used to refer to Israelites. It probably did not have nearly the harsh connotation that the word has today. If Jesus had used "pig," that would truly have been a derogatory reference in the Jewish culture.
16. Brigham Young Papers, Church Archives, 5 February 1852; as quoted in *Encyclopedia of Mormonism, Vol. I*, p. 126.
17. *Ibid.*, p. 125.
18. I was never able to fully discuss the LDS religion with Jesse. The last time I saw him and his wife, Flo, was at my college graduation ceremony. Since then we've lost track of one another. The years slip by so rapidly. I'm not very good at keeping in touch, and evidently neither is Jesse.

## 19. The Road Back

1. Not her real name. The letter that follows is of my own creation; it was inserted to summarize the sentiment among the missionaries that had worked with me.
2. I thought it was interesting that a "fireside" was a meeting held generally on Sunday evenings after normal church meetings where there is usually no fire or fireplace involved.

3. *No More Strangers, Vol. 3,* pp. 54-59.
4. "A Telephone Listing Changed Minister's Life." *Church News,* 30 January 1971, p. 10.
5. *Doctrine and Covenants,* Official Declaration—2; The Church of Jesus Christ of Latter-day Saints, 1981, pp. 293-294.
6. See *Brother to Brother.*
7. *A Soul So Rebellious,* pp. 67-78.
8. Short, *North Americans of Antiquity,* 1880, p. 515; as quoted in *Book of Mormon Message and Evidences,* p. 142.
9. *Kukulcan, The Bearded Conqueror,* 1941, p. 149; as quoted in *Ibid.,* p. 144.
10. *The Messiah in Ancient America,* p. 19.
11. *Ibid.,* p. 2.
12. *Ibid.,* p. 3.

## 20. Peace

1. *Autobiography of Parley P. Pratt,* p. 32.

# Bibliography

*ABC's of the Bible*. Pleasantville, New York/Montreal: The Reader's Digest Association, 1991.

Allen, Joseph L. *Exploring the Lands of the Book of Mormon*. Provo, Utah: Brigham Young University Print Services, 1989.

Alward, Benjamin. *Know the Bible*. Salt Lake City: Deseret Book, 1954.

Anderson, Richard Lloyd. *Investigating the Book of Mormon Witnesses*. Salt Lake City: Deseret Book, 1981.

Andrus, Hyrum L. and Helen Mae (compilers). *They Knew the Prophet*. Salt Lake City: Bookcraft, 1974.

Bach, Marcus. *Faith and My Friends*. Indianapolis/New York: Bobbs-Merrill, 1951.

Backman, Milton V. *Joseph Smith's First Vision*. Salt Lake City: Bookcraft, 1971.

Barclay, William. *Introducing the Bible*. Nashville: Abingdon Press, 1972.

Barker, James L. *Apostasy from the Divine Church*. Salt Lake City: Deseret News Press, 1960.

Barrett, Ivan J. *Joseph Smith and the Restoration—A History of the LDS Church to 1846*. Provo, Utah: Brigham Young Press, 1973.

*Biblical Archaeology Review*. Washington, D.C.: Biblical Archaeology Society. Harper, James E. Nov/Dec. 1993:44. Lehmann, Manfred R. Nov/Dec. 1993:39.

Biederwolf, William Edward. *Mormonism Under the Searchlight*. Grand Rapids, Michigan: Wm. B. Eerdmans Publishing, 1956.

*The Book of Mormon*. Salt Lake City: The Church of Jesus Christ of Latter-day Saints, 1981.

Brooks, Melvin R. *LDS Reference Encyclopedia*. Salt Lake City: Bookcraft, 1960.

Brown, Robert L. and Rosemary. *They Lie in Wait to Deceive.* Mesa, Arizona: Brownsworth Publishing, 1984.

Bushman, Richard L. *Joseph Smith and the Beginnings of Mormonism.* Chicago: University of Illinois Press, 1984.

Cannon, George Q. *Life of Joseph Smith the Prophet.* Salt Lake City: Deseret Book, 1986.

Carter, Kate B. *The Story of the Negro Pioneer.* Salt Lake City: Daughters of Utah Pioneers, 1965.

Cheesman, Paul R. *Ancient Writing on Metal Plates.* Bountiful, Utah: Horizon Publishers, 1985.

Cheesman, Paul R. *The Keystone of Mormonism.* Salt Lake City: Deseret Book, 1973.

Cheesman, Paul R. *These Early Americans.* Salt Lake City: Deseret Book, 1974.

Cheesman, Paul R. *The World of the Book of Mormon.* Salt Lake City: Deseret Book, 1978.

*Church News.* Salt Lake City: supplement of *The Deseret News.* 22 June 1974:10; 16 Sep. 1984; 4 May 1991; Bennett, Eldean. "Conversion Hard for Jewish Rabbi." 8 November 1975, p. 13; Blackinton, Pat. "Former Monk Describes Route to LDS Conversion." 11 Aug. 1979, pp. 12-13; McKellar, Joyce. (Date unknown); Peters, Colleen. "Nun Disturbed by Family's Baptisms, Then Joins Ranks." 17 Sep. 1977, p. 12; Woodford, Brian. "A Telephone Listing Changed Minister's Life." 30 Jan. 1971, p. 10.

Crowther, Duane S. *Prophecy, Key to the Future.* Salt Lake City: Bookcraft, 1963.

*The [Provo] Daily Herald.* Provo, Utah: Scripps League Newspapers: 6 October 1990, p. 1.

*Doctrine and Covenants.* Salt Lake City: The Church of Jesus Christ of Latter-day Saints. 1981.

Doxey, Roy W. *Prophecies and Prophetic Promises from the Doctrine and Covenants.* Salt Lake City: Deseret Book, 1969.

Ehat, Andrew F. and Cook, Lyndon W. *The Words of Joseph Smith.* Salt Lake City: Bookcraft, 1980.

*Ensign.* Salt Lake City: The Church of Jesus Christ of Latter-day Saints. "Ancient Gifts for a New Dispensation." January 1993, pp. 11-13. "Catholics Honor Church." Feb. 1988, pp. 73-74. "Foundation Honors Welfare System." May 1992, p. 112. Spangler, Jerry D. "Jane Johnston Methodist Minister to Mormon Pioneer." Apr. 1981, pp. 65, 68.

Evans, John Henry. *Joseph Smith An American Prophet.* New York: MacMillan, 1946.

Farnsworth, Dewey. *The Americas Before Columbus.* El Paso: Farnsworth Publishing, 1947

Gibson, Stephen W. *From Clergy to Convert.* Salt Lake City: Bookcraft, 1983.

*Gold Plates Used Anciently.* Salt Lake City: The Church of Jesus Christ of Latter-day Saints, 1967.

Gorton, H. Clay. *The Legacy of the Brass Plates of Laban.* Bountiful, Utah: Horizon Publishers, 1994.

Harris, Franklin S., Jr. *The Book of Mormon Message and Evidences.* Salt Lake City: Deseret News Press, 1953.

Held, Robert. *Inquisition.* Florence, Italy: Qua D'Arno Publishers, 1985.

Hill, Donna. *Joseph Smith: the First Mormon.* Garden City, New York: Doubleday, 1977.

*The Holy Bible.* Salt Lake City: The Church of Jesus Christ of Latter-day Saints, 1979.

Howells, Rulon S. *His Many Mansions.* Hollywood, CA: Murray & Gee, 1944.

Hunter, Milton R. *Christ in Ancient America, Vol. II.* Salt Lake City: Deseret Book, 1959.

Hunter, Milton R. and Ferguson, Thomas Stuart. *Ancient America and the Book of Mormon.* Oakland, CA: Kolob Book, 1957.

*The Improvement Era (also Era, and New Era).* Salt Lake City: The Church of Jesus Christ of Latter-day Saints. Feb., 1972; Bahlinger, Heidi as told to Edwin O. Haroldsen, "A German Girl's Prayer Answered." Apr., 1975, pp. 11-12; Cannon, Robert L. "My Confronttion with Mormonism." Sept., 1970, pp. 24-25; "Booker T. Washington's Views of the Mormons." Nov., 1970, pp. 62-63; Jones, Helen Hinkley, "A Writer Looks at the Book of Mormon." *The Improvement Era.* Nov., 1960, pp. 798-801; Welch, John W. "Chiasmus in the Book of Mormon." *New Era.* Feb., 1972, pp. 6-11.

*Insights, An Ancient Window.* Foundation for Ancient Research & Mormon Studies. February 1986.

Jakeman, M. Wells. *Stela 5, Izapa Chiapas, Mexico.* Provo, Utah: The University Archaeological Society, 1958.

Jones, Gracia N. *Emma's Glory and Sacrifice.* Hurricane, Utah: Homestead Publishers and Distributers, 1987.

Kirkham, Francis W. *A New Witness for Christ in America.* Salt Lake City: Utah Printing, 1959.

Larsen, Wayne A. and Rencher, Alvin C. "Who Wrote the Book of Mormon? An Analysis of Wordprints." pp. 157-188.

*LDS Bible Dictionary.* King James Version of the Holy Bible. Salt Lake City: The Church of Jesus Christ of Latter-day Saints, 1979.

Ludlow, Daniel H. *The Dead Sea Scrolls* audio tape. Salt Lake City: Deseret Book, 1991.

Ludlow, Daniel H. *Encyclopedia of Mormonism.* New York: MacMillan Publishing, 1992.

Ludquist, John M. and Ricks, Stephen D. *By Study and Also By Faith.* Salt Lake City: Deseret Book and Foundation for Ancient Research and Mormon Studies (FARMS), 1990.

Lyon, T. Edgar. *Apostasy to Restoration.* Salt Lake City: Deseret Book, 1960.

Mabey, Rendell N. and Allred, Gordon T. *Brother to Brother.* Salt Lake City: Bookcraft, 1984.

Martin, Walter R.. *Mormonism*. Grand Rapids, Michigan: Zondervan Publishing House, 1957.

McConkie, Bruce R. *Mormon Doctrine*. Salt Lake City: Bookcraft, 1979.

Mulder, William and Mortensen, A. Russell. *Among the Mormons*. Lincoln, Nebraska: University of Nebraska Press, 1958.

*Mysteries of the Ancient Americas*. Pleasantville, New York/ Montreal: The Reader's Digest Association, 1986.

Nervig, Casper B. *Christian Truth and Religious Delusions*. Minneapolis: Augsburg Publishing House, 1944.

Nibley, Hugh. *Lehi in the Desert and The World of the Jaredites*. Salt Lake City: Bookcraft, 1952.

Nibley, Hugh. *Since Cumorah*. Salt Lake City: Deseret Book, 1973.

Norman, Garth V. *Izapa Sculpture*. Provo, Utah: New World Archaeological Foundation, 1976.

Parry, Donald W. *The Book of Mormon Text Reformatted According to Parallelistic Patterns*. Provo, Utah: Foundation for Ancient Research and Mormon Studies (FARMS), 1992.

Parry, Donald W. *Poetic Parallelisms in the Book of Mormon, Supplement*. Provo, Utah: Foundation for Ancient Research and Mormon Studies (FARMS), 1992.

Peloubet, F. N. and Adams, Alice D. *Peloubet's Bible Dictionary*. Philadelphia: John C. Winston, 1947.

*Pearl of Great Price*. Salt Lake City: The Church of Jesus Christ of Latter-day Saints, 1981.

Pratt, Parley P. *Autobiography of Parley P. Pratt*. Salt Lake City: Deseret Book, 1985.

Rector, Hartman and Connie. *No More Strangers*. Salt Lake City: Bookcraft, 1971.

Reynolds, Noel B. *Book of Mormon Authorship*. Provo, Utah: Bookcraft, 1982.

Roberts, Brigham H. *History of The Church of Jesus Christ of Latter-day Saints.* Salt Lake City: Deseret Book, 1978.

Rosten, Leo. *A Guide to the Religions of America.* New York: Simon and Schuster, 1955.

Scharffs, Gilbert W. *The Truth About the "The God Makers."* Salt Lake City: Publishers Press, 1986.

Skousen, Cleon. *Prophecy and Modern Times.* Salt Lake City: Deseret Book, 1948.

Smith, George Albert. *Essentials in Church History.* Salt Lake City: Deseret Book, 1950.

Smith, Joseph—History. *Pearl of Great Price.* The Church of Jesus Christ of Latter-day Saints, 1981.

Smith, Joseph. *Journal of Joseph.* Compiled by Leland R. Nelson. Mapleton, Utah: 1979.

Smith, Joseph. *Lectures on Faith.* Compiled by N. B. Lundwall. Salt Lake City: 1935.

Smith, Joseph Fielding. *Teachings of the Prophet Joseph Smith.* Salt Lake City: The Deseret News Press, 1954.

Smith, Lucy Mac. *History of Joseph Smith.* Salt Lake City: Bookcraft, 1958.

Sorenson, John L. *An Ancient American Setting for the Book of Mormon.* Salt Lake City: Deseret Book, 1985.

Spencer, Orson. *Letters Exhibiting the Most Prominent Doctrines of The Church of Jesus Christ of Latter-day Saints.* Salt Lake City: George Q. Cannon & Sons, 1891.

Sperry, Sidney B. *Our Book of Mormon,* Salt Lake City: Stevens & Wallis. 1947: 125-133.

Stewart, John J. *The Glory of Mormonism.* Salt Lake City: Mercury Publishing, 1963.

Sturlaugson, Mary Frances. *A Soul So Rebellious.* Salt Lake City: Deseret Book, 1981.

Talmage, James E. *Articles of Faith.* Boston: University Press, 1959.

Talmage, James E. *Jesus the Christ.* Salt Lake City: Deseret Book, 1949.

Talmage, James E. *The Great Apostasy.* Salt Lake City: Deseret News Press, 1910.

Top, Brent L. *The Life Before.* Salt Lake City: Bookcraft, 1988.

Tvedtnes, John A. *Preliminary Report of the Isaiah Variants in the Book of Mormon,* Provo, Utah: Foundation for Ancient Research and the Book of Mormon (FARMS), 1984.

*USA Today.* 5 March 1986.

Warren, Bruce W. and Ferguson, Thomas Stuart. *The Messiah in Ancient America.* Provo, Utah: Book of Mormon Research Foundation, 1987.

Welch, John W. "Chiasmus in the Book of Mormon." p. 51. Richards, LeGrand. *A Marvelous Work and a Wonder.* Salt Lake City, Utah: Deseret Book, 1978.

Welch, John W. "Study, Faith and the Book of Mormon." *BYU Today.* Sept. 1988: p. 20.

*Welfare Service Resource Handbook.* The Church of Jesus Christ of Latter-day Saints, 1980.

*The World Book Encyclopedia.* Chicago: Field Enterprises Educational Corporation, 1963.

*The Zarahemla Record.* Angela Crowell. "Hebraisms in the Book of Mormon." Summer and Fall 1982, p. 4; from Foundation for Ancient Research & Mormon Studies reprint.

# Index

    characterization in 183
    chiasma in 92-93, 178
    codices 182
    cognate accusatives in 182, Note
        16:33/233
    compound prepositions in 182,
        Note 16:33/233
    conversions 80, 101-102, 175-176
    cultural components, customs 180
    description of 51, 73-75
    epistles 181, Note 16:32/232
        errors in 80
    establishes truth of Bible 135
    "eth" suffixes 183
    fascinating facts 183
    fruit of the prophet 8-9, 80
    filtering agent 186
    Finger, Charles comments 91
    forgotten prophets in 181
    genealogy list in 181, Note
        16:32/232
    gold plates 51, 73
    hidden 79
    inspiring 186
    Isaiah in 91-93, 181
    Jones, Helen evaluation 177
    keystone 52, 80, 170, 176
    King James style 91
    lamentation in 181, Note
        16:32/233
    languages 186
    legends 182
    literary devices and forms in 92-
        93, 177-182, Notes 16:32,
        33/232-233
    "literary masterpiece" 90
    Lord's Prayer in 94, Note 9:23/224
    lost Bible scriptures in 181
    Malachi quoted in 94
    Mesoamerican setting 161-162
    mimation in 181, Note 16:32/233

    money in 180, Note 16:22/232
    moral teachings 172
    Moroni's promise 174
    most correct book 80
    New Yorker comment 177
    nunation 181, Note 16:32/233
    parallelisms in 178, 181-182
    "plagiarized" 84-85, 95
    predictions about 173
    prophetic perfect in 182, Note
        16:33/233
    proverbs, aphorisms in 179
    psalms in 177, 181, Note
        16:32/233
    qasids in 182, Note 16:33/233
    research about 177
    reformed Egyptian in 162-163
    repeating dictation 184-185
    "satanic" 172
    scriptures of Egypt's Joseph 181
    sealed 79
    Sermon on the Mount in 85, 93-94
    sermons, debates, discourses,
        oratory in 179
    similar to Bible 73
    Spaulding, F. S. comments
        172-173
    Spaulding, Solomon 84, 87-90
    Spencer's appraisal 99
    spiritual elements in 179
    stick of Joseph 173
    stories in 180
    theme of 177, 185-186
    time needed to translate 185
    titles for Jesus Christ in 184
    translation of 80, 209
    Twain, Mark comment 185-186
    unique book 80, 213
    unnamed persons in 184
    Wallace, Henry comments 174